MILTON H. ERICKSON, M.D.: AN AMERICAN HEALER

Ida Libby Dengrove
1976

MILTON H. ERICKSON, M.D.
AN AMERICAN HEALER

Edited by Betty Alice Erickson, M.S.
and Bradford Keeney Ph.D.

RINGING ROCKS PRESS

in association with

LEETE'S ISLAND BOOKS

THANKS TO:

❧ The *American Journal of Clinical Hypnosis* for permission to reprint the 1965 paper by Milton H. Erickson on page 217.

❧ Farrar, Straus and Giroux, LLC, New York, for permission to reprint an excerpt from "Poetry" by Pablo Nerudo on page 337. Originally published in an anthology of Neruda's poetry, entitled *Ilsla Negra,* the poem was translated by Alastair Reid and copyrighted by him in 1981. (ISBN: 0374517347)

❧ Maypop Books, Athens, GA. for permission to reprint The Rumi quote on page 347, translated by Coleman Barks from his book, *Delicious laughter: rambunctious teaching stories from the Mathnawi of Jelaluddin Rumi,* published in 1990. (ISBN: 0961891610)

❧ Dr. Wendel Ray, Professor of Family Therapy, University of Louisiana & former director of the Mental Research Institute, who on behalf of the John Weakland Archive granted permission to use the DVD and transcript.

RINGING ROCKS FOUNDATION explores the world documenting and conserving healing practices and spiritual traditions.

PUBLISHED BY
Ringing Rocks Press
3190 West Highway 89A, Suite 100
Sedona, Arizona 86336
Tel: (928) 282-1298
Fax (928) 282-1327

IN ASSOCIATION WITH
Leete's Island Books
Post Office Box One
Sedgewick, Maine 04676 USA

DISTRIBUTION
Independent Publishers Group
814 North Franklin Street
Chicago, Ilinois 60610 USA
(800) 888-4741 or
www.frontdesk@ipgbook.com

PHOTO CREDITS
Courtesy of the Erickson Family

Designed and produced by Karen Davidson
Davidson Design, Inc., Lake Placid, NY

Library of Congress Control Number: 2005906727
ISBN: 0-918172-55-1

Printed in the U.S.A.

MILTON H. ERICKSON, M.D.: AN AMERICAN HEALER

Mrs. Elizabeth Moore Erickson

I AM SO PLEASED to write the preface for the first book written by a member of the family about Milton Erickson. This book is done from a different perspective than the many others about my late husband—it talks about him, the man, rather than his psychotherapeutic techniques.

Milton had so many facets. Besides being a wonderful husband and father, he was a physician, a scientifically-based researcher, the most influential hypnotist of the twentieth century, a world famous psychiatrist and psychotherapist, and a man always deeply interested in anthropology and in trance states in cultures around the world.

He revolutionized psychotherapy with so many new and different perspectives that have since become fundamental concepts in the professional world as well as for people who are not in mental health or medical fields. His idea that the unconscious was a benign and helpful part of the person was revolutionary when he began his career. Now, most people acknowledge that concept without question and without even knowing that Milton was virtually the first to believe and teach it.

Milton was unafraid to challenge habitual perceptions—his own as well as those of others. He strongly believed that no psychological theory could possibly encompass the enormous diversities that human beings present. Therefore methods of dealing with people and their problems have to be individually tailored. Theories about people's thinking and behaviors are limiting and can lock a person into perceptions and responses that aren't accurate.

He used any aspect of patients' lives and of the systems around them to help them reach their productive goals. He was incredibly creative. Some of his interventions in psychological work have become legendary.

4

I think one of his most important contributions was his idea that people have resources within them, the ability to heal their own pain and solve their own problems in ways they do not have to understand cognitively. It wasn't important to Milton that anyone, even the person, "understand" how productive changes and growth occur—it was only important that it happened.

There is much we don't know about people. Physical processes are easily studied. We can see, touch, examine, measure, and photograph a great many aspects of ourselves, but we still don't know how to study the human mind in those definitive ways. Even less is known about the brain's processes. How Milton would have enjoyed participating in the next level of research, the scientific explorations of the complexities of the human mind.

Milton is one of the most studied people in the field of hypnosis and psychotherapy. Despite the hundreds of thousands of words that have been written analyzing his therapeutic methods and words, and the miles and miles of film and audio and video tapes of him, I've never heard anyone say that they completely understand how he did exactly what he did.

Everyone does agree that Milton communicated in ways that were heard deeply and on levels very different than ordinary communication. Almost three decades after his death, people are still approaching family members and saying, "Dr. Erickson changed my life!" Then they quote the exact words they remember Milton saying. Even people who never have met him often say just studying his work has changed their lives in ways they couldn't have imagined. They have felt as if his words—even words printed or recorded on tape—were speaking directly to them.

Milton was adamant that he not be regarded as a guru, a mystic, or a person who did magical things. He insisted that everything he did was a result of observing the other person carefully and responding to that person's own communications. He believed there were explanations that would eventually be supported by research and science, and that eventually, we would be able to describe the inner workings of the mind much more fully than we can today.

I think Milton's work will continue to be studied by more and more people. I also think that as the ability to do research on the mind and the processes of the brain progresses, more of what he did with hypnosis and with psychotherapy will become clearer.

I first met Milton when I attended a scientific meeting as a university undergraduate. I then worked for him as a research assistant the summer before my senior year. We eloped the day I graduated and

I became his wife and an instant mother to his three small children. Every young bride dreams about her future, and I knew Milton was a remarkable man. But I could never have imagined the life we made together! From the beginning, I helped him with his research. This was a very special connection between us separate from our day-to-day life. We wrote scientific articles together and after we moved to Arizona, I helped manage his practice. We always met fascinating people—colleagues, students, and just people along the way. We worked, we traveled, and we had a wonderful life! Most importantly, we raised our family of eight children together.

Milton and I knew lives are made of small actions. We decided deliberately to remember and use many of those events that exemplified the kind of life we wanted to have to teach our children. They didn't have to be big, just meaningful—the kind of thing that can occur anywhere and with anybody.

For the first several years of our marriage, the family vacationed in a small cottage on the shore of Lake Huron. The children learned to swim there and Milton spent countless hours teaching even the younger ones how to skip stones across the water when the lake was smooth and quiet. Close by, there was a small general store owned by a husband and wife. Their adult son who was mentally handicapped worked with them.

Every time Milton and I went to the little store, the young man would chat with us. Every conversation ended the same. "Isn't the lake beautiful?" he would say as he walked us to the door. We would step outside and he would continue talking about how he never tired of looking at the lake. It was always different, he would tell us as he gazed admiringly at a sight we knew he'd seen every day of his life. Sometimes one of his parents would join us and we would all admire the magnificent scene.

Milton and I talked about how that family had learned such an important lesson so well. Neither the young man's handicap nor the daily and commonplace sight of the lake, literally at their front door, prevented them from finding true enjoyment in the moments of their lives. They never tired of the beauty or of sharing that beauty with others.

Sometimes even more fleeting encounters held the same inspiration. Once in a small trading post in New Mexico, Milton bought a ring for me set with a piece of clear obsidian with milky occlusions. Neither of us had seen that kind of obsidian before and we asked the man behind the counter about it. He was delighted to show us the large rock he'd cut the gem from. He told us all about obsidian, where he'd found the rock, and how rare that particular shade was. We were fascinated. As we were walking out the door, I looked up at Milton and said happily, "Don't we meet the nicest people!" The man hurried from behind the counter to catch up with us and said, "And you always will!" That ring became my favorite object to look at when Milton asked me to demonstrate self-hypnosis.

The only thing Milton and I knew for sure, over the years, was that our lives would always change. We moved to Arizona for his health and our two youngest children were born there. Milton's career also took a different direction. Always interested in teaching, he and a few colleagues began producing Seminars on Hypnosis and presented workshops all over the country. Seminars became the predecessor to the American Society of Clinical Hypnosis which Milton founded because he felt there was a need for a professional hypnosis organization that would welcome clinicians. Much of the income from Seminars was dedicated to the formation of the educational arm of the American Society of Clinical Hypnosis (ASCH). Milton became its founding president and was editor of its journal for 10 years. I felt as though our house was an office for ASCH with our dining room table the publishing center for the journal. We had several children still at home, school activities, Milton's patients sitting in our living room waiting for their appointments and always our family dog who also enjoyed the constant activity. I look back and wonder how we did it! But we not only did do it, we enjoyed it.

Milton loved life so much. He was much more romantic than people tend to think. We were married by a justice of the peace and I didn't have a formal wedding. Milton always thought orchids were very special flowers and he wanted me to have them for my wedding. We searched throughout the little town we'd driven to, but the florists had only gardenias so I wore a corsage of gardenias that I still have in my cedar chest. Milton never forgot, though, and every anniversary, he gave me a beautiful orchid corsage.

He always loved puzzles and riddles and practical jokes and puns. He would present puzzles and riddles and refuse to give the answer until he was convinced the listener really couldn't figure it out. Even then, he would just give bigger and broader hints until the person finally solved it.

He insisted on telling long involved "shaggy dog" stories to anyone he could make listen. For years, he carried a little notebook and if he heard a good joke or pun, he would pull out the notebook and jot it down. He never understood why people were surprised by this habit. After his death, I collected some of his favorite jokes and put them in another little book which I kept.

When his health was good, especially in the early years, we often had small dinner parties. We both liked that—we loved the conversations that would develop and the sometimes lasting friendships we built. Some of our friendships began with a professional relationship and were broken only by death. Gregory Bateson, Margaret Mead, Aldous Huxley and his wife as well as his brother Julian, and so many others all began as colleagues and ended as friends. I still have many people on my Christmas card list whom we met that way.

There were also many people we considered friends even though it wasn't the usual relationship. One of those was a Detroit newspaper writer, H.C.L. Jackson, who authored a regular column. Milton had a long correspondence friendship with Mr. Jackson and contributed little stories to the column for years under the name "Eric the Badger." Every year, the articles were put into book form. We always got an autographed copy and everybody in the family read each book over and over.

Mr. Jackson became part of our family lore even though we didn't socialize much and our children never met him. I remember he once wrote about his favorite breakfast, an egg, fried in a hole cut from the center of a slice of bread. We decided to try it and liked the combination of fried bread and egg. Our family ate what we called Jacksons for breakfast for many years. Even some of the grandchildren ate Jacksons and knew the story of how that breakfast was "invented."

Mr. Jackson, in that small involvement with our family, became part of our lives in ways he couldn't have ever anticipated. He even was a part of the lives of people born long after his death. That pleased both Milton and me.

Milton was proud of many things in his life. He loved his plants and took great pride in them. He had a large collection of cactus plants before I met him and he continued collecting cacti our entire life together. Of all the plants we had, I think his favorite was the night-blooming cereus—the beautiful blossoms bloomed only one night and then wilted when the first ray of sunshine hit them. When he was older and more confined to the house, we used to bring them in the house for him. He loved showing those huge delicate flowers to visitors.

We had a tall date tree in our backyard when we first moved to Phoenix. When the tree blossomed but no dates appeared, we discovered we only had the female tree. So we had to buy pollen and fertilize the flowers by hand. We covered the maturing dates with bags to protect them from birds, then we picked them and pasteurized or cured them in the oven. Finally we had wonderful sweet homegrown dates. Milton loved those dates. He saw the work that we did to get the dates as just part of the final accomplishment.

He felt that any amount of work was worth a result that was really wanted. He worked very hard to make the residuals of his paralysis from polio an inconvenience rather than a handicap.

Although he used a cane his entire adult life, he could keep up with almost anybody! He rode a bicycle, went camping, and was always pleased when people seemed to forget that he walked with a limp. He was examined by his neurologist after what was originally diagnosed as a second bout with a different strain of infantile paralysis, but what was actually understood later to be post-polio syndrome. The physician was astonished that Milton was able to stand so straight and with such level shoulders. He didn't know the hard work that Milton had put into that achievement.

Milton was also very proud of professional accomplishments. He was instrumental in turning hypnosis into a respected medical, dental, and therapeutic tool and lived to see it widely accepted and taught in medical schools all over the United States.

Students who gathered in the office were another source of great satisfaction to him. Milton took such delight in their accomplishments! Many of those who studied with him, especially in his later years, are well known—Jay Haley, Jeffrey Zeig, Ernest Rossi, Stephen Lankton. There were so many more. From the time I first met him until his death, he had students seeking him out to study with him.

I think it took a long time for Milton to realize fully just how influential he had become in both hypnosis and in psychotherapy. I think he finally knew, but I'm pretty sure he would be a bit surprised at just how famous he has become.

Sometimes I wonder what he would have been able to do if his health had been better. He had such creative vision, such energy, such integrity, and such intelligence! He had so much drive and so much curiosity about everything. He studied people and how they acted and learned and behaved his whole life.

Marrying Milton was a very big decision for me. I was young and my parents wanted me to wait until I was older. I didn't want to wait, however. I know I never regretted our decision to marry for a single day. I know Milton never did either.

In 1948, when he became so sick, we decided that his best chance for his life was to move from Michigan to Arizona. He went on the train where he could rest in a sleeping car. We hired two young medical interns to care for him during the trip and take him to the hospital when the train arrived in Phoenix. I followed with the four youngest children in our car. I didn't know for certain if he would even be alive when I got to Arizona.

I remember thinking then, that I would rather have had the 12 years with him than a lifetime with anyone else. I had over 40 years with Milton and he's been gone for over 25. But I have never lost that thought that I still would rather have had any amount of time with Milton than a lifetime with anyone else—I was just lucky to have had him for so long.

BRADFORD KEENEY

ALTHOUGH MANY PSYCHOTHERAPISTS have made positive contributions to the lives of those seeking their help and to the profession's
theoretical hypotheses for understanding human experience, no
Western-trained psychiatrist, psychologist, social worker, or therapist
has ever been as prodigious a people helper as Milton H. Erickson,
M.D. Founder of the renaissance of contemporary therapeutic
hypnosis and the inspiration to numerous orientations to psychotherapy, particularly brief strategic therapy and the communications
approach to family therapy, Erickson was the pioneer explorer of
how learning, growth, and evocation of human potential can be
facilitated through naturalistic, communicational means.

He was born on December 5, 1901, in what is now the ghost
town of Aurum, Nevada. Then his parents traveled across country in
a covered wagon part of the way back to a rural farm in Wisconsin.
In his adult years, after he had become a medical doctor, psychiatrist,
and psychologist, Erickson moved back west, settling in Phoenix,
Arizona, largely for health reasons, where he maintained a clinical
and teaching practice in his home.

Severely color blind, he was able to truly enjoy only the color
purple. Tone deaf, arrhythmic, dyslexic, and paralyzed with polio at
age 17, he overcame his deficiencies—which he called the
"roughage" of life—and transformed them into resources. He used
himself as a scientific instrument, whose observational skills were less
contaminated by theoretical assumptions than those of most social
scientists. Thus, he was able to notice and take part in the multiplicity
and complexity of communicational process in a way rarely experienced by others. For instance, he learned how to hypnotize people
by indirect means—sometimes while talking about raising crops or
by not talking at all, using only carefully orchestrated gestures.

As the renowned anthropologist Gregory Bateson put it, Erickson

was the Mozart of psychotherapy. Students and teachers of Ericksonian-inspired approaches characteristically only tap into a single aspect of his work. Rarely does anyone exemplify the diversity of therapeutic techniques or the charismatic impact of Erickson's presence.

Today's ongoing proliferation of therapeutic schools, including postmodern orientations, typically fail to appreciate or recognize the extent to which Erickson evolved ways of participating with others to facilitate their growth. To invoke Bateson's music analogy, it is as if most therapists are still trying to figure out how to hear and play a single musical scale, rendering them deficient in discriminating (and performing) skills to discern the advanced musicality of a Mozart.

When Milton Erickson began his internship in 1928 at the Colorado General Hospital, he was forbidden to even mention hypnosis. If he brought it up, his superiors threatened to dismiss him and block his application for a state license to practice. Later, he differentiated his practice and understanding of hypnosis from that of his mentor, the renowned behaviorist Clark Hull. Erickson stepped away from the academic definition of "psychological science" that attempted to generate standardized principles and procedures that applied to all human subjects and clients. Erickson, believing that every individual was unique, held that each client required a particular therapeutic strategy and hypnotic interaction.

Furthermore, he proposed that all human beings had their own unique forms of consciousness and trance states. He avoided using general principles generated by "scientific" models of therapy and hypnosis, regarding them as products of an "absurd" and "futile" endeavor that disregards "… the subject as a person, putting him on a par with inanimate laboratory apparatus …" (Erickson, 1952). Instead, Erickson preferred to meet each client with an open mind and minimal assumptions, relying upon his own observations of people in real-time encounters.

Not surprisingly, Hull and his so-called "scientific" view of hypnosis went in one direction while Erickson created an approach that he called "clinical." In 1957, Erickson was the founding president of the American Society of Clinical Hypnosis, an organization that provided a clinical alternative for hypnosis, dedicating it as distinct from the laboratory orientations that emphasized generalities rather than particularities of both trance and its induction.

Erickson, however, was radically empirical; his work was based on his careful observations rather than theoretical assumptions. Like the early horse and buggy doctors who were called "empirics," he

The last meeting of two old friends, MHE with Gregory Bateson at home on Hayward in Phoenix, 1977.

allowed his observations to guide what he did with his clients. Ironically, this approach was more "objective"—that is, tied to observables—than the scientific models and theories of psychological (and psychiatric) science. The latter were more inferential, relying upon statistical averages that attempted to define the "norm" and then persuade practitioners to treat everyone as if they were the same (or should be the same).

Erickson, eschewing a template approach to therapeutic practice, was not surprisingly misunderstood by many of his contemporaries. As they observed him working in unpredictable ways, with the unique situation of each client's resources and challenges directing how he helped them, they sometimes proclaimed that he wasn't scientific. His unexplainable outcomes were acknowledged and dismissed by critics and advocates alike as being "mystical" or "intuitive." Such judgments overlooked the fine-tuned instrumentality of Erickson's disciplined observation and analysis of a client's manner of communication. Frustrated by such professional blindness to his skills and empirically-based work, Erickson went out of his way to declare that he wasn't a mystic, but a disciplined empiricist. In the same spirit, his students and family tried to define him as "scientific" rather than "mystical." They would have been more accurate if they called him an "empiric" who rejected the definitions and outcomes of psychological science's theory making and template prescriptions.

When viewed in the multi-cultural context of the world's diverse helping traditions, the evolution of Milton Erickson's resourceful conduct can be seen to be similar to that of shamans, healers, and the medicine people of indigenous cultures. They begin their journey with a personal crisis, often physical in nature, and set forth to find their own means of overcoming it. In the victory of learning how to bring themselves back to life, so to speak, they learn the skills that enable them to help others survive, endure, and thrive. Erickson's battles to overcome physical limitations arguably constituted his first school for learning how to be a skilled observer and communicator. As a teenager with life-threatening polio, he had to relearn how to perceive and use his body. Stricken again in 1952, he spent much of the rest of his life in a wheelchair. A lifetime of physical ailments and chronic pain taught him how to draw upon his inner resources.

Like shamans who take an odyssey into the wilderness to learn more about how to access their own inner strengths, Erickson went on a legendary canoe trip. Barely able to lift his canoe when he began in the summer of 1921, he returned 1,200 miles later with great physical strength (able to swim a mile and carry his boat) along with some finely developed bartering skills. In the course of a long life, his numerous explorations of states of consciousness ranged from developing methods of personal pain control, to learning how to sleep in the midst of noise during building construction, to being in and out of trance during therapy with others, to explorations of deep trance with Aldous Huxley.

Many shamans and healers, like most psychotherapists, lack the skills of empirical observation and flexible participation that characterized Erickson's work. But the most developed shamans and healers, like Erickson, emphasize utilizing whatever the client or patient brings them. Accepting the other's presenting communication as a starting point, they create a communicational climate that enables the client to access and follow his or her own internal strengths and resources. They access and foster rather than impart new information. Believing that the client has his or her own "inner doctor," as Albert Schweitzer put it, enables healers to be more humble and less missionary-like in their efforts to help. The wisest shamans, like Erickson, believe that they have little to do with successful outcomes. They see their role as encouraging clients to find their own ways, sometimes by shining a flashlight on the trail, other times by tripping them as a means of getting them to move forward.

In Erickson's latter years, people began paying as much attention to his psychotherapeutic skills as they did to his hypnotic work. Numerous clinicians subsequently built their own models of therapy based on some fragment of Erickson's thoughts and skills, leaving the vast richness of his clinical work seldom realized or conveyed.

It is my personal belief that the body of Milton Erickson's work comprises the richest source material for understanding therapeutic process—more so than the collected works of most other therapeutic traditions. Therapists have largely concerned themselves with making imaginative guesses about human experience, usually emphasizing pathology and dysfunction, and they have filled numerous books with their assumptions and hypotheses. However, Erickson held on to an Occam's razor, sharpened by what he observed. He was led by observables and nothing but the observables. And then through experimentation and tinkering, he became an accomplished communicator, a master of moving inside the webs of human interaction.

In the chapters that follow, different aspects of Erickson's life will be presented, beginning with Betty Alice Erickson's and Roxanna Erickson Klein's reflections on their father, followed by further remembrances and stories by Allan Erickson, a mathematician and former professional cryptoanalyst. Like her father, Betty Alice is in full-time therapeutic practice, aiming to help her clients access their inner strengths and processes of learning and growth. In my many conversations with both the students and offspring of Milton Erickson, I have found Betty Alice's perspective to be remarkably attuned to the work of her father.

The subsequent chapters present archival materials from Erickson's life, including pages from his diary made during his canoe trip. In addition, excerpts from his correspondence with his son Allan and his daughter-in-law Luanne are included, showing how he creatively communicated with family members. Following these chapters, a gallery of family photographs with dates and captions provided by the three family contributors, Allan, Roxanna, and Betty Alice, chronicles his life from early childhood to his latter years.

The text of a clinical case consultation that Erickson conducted in November 1958 is presented along with an accompanying DVD of the original film so that his work may be observed more closely. In addition, Erickson's remarkable essay, "A Special Inquiry with Aldous Huxley into the Nature and Character of Various States of Consciousness," is included to show how relevant his work is to anyone interested in the furthest reaches of the human mind.

When looking at the reactions of therapists to Erickson's body of work, we too often find ignorance. Many clinicians have not studied his work and continue to go down a dead end similar to the one prescribed by Clark Hull and other so-called scientific models of psychology. These practitioners, teachers, and researchers emphasize standardization of assessment, intervention, teaching, and learning. They worship generalizations that are assumed to be applicable to the masses. This approach has led to the contemporary emphasis upon over-concretizing abstract diagnostic categories of pathology and the addictive prescribing of pharmacological substances. Erickson's way, the path of communicational and interactional details and particularities, stands as an alternative to such a simple-minded scientism, and prefers an older science of careful empirical observation accompanied by carefully accurate record-keeping. With respect to the latter, Erickson's clinical notes were examples of highly disciplined empirical observation. To assure their accuracy, he sometimes asked his clients to read them and make any corrections.

I believe that the essence of Erickson's work is found in his unique "presence" in the therapeutic moment. Often in trance, Erickson was able to make an interpersonal connection that had the effect of facilitating the personal accessing and triggering of inner resources, cognitive and contextual reconstruction, personal learning, hope, and growth. His presence was more like that of a wise shaman, tuned in completely to the healing situation, than that of a scientific medical doctor, trained to be disconnected from the possibility of entering into any meaningful relational moment.

In 1976, when Erickson's clinical work was developing a large audience, I asked Gregory Bateson what he thought of the many books and talks that were coming out about Erickson. With a British intellectual air, he replied that he despised what he had seen and heard about, lamenting his decision to send clinicians to Erickson. When I asked him to elaborate, he said that they ignored the systemic complexity and integrity of Erickson's work. More specifically, Erickson had a way of entering a system that allowed him to be part of the "weave of the total complex" rather than as an ego separate from the system. This enabled his action to arise within the weave and be harmonious with it. He went on to say that the people studying Erickson brought with them the traditional Western epistemology of an outside observer operating on the other, leading them to believe that they could create and use a "bag of tricks" and have "power" over others. Bateson loathed that kind of power game. In other words, Bateson saw Erickson as an effective practitioner of systemic wisdom, but believed that many of his observers inappropriately construed and reduced his orientation to various simplistic techniques. From Bateson's perspective, they threw away his "systemic presence" in favor of a tool kit of behavioral and linguistic skills which they used in an effort to replicate his therapeutic way of working.

The final section of the book presents the personal comments of friends and colleagues who remember Erickson, the healer. Stephen Gilligan, Ph.D., describes Erickson as being like "an incredible wizard, an amazing healer, and a funny old man" whose "hypnotic presence was really very strong—like an old shaman." Knowing Gilligan's work, I know that he does not mean that Erickson had a magic stone inside his pocket, that when rubbed enabled him to have amazing insights as to what he should say and do with clients. Erickson, like the great indigenous shamans, practitioners of Chinese medicine, and master yogis, was a highly disciplined human being with tremendous sensitivity, awareness, creativity, and respect for others.

Genuine shamans are not magicians. They are finely tuned instruments, made that way by intense effort and the lifelong pursuit of communicational interplay. Erickson was neither a magician nor an advocate of social science's pursuit of standardized techniques and understandings. He was an empirical scientist, a naturalist who carefully and patiently and wisely observed nature, human and otherwise, like the old medicine men and women of Native America. Nature, rather than textbooks, was his teacher. His suffering and limitations were his resources. His odysseys, experienced and prescribed, were paradoxical ways of going inside while paying careful attention to the outside.

Milton Erickson's place in history is less likely to be in the company of Freud, Jung, Skinner, Perls, and Rogers, theorists who published many assumptions, generalizations, and grand theories. Erickson was more like the old shamans, who instead of asking why, said, "Show me." When questioned, he often replied, without words, "Let me show you, doing so indirectly, so you may surprise yourself with your own learning."

When he talked, and he talked a lot, it wasn't necessarily what he said, but how his saying was interwoven with the other's responses, that made a difference. His deeds, interactions, outcomes, and ponderings over what he and others did in relation to one another comprise his legacy. He leaves us unable to settle for any particular approach to helping others, but open to doing anything that can help another person live in a good way. As he once summarized his work, "The thing to do is to get your patient, any way you wish, any way you can, to do something" (Zeig, 1980, p. 143).

The Dalai Lama typically brings an official rainmaker with him when he conducts an important ceremony. Climatic conditions must be right to bring forth the potential of a ceremonial enactment. One of these rainmakers, the Venerable Ngagpa Yeshe Dorje Rinpoche, was described by the Dalai Lama as follows: "Wandering from place to place, he would meditate in caves and remote places, dependent upon the support of the local people. They in turn would request him to perform rituals for their welfare. His particular skill, the prevention and summoning of rain, has special value in Tibet, where drought on the one hand and violent hailstorms on the other could have a drastic effect on people's lives" (Marsha Woolf and Karen Blanc, *The Rainmaker*, Boston: Sigo Press, p. xi).

Milton H. Erickson served as a kind of "rainmaker" for his clients. His job was to create a climate that would help bring forth the natural growth and transformational processes of those who came to him asking for help. As he described this aspect of his work: "It is the patient who does the therapy. The therapist only furnishes the climate, the weather. That's all. The patient has to do all the work" (Zeig, 1980, p. 148).

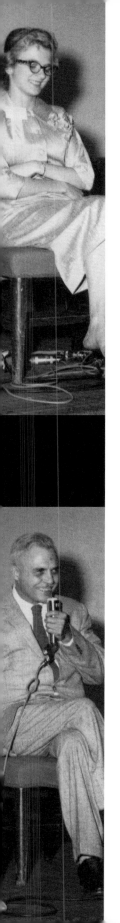

CHAPTER ONE

BETTY ALICE ERICKSON

AN AMERICAN HEALER

Dr. Milton H. Erickson, my father, was one of the most unique human beings who ever lived. His training as a psychiatrist taught him that although a person's unconscious might be filled with demons and conflicting innate desires, it also motivated people. Psychotherapy, at that time, was structured either with the patient listening to the physician who helped the patient understand the unconscious motivations that created dysfunction, or, with the therapist listening to the patient until the patient understood his own unconscious drives.

Dad almost single-handedly revolutionized the field, encouraging it to move to an emphasis on wellness and the inherent potential within. He believed the natural state of a human being was to be "healthy, wealthy, and wise," and to experience life as a joyous event. To begin to understand how he healed requires appreciating his unswerving belief in the basic goodness of humanity.

Dad enthusiastically inspired people to reach, to strive for their own personal pinnacles of wholeness. He had a fervent belief in the positive spirit of each individual. I remember him telling my mother once, "If people can build the pyramids and Machu Picchu, they can do anything." He wasn't talking about the physical labor—he was referring to the human spirit, to people's creative vision and abilities to imagine new meanings for life.

This perspective along with his prodigious understanding of human nature was more than enough to make him a revolutionary figure in the mental health profession. But he also became one of the greatest healers ever—and certainly one of the most original healers in the Western world. He used words and tasks, rituals and connections; he used compassion and the therapeutic relationship to initiate the patient's own healing abilities. He saw his work with his patients most often as a cooperative journey—he was sometimes the leader but the efforts belonged to the patient.

His understanding of human nature, developed during his own illnesses and pains, guided him in mastering this art of helping people to change themselves. He had an uncanny way of connecting with the true aspect of each person—the part that was essential, positive,

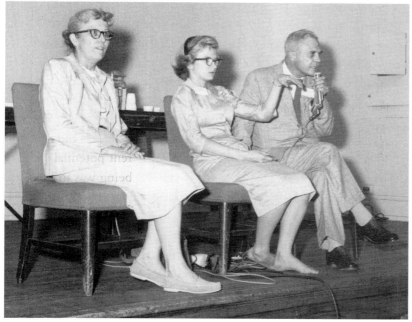

1958 workshop in Milwaukee using sister Bertha and daughter Betty Alice as subjects.

healthy, and growth oriented. He had a remarkable ability to assess people by merely being in their presence. He attributed this acumen in understanding things about people, that they themselves may not have even realized, to his finely honed abilities to observe. He observed how they looked, how they moved, sat, spoke, smiled, responded—everything about them. People give information, they communicate in all sorts of ways and he was a master at observing them through those various ways.

Dad was fully aware of the vast spectrum of human behavior. He knew there was evil, psychosis, and true psychopathology in the world, but he was convinced that the natural state of humans is to live a productive and wholesome life with meaning in it, and to help other people do the same. He always believed that, deep down, most people want to become all that they are capable of being. Each of us wants to reach for the sun and the stars.

He also knew that sometimes, even lots of times, people get into situations where obstacles prevent them from developing in this natural way. These obstacles often spring from faulty or incomplete learning. The goal of psychotherapy was to help them complete learning and recognize options and alternatives.

Often he used the analogy of the flower growing through a crack in the sidewalk: People can triumph, despite footsteps trampling over them, regardless of the poor soil they can still grow and flourish. But he also believed that people, like those plants, had to work hard. He used to say, "If a chicken is trying to get out of its egg, you can't help it too much. If you do, the chicken won't develop its own strength to get through the barrier that separates it from having a life."

People had different perceptions of his work. They looked at the language patterns and the structure of his narratives, the complexity of his communications, his clinical acumen, and his hypnotic skills. Very few looked at the metaphor of love that was so present in his work and his presence with his patients. He was able to give incredible love and would bring this forth as people opened themselves to receive it.

When patients and students first became acquainted with him, many thought Milton H. Erickson, M.D., was scary and fear-invoking. This always amused me, as a kid, because there was nothing to be scared of. In fact, he was fierce only in regard to what he held was right and wrong. People would say they felt he could see right through them. Even as a child, I thought only those people who were afraid of themselves were fearful of him. In fact, he was a good father, strict but not inappropriately so—he was a father in just the same way he was a person. There was no sloppy sentimentality, but there was abundant love. That love enabled others to experience his faith in the goodness of people, including in themselves.

It took enormous effort to do the kind of work he did. Let me try to explain what I saw in this way: When you sit or read a newspaper or watch television or some activity like that, your everyday self is present without noticeable change. But when Dad connected with people, he went through an alteration of his whole being. I would sometimes sit in on his sessions with people to demonstrate hypnosis. During those times in his office, I noticed he would undergo a change. He became "different." He was much more "present" in the clinical situation than people are in ordinary activities. As I sat and observed this firsthand, it felt as though I could feel energy, a creative essence that came from him.

I was also always struck with how deeply he observed others. When Dad listened, he really listened to you. His listening was so profound that sometimes people thought he'd said what he'd never said. I think it was Jay Haley, one of the founders of brief and strategic therapy ("problem-solving therapy,") who once said, "Erickson never praised." As a girl, I heard that and thought, "That's nonsense. Daddy praises all the time."

Sometime later, I was living in Phoenix. Dad liked to garden and it was my children's turn to help with this. We used to go over to the house three or four times a week. Dad would come outside in his wheelchair, while David, Michael, and Kimberly , who were 12, 11, and 10, respectively, weeded and planted. Daddy liked compost and, accordingly, they had to work with the compost Dad and Mom had made. I would sit there, observing, glad I'd already done my share of gardening, glad it wasn't my turn.

I listened very carefully to the conversations the children and their grandfather had. On the way home, I would ask all three, "Did Grandpa praise you?" They would all say he had and then tell me exactly what their grandfather had said to them. "Grandpa said I did a good job!" and "He told me I weeded better than anybody." "Grandpa said I grew wonderful carrots." I would listen to my children telling me things that Dad had never said. It was amazing how convinced they were that he had praised them.

I spent a lot of time that summer watching and trying to understand what was occurring. What he did was to listen to them with intense interest. He would ask questions and then really focus on them and hear their answer. What they heard was praise for them—and it was, but it was from them to them. Dad would listen and they would feel him listening with such intensity that they would feel it as praise for them, as it really was. They would "remember" words that had never been uttered, and then make those words into the exact words that would fit best within them. Dad connected with them at the very deepest part of their being.

A family friend once said that when she told Dad something painful and deeply personal, he held her hand as they put their heads together and wept. She said they wept together for several minutes. We family members internally shook our heads and said to ourselves, "Never happened. Daddy simply did not respond like that." Clearly, no one except this woman and Dad were in the room. I think that it is another example of how Dad listened so intently and with such loving support. I think she, like my children, heard and felt what he was offering, but, in actuality, the physical events did not occur.

This is a special way of being, a way that is deeply meaningful to others, and, in the broadest sense of the word, spiritual. In this spirituality, Dad saw what was needed inside another and was, by his own connection to that deep part of them, able to help them access and bring forth that piece within themselves. That is healing—helping from within. Treatment is helping from the outside. Dad healed.

This spirituality was part of why he saw and believed in the best in most humans. He was in awe of the magnificence of human nature, our natural world. He taught that to many people, certainly to me. He paid attention to the cycles of nature—when it was time to plant, time to grow, and time to reap. He recognized the cycle of humans—when it is time to grow, time to separate, time to give to others, and time to retreat. He pondered the complexity of what the world really is and how it all fits together. He was more an empiricist, like a naturalist, a field scientist dedicated to accurate and clear observations of nature and people. He was definitely not a dreamy mystic with rhapsodic metaphors for imagined worlds from another realm. He was fully present in this world, the world of stars, mountains, plants, animals, rain, and sunshine and engaged it all, without compromise, with all his senses. He wanted to behold life in a direct way, deeply in touch with the world. I think this orientation alone led him to a profound belief in the connection between people and the processes and cycles of nature.

My brother, Lance, grew up with a heart defect. He gave a talk once where he said that from the time he was a small boy, he and Dad used to go out and look at trees. They would look at how high the trees were and find the biggest and the tallest trees around. Then they would talk about how long a time that particular tree had lived and how it had taken its energy from the ground and the sun, and then how it had nurtured the squirrels and the birds that had made their homes on and within that tree. If this is looked at psychothera-peutically, Dad was connecting Lance with the idea and suggestion, "Live for a long time, live a long life and live well."

They talked about this to such an extent that Lance said all his life, he has always almost automatically scanned the landscape to find the oldest tree around, the biggest and tallest trees in sight.

No one can scientifically prove that these conversations and thoughts affected my brother's life expectancy, but they certainly didn't hurt. Dad was connected with nature and he used it as a part of his world of communication and even healing.

From time immemorial, medicine men and women, shamans and healers from myriad cultures around the world have also used nature as a teacher, as a healing metaphor, and as a transforming resource for those who came to them for help. In this sense, my father shares the traditions of many of the world's indigenous healers.

From the time we were children, and throughout our lives, Daddy used to tell us stories. They were parenting stories, inspirational stories, stories that connected people with each other and with nature. The stories were about us, but they were not about us. They were about our family, our relationships, our place in our life cycle, and they weren't about that at all. Sometimes, they were just stories with no apparent reason.

In many of Dad's stories, the central character was a frog named White Tummy. He had a green back and a white tummy, and that was his name. White Tummy lived in the middle of the forest in a pond with lily pads and he would sit on a lily pad and wait for flies to come by. Red flies, blue flies, green flies, yellow flies, and once in a while, his very favorite fly, a big fat juicy purple fly! I can recall Dad saying slowly and purposefully, "As White Tummy was sitting there in the pond, with the warm sun on his green back and the cool water underneath his lily pad, he...." Today, I know this was, without question, a hypnotic induction beginning the story.

Many good stories begin with a hypnotic induction—"Once upon a time, a long time ago, in a magic land, there lived a beautiful princess ...." Dad used this way of storytelling, which is probably as old as mankind, and we listened raptly to the stories and took them within us as people always have.

White Tummy, living in the forest with all the other land and pond creatures, also emphasized Dad's connection with and respect for nature. We always had homemade bird feeders in the yard. Dad was always interested in birds, and particularly in their migration. Geese migration, because of the birds' "V" pattern was especially interesting. Whenever migrations were taking place, Dad wanted us to go to the yard where we would watch and wonder just how they did it and marvel at how far birds flew. Sacred connections in nature are another thing so associated and respected with indigenous healers and their wisdom traditions, and with my father.

When I was a child in Michigan, we would go to a summer cabin on Lake Huron. I remember Dad teaching me to skip stones on the lake. He also used to take us children out in the woods. Once we saw an albino frog and Dad made sure each of us got a good look. He spent a long time explaining to me what a remarkable creature an albino frog was and what incredible obstacles it had to overcome to reach adulthood. To me, that reverent respect for life, for the hard work to overcome difficulties, some of which are not of our own making, for the things that really constitute the world and life, for all of that, is very spiritual. Dad's deep interest in anthropology and different cultures also speaks to that recognition of importance to all expressions of life.

He also really enjoyed plants and gardening. When I was little, we had a big vegetable garden, a physical place for growing food for the family. As Dad got older and more frail, planting vegetables became more sporadic. But he always had plants.

The vegetable garden in Michigan, when I was little, was also an opportunity for hard work—a value Dad absolutely believed in. I don't know how big it really was, but it seemed huge to me. My older brothers and my older sister and I used to do work in it, commensurate with our ages. We had to plant it, weed it, and keep it free from harmful insects. I remember corn and potatoes, beans and tomatoes, all sorts of vegetables.

The other type of garden Dad always had was of plants he just enjoyed. The window sills of his and Mom's bedroom in Michigan were filled with pots of cactus plants. He also grew many varieties of cacti on our screened-in front porch there. My brothers would often catch turtles in the creek that was close by. They would bring them home and the turtles would live on the porch among the cactus pots for a while. I remember watching how the turtles walked and how they hid in their shells. Dad would tell me that they were unchanged from the days of the dinosaurs and then we'd talk about dinosaurs. After a while, the turtles would be returned to the creek where they really lived.

Dad loved plants that reminded him of people. There is a succulent with the popular name "Live Forever." It's a small squatty plant with fat little leaves that you can leave a thumbprint in if you press it hard. Or you can peel a leaf and make "frog's tongues"—a moist little pad that a child can stick bugs to, and imagine it's like a frog's tongue. Dad brought a few clippings of this plant from his parents' home in Wisconsin to our home in Eloise, the County Hospital where Dad worked as a psychiatrist. Dad had Bert and Lance plant the clippings along the sides of "I Building" the huge building we lived in. They grew and spread. Eventually there were hundreds of those plants beginning to form a frame around the building. They had all originated from the clippings from Grandmother's garden.

When we moved to Arizona for Dad's health, some of the cacti moved with us. Dad didn't work that whole first summer. He was recuperating from a debilitating illness which was probably caused by an extreme allergic reaction to an anti-tetanus shot he'd needed after he'd fallen off his bike. Even though we were going to stay in that house for just the summer, Dad still planted cacti in the yard.

As an adult, my brother Bert went to Aurum, Nevada, where Dad was born. The old silver-mining town has long been abandoned but Bert found it and brought home a couple leaves from a prickly pear cactus. We planted those leaves and eventually they grew into a gigantic plant. Daddy loved it. After his death, I planted several cuttings from it where we'd scattered his ashes. Although the cactus grows naturally nearby, for some reason it doesn't flourish where his ashes are.

Dad also had cacti planted in front of the little house where his students met. He used to ask them, "How can you have 10 items in five rows of four each? You saw the answer when you came in the house, but you didn't know you'd seen it." He wouldn't tell them the answer—he wanted them to notice the cacti planted in the shape of a star at the front door. One cactus was placed at each of the intersections of the lines that make a five-pointed star—five lines each with four intersections—five rows of four each. He wouldn't tell them because he wanted them to observe carefully and to think broadly.

My brother Bert, who loves nature in the same way Dad did, now has one of Dad's favorite books. It's called *Fantastic Trees* by Edwin Menninger, brother of Karl Menninger of the renowned Menninger Clinic. Some of the chapter titles are wonderful: "Trees with Peculiar Parts and Trees that are Peculiar All Over" and "Trees that Flap their Leaves" are just two. Dad was fascinated with this book and showed it to a lot of people. Consequently, and because people knew he especially liked trees, people from all over the world sent him pictures of trees and little articles about trees. He treasured those pictures and articles. During his life in Arizona, he often sent people to the Botanical Gardens with specific instructions to find the Boojum Tree. He would give the hint that the tree looked like no other. It actually looks like an upside-down carrot and is fascinating.

Bert told me that when he was about four years old some of the other physicians on staff had told Dad he couldn't climb an enormous tree. Bert watched as Dad climbed to the top. He says he then called to Dad, "I want to throw you a ball. See if you can catch it." Dad replied, "Toss me an apple." Bert did, Dad caught the apple and ate it. This became one of Bert's most vivid childhood memories. Even though his father walked with a cane and had to rubber-band his feet to his bicycle pedals, he could still climb a tree and catch an apple that his son threw to him. As difficult as it must have been, Dad accepted the challenge and then made it even better.

Climbing trees gives most mothers trepidation. Nevertheless, Dad told Mama that it was a good thing for us to climb trees. Children learn lessons that way; they learn to stretch their abilities and learn their limitations. They are connected to nature and the worst that will happen is that they will fall out of the tree as hundreds of thousands of children have done since the beginning of time. Any risk is far outweighed by the adventure. I don't remember Dad ever talking to me about climbing trees, but somehow I learned the wonder of it. I remember climbing up in a tree so high that sometimes I was afraid to come down and I remember wondering, when I was in a tree, if I was quiet enough, how long would it take the birds to feel safe enough to land next to me?

When my own children were small, we had picnics, actually sitting on a very fat branch of a friendly tree near our home. We'd sit and eat our lunch and talk about the world. The idea to do this must have sprung from some un-remembered message from Daddy that tree-climbing has many benefits.

Dad liked to point out how trees adapt to virtually every place and climate on the globe. They nurture and support much of the rest of the world's life. He wanted us all—patients, students, friends, and family—to see, to understand on a deep level that different plants required different things. What worked for one might not work for another. People are a part of nature, different from, yet no different from all the other plants, animals, and living things of the earth. Over and over, he wanted us all to learn that. And this is how he treated everyone, including his patients—with total respect for their uniqueness.

On Cypress Street, Dad planted a bay tree in the back yard and gave everybody leaves for cooking. We didn't have as many cacti as before, but we had two great big pecan trees. We children picked up the pecans, shelled them, ate some, Mom baked with them, and we gave away the rest. There was also a date palm that Daddy truly liked. We only had the female tree, so when we first moved there, Lance would climb up on a tall ladder to fertilize the blossoms. As years went by, Allan took over that job.

At the last house he lived in, Dad had many plants. I think one of the reasons Mom and Dad bought the house is the huge Palo Verde tree in the yard. This desert-loving tree is unusual in that it has greenish bark and very skinny leaves. The one in the yard was larger than others that have officially claimed the record, perhaps because it's sheltered from the desert winds. It is also home to several bird feeders.

There is also a pomegranate tree, a wonderful grapefruit tree that has had orange-bearing limbs spliced onto it and many night-blooming cereus plants. Dad took such joy in those beautiful blossoms. When he was too frail to be wheeled out into the yard, he took equal delight in seeing the cut flowers brought him. During his life and after his death, there were many trees planted in his honor in so many parts of the world—throughout the United States with special gardens in New York, Israel and Japan, France, Germany, and many other places.

One of Dad's favorite assignments for students and patients was to walk up Squaw Peak, a little mountain by our home. The trail is rather steep, but almost anyone can complete the hike. Dad would often tell them they were to climb the mountain and watch the sunrise, or the sunset. This is another example of his quiet spirituality and of the great respect with which he saw nature. If anyone climbs any difficult trail and watches a sunrise or a sunset, changes happen. The beauty, magnificence, and wonder of the world are naturally transforming. Additionally, when people see nature after an arduous hike, the significance and insignificance of mankind, the importance and unimportance of our problems changes.

Squaw Peak was so important to Dad that we scattered his ashes there over an area that can be seen from the house. While the family and Jeffrey Zeig were climbing slowly up the trail with my mother, my brother Robert went to the top with the canister of ashes and held them high in the air. Hundreds and hundreds of people had hiked that trail because of Daddy. He'd been in a wheelchair the whole time he'd lived near it and even though some of his students had pushed and carried him in his wheelchair most of the way up, he'd never reached the summit. Now he had.

Robert brought the ashes back down to the spot we'd selected and I scattered them. With each handful, I named either Mama or one of his children. The only other person I named was my sister Roxie's oldest daughter Laurel, who was just a baby then. She had come to Phoenix with her mother when Dad was in the hospital, and she kept all our spirits up. She also symbolized new and ongoing life. I think our simple ceremony for Dad's ashes further symbolized the modest and deep spirituality he embodied and how he passed it on to us all by the way he lived, without using words.

Dad focused his attention on the rich tapestry of life. I think it's fair to say part of his spirituality was his way of observing, learning, celebrating, and interacting with life itself. He never said these things but it is what I have come to understand. Each of us children may have a different view, and I have no doubt that each different view and understanding would greatly please him. I see him appreciating life as a weaving together of everything. Like any weaving, it's imperfect, sometimes by accident, and sometimes in the same way a Navajo rug weaver deliberately makes an error so as not to offend the gods. He loved that metaphor about Navajo rugs and I love it too. That's what I think Dad's spirituality really was—being in tune with, in harmony with all the goodness that is around, recognizing that it's not perfect and that you are not perfect, but emphasizing the overall goodness and beauty around all of us all the time.

Dad always had a lot of interest in the Native American Indian traditions of the Southwest. This wasn't just because we lived in Phoenix. His honeymoon with my mother was a driving trip through the Southwest. When they got married in 1936, there were even larger areas of the Southwest with little population. On their honeymoon, they went to many of the trading posts—sometimes the only place where people gathered. This was the beginning of Mom's collection of Indian jewelry. She has a genuine medicine bag that she bought on that trip. Neither Dad nor Mom was just interested in buying items; they were far more interested in the people and in learning about the circumstances that made them who they were. All their life together, they liked to go to unusual places and meet the people who lived there, not just those who worked there, but the people who were part of life in that area.

Their enjoyment of jewelry crafted by Native Americans lasted throughout their married life. Once just a few years before Dad's death, when I was visiting, I saw a beautiful squash blossom necklace set with red coral on one side and turquoise on the other. It was expensive and cost far more money than I had with me so I begged the man to hold it. I went home, described it to Dad and he told me to go back and purchase it.

Later that evening he called Mom into the front room and said he was going to give her birthday present early. She sat down in front of his wheelchair and closed her eyes. Dad told her she couldn't touch the birthday present; she could only look at it. He put the necklace on her with the coral side foremost and told her to open her eyes. After she'd seen the lovely red coral necklace, he told her to close her eyes again. He turned the necklace over, announced, "Now I am giving you an early Mother's Day present," and told her to open her eyes to see the blue turquoise necklace. He really enjoyed that kind of loving teasing.

Dad integrated all that he learned in his experiences with life into other parts of his life. Every event was an opportunity to learn. One well-known story about his adolescence is useful in understanding how he used even adversity to help himself and others. As a boy of 17, he was stricken with infantile paralysis and was almost completely paralyzed. Throughout his life, he gave a great deal of credit for his recovery to a nurse who used the Sister Kenny method of treatment: placing scalding hot blankets on the afflicted areas and allowing the blankets to cool. This was repeated over and over before she moved his arms and legs in a pattern of exercises. I don't know what the medical rationale was—probably increasing the circulation. Dad felt it not only saved his life; the treatment saved what muscles were saved.

As he recovered, he knew he had to learn how to walk and be independent. He would have done literally anything for that, I think, and he did. The story has been told many times how he watched his youngest sister, who was just learning to walk and analyzed the countless movements people make to walk without conscious thought or even remembering how to do it.

What's not so well known is that Dad also decided he needed to strengthen his chest and arm muscles. He would go out into the yard of his home in his wheelchair. Then he would fall out of his wheelchair and literally crawl over the ground for as long as he could. After he had gone as far as he could, he had to turn around and crawl back to his wheelchair. I am still in awe of that kind of determination.

During his recovery, Dad and a friend decided to take a canoe trip during the summer, going from a series of lakes by Madison, Wisconsin to the Milwaukee River to the Missouri, then to the junction of the Mississippi River at St. Louis and returning to his starting point by paddling back against the current. He took only five dollars, a change of clothes, and some books to study for his next year of college. As he prepared to leave, his friend backed out and Dad decided not to tell his parents because he was afraid they wouldn't let him go alone. I am sure they wouldn't have.

He could walk only with difficulty and his canoe had to be carried for him when he first started. At the beginning of the trip, when he had to portage the canoe, he would sometimes just sit there and wait for a passerby to ask him what he was doing. He would tell them he was on a canoe trip to strengthen himself and they would ask if he needed help with his canoe. He said he learned that people enjoyed helping more if they volunteered the help rather than being asked for it. Sometimes, if no one came upon him within a short time, he would crawl over the land, dragging the canoe behind him. When he got to the water, he would push the canoe in until it floated and then flop himself into it. Again, I am in such awe of his determination! What a lesson for everyone!

He earned his keep, so to speak, by making friends with people along the way who wondered what this young man was doing paddling all alone in a canoe. Daddy had very dark eyes and hair and his dark skin became very tanned. He was often mistaken for a Native American Indian. He and the acquaintances would strike up a conversation and they would all tell their stories. Sometimes Dad would offer to work, or to clean fish or untangle fishing lines. Sometimes he would be paid a small amount and sometimes not.

Sometimes he would be invited to eat with them or they would give him some of their fish. He always refused the "good" fish and accepted only those kinds that were not marketable. He knew fishermen earned their living selling the better quality fish.

The last page of his diary says, "Paddled up to boathouse. The end of a 1,200 mile canoe trip—1,000 miles paddled—200 miles on steamers—worked my way—studied hard—had a good time—improved about 500% physically.... I'm proud of my trip. 'Something attempted, something done has earned a night's repose.' My each night's repose was earned."

He still had his original $5.00 and could walk, carrying his canoe on his shoulders.

This pilgrimage was a turning point in his life. It was so incredibly difficult—there were times when he was in enormous pain from cramps in his muscles, the weather was sometimes miserable—but he gained so much. Not only did he change himself physically and emotionally and learn to the depths of his being that people can do whatever they really want to do, but he nurtured his reverence for the human spirit, and for the intertwined nature of the earth and its creatures. He wrote in his diary, "Just now a beautiful delicate Mayfly alighted on my hand to molt—the prettiest little creature I ever saw—the work of God."

I've been told that a pilgrimage that involves overcoming a sickness or a physical challenge is at the heart of life experiences of shamans and healers in other cultures. I don't know if Dad knew about that at the time he undertook his journey. But I do know that trip was a fundamental and large step toward him becoming a great healer and a great human being.

I don't remember being told the story of his canoe trip until I was a teenager and asked about it. Dad didn't talk much about things like that without specific questions. I think he also knew what we all learn when we have our own families—that children are often not greatly interested in the fact that their parents had a life before they were born. When he did answer my questions, I do remember being fascinated at the drive that made him set out all alone to do something so different and so very hard.

On another level, I think the essence of the story was communicated to us in some way. Many of my brothers and sisters, as well as some of the grandchildren have made journeys that were unusual much as the canoe trip was unusual. We undertook our own personal "rites of passage" without having the story held up as an example. Bert went on a canoe trip on his honeymoon with his wife, Lillian. Roxie lived in Mexico and perfected her Spanish while she traveled around. I sold all my possessions and immigrated to Australia. When Allan was 17, he bicycled from Arkansas to Phoenix in just over two weeks. His daughter Nicole backpacked around the world. It's almost as though the journey Dad took was passed on to some of us without him saying many words about it.

When I immigrated to Australia, I had finished college and was working as a teacher. I thought about what else I could do without speaking another language. I wrote the Department of Education in Australia and they responded that they would interview me for a job. I landed in Sydney on a Sunday morning, after a wonderful trip throughout the South Pacific, and went to the YWCA because I knew it would be open and I could afford it. I had no Australian money; everything was closed so I could neither eat nor change money. I lay on my bed and cried for about an hour. Then I sat up and thought, "If I can live through this, I can do anything." The next morning, I called the Department of Education. They were quite surprised to hear from me, but they hired me.

When I left the States, my father talked at great length about the wonderful adventures I would have, how much I would learn, and how glad I would be that I had experienced it. To this day, I still do things because I will be glad I experienced them. That line, that piece of information, fit exactly into the way my mind works and I know Dad knew that.

It was an amazing experience being the daughter of Milton Erickson. I am still becoming aware of how fortunate I was and of things I learned without knowing I learned them. I was only about three years old when I first met the legendary anthropologist Gregory Bateson. He and his wife, Margaret Mead (of equal legend), were interested in Dad's and Mom's perspective on hypnosis, and they all developed a friendship over the years. When I first saw Bateson, I asked him where he was from. He had just returned from a trip to Australia and said he was from Australia. I then announced that when I grew up I was going to Australia.

Bateson was a very tall man and I asked him to put me on his shoulders and walk around with me. He very politely agreed and asked, "Why do you like to be up there?"

"Because everything looks different," I replied.

When he had put me down, I asked him to bend over and look through his legs. He joined me doing that and we discussed how different the world looked from different angles. Bateson and I did this many times.

What a wonderful man Gregory Bateson was, to be so kind, so respectful, and to take such time and care to expand a little girl's horizons. No one will ever know for sure if that interaction influenced my adult behavior, if it had any part in my choice to immigrate to Australia. But I think that, like my father, Bateson was able to reach inside another person and help that person become a richer human being.

Dad brought the world into our home in many different ways. Traveling was much more difficult then, so some of his wanderlust was satisfied by the many foreign visitors we welcomed into our home. Dad was interested in anthropological studies his whole life and that was something he would frequently initiate conversations about.

We had a lot of books in the house. In the dining room, one book case held the *Encyclopedia Britannica*; Daddy had written the article on hypnosis for it. Next to that was *Collier's Children's Encyclopedia*.

I know Allan and I read through all the volumes. We didn't "have" to read them; there was no consequence if we didn't. There was just this air of, "Why wouldn't you read such interesting things!" We didn't read every word, but once you get started on something like this, there is an enormous amount to interest anybody.

In Dad's office, one book case held his special books. There were many old books on hypnosis there. Even then he was regarded as the world's greatest authority on hypnosis. For him, hypnosis was a state of heightened awareness with increased suggestibility, an altered state allowing communication with the unconscious. Heightened awareness is probably the most important part of a trance state, because the subject is then able to focus more effectively on his or her self and goal. I'm sure some who read this will quarrel with my definition of how Dad saw hypnosis, but that's how he defined it to me and how I think he understood it.

One of Dad's mantras in teaching and in life was, "Observe, observe, observe." From this perspective alone, it is valuable for the hypnotist to be in a trance. The hypnotist has a heightened and enlightened awareness not only of the connection between the hypnotist and the subject, but he or she is able to really observe and have much more awareness of the many subliminal signals, the communicative cues that people constantly give without conscious awareness. Being in a trance state enables anyone to be more observant and more connected. That is why Dad was so often in a trance state of hypnosis when he worked with his patients.

For him, hypnosis extended to both sides of the therapeutic relationship, embracing both the patient and the doctor. Of this, I am absolutely certain. I think he was unique in holding this particular view and was probably one of the very first to think and practice this way. Today, many hypnotists recognize that the operator, the facilitator, the hypnotist needs to be in a trance to facilitate a good trance with a subject—or at least to be deeply connected with the subject.

Dad saw his work as an innovative hypnotist as part of being a

good doctor, which he was first and foremost. He didn'
medically, *per se*, because he was a psychiatrist. But he al
clinical awareness of medical conditions and recognized
people present, both physically and psychologically, are ɪ
complex system. His superior medical acumen and diagɪ
never left him. Jay Haley once called him a "wise old co
doctor," with all that implies and means, and I agree wit

Diagnosis—knowing what was going on with another
for Dad a natural consequence of the enhanced state he aɪ
being in a trance. There are medical diagnoses and psychological diagnoses. But he also appreciated that diagnosis is not always where one
should start. Diagnosis is just a part of the complex of the whole
framework of looking at people. At times, it may be important, but it is
never as relevant as the journey toward good health. It doesn't do any
pragmatic good to know the differences between a sprained ankle, a
broken ankle or just an over-stretched ankle. What is good is to know
how to make the ankle better and stronger. That was Dad's general
overall perspective. Even though he knew that a diagnosis can sometimes help chart the course toward treatment leading to good health,
he was far more interested in the process of helping people reach their
own health, their own personal potential, and ultimate growth.

Enhanced awareness means to observe clearly without your own
"spectacles" getting in the way. Most people see only a part of another
person and even that through their own biases. And most aren't very
observant at all. For example, if a man shaves off his mustache, people
often say, "Gosh, you look different," without knowing what is different
if they even notice anything. Most people concentrate on a large field
of vision and forget to look at details. Dad was a master at noticing
details. Details are, after all, what make up the whole.

He served on the Draft Board during World War II, and the idea of
developing a therapeutic state of enhanced awareness grew even more
important then. I remember him talking about that part of his career
later in his life. He interviewed physically healthy young men, each for

just a few minutes, to assess whether they were good candidates for the military. Perhaps this was one of the actual beginnings of brief therapy.

The young men would come into his office wearing only a towel. This was in the days when cigarette smoking was commonplace. Dad had placed a pack of cigarettes and some matches invitingly on his desk and the interview chair in a way that was awkward for face-to-face conversation. He sat behind the desk as each man entered. Turning the chair to talk more comfortably was regarded as a good sign. Reaching for the cigarettes was not a favorable indication. These two things began his assessment.

Seeing literally thousands of young men truly honed Dad's abilities to make inferences. He once told me that if a man came in with a tattoo that said "Mom" or "Mother," Dad was virtually certain he had a juvenile record. He would say, "What were you arrested for?" and the young man would think, "Wow! How does he know?" not realizing Dad had seen thousands of young men, and the ones with a tattoo saying "Mom" had almost always been in trouble with the law.

He had another story he liked. A fellow came in with his toenails painted bright red. Dad talked to him and talked to him. The man seemed perfectly normal—except in the 1940s, perfectly normal young men did not wear red polish on their toenails. Finally Daddy broke down and asked him directly, "Why are your toenails painted red?" The guy blushed and replied, "I was napping on the couch yesterday with bare feet and my little sister thought it would be funny. She was so tickled with how she'd gotten one over on me, I just left them." This reinforced to my father that he should always have an open mind, ready to change in an instant should new information be received. He kept that very valuable trait his whole life.

Working with the Draft Board also gave Dad a very wide view of what was normal—these men came from every style of home and upbringing and most of them were normal. It also enhanced his admiration of the human spirit. The men came in willing to give their lives for their country. Almost all of them tried to convince the doctor that they were good candidates for that risk.

Dad first became interested in hypnosis as a youngster. He didn't begin serious study until he was in college, deciding he needed more academic learning before he began working with it. He was trained in the traditional way of classic authoritative hypnosis. My sister Roxanna Klein and I once decided to write an article to explain why he moved from that to the more cooperative and indirect induction methods that he used almost exclusively in later years.

The article kept changing as we were writing, and we discovered we were focusing on mistakes he'd made as he learned. There were five of us who worked with him from the time he began his career until his death. Roxie and I were two; the others were my mother, Elizabeth Moore Erickson, my sister-in-law, Lillian Erickson, and Dad's sister, Bertha Erickson Gallun. Collectively, we were part of his entire 60-year career, and we each had long spans of time working with him.

All of us, except Roxie, remembered a particular time when Dad had done something "wrong" and it had affected us significantly. Three of us remembered that event very clearly, decades after the occurrence. In my own event, I had blocked my trance from my memory, although I clearly recalled things right before and after the demonstration. I then made certain to let Dad know in a "casual conversation" that I had "lost" a certain hypnotic ability. He spent quite some time convincing me that I needed to re-learn this ability and then re-teaching me. Each time such a mistake occurred with one of us, we noticed he significantly changed his way of doing hypnosis to avoid that error again.

Roxie reaped the benefit of Dad's perfecting of his skills. The trance she remembers most clearly was surprising, effective, and it clearly pulled together what he'd learned about hypnotic communication.

In his work, in his whole life, Dad recognized that all great story-tellers, therapists, parents and teachers, children, all practitioners of effective human communication use the principles of hypnosis. Part of that is making a good relational connection, listening and suggesting. Obviously there is much more to hypnosis, but the underlying concepts contain these behaviors.

One of Dad's incredible assets was his ability to offer a sincere invitation to other people to make a special connection with him. This presence, this connection is not really psychotherapy but it is the basis of healing. It was Dad accessing his pure unalloyed love for people and his belief in them, setting this love and belief, so to speak, between them. If they took this from him, the connection took place. If they didn't, that was all right too, because the connection was still there. Dad really knew that the true joy is in the offering. There was no "you have to take it, I want you to take it," or even, "I'll notice if you take it." This made it totally safe for the other person to take, to feel, to sample, to touch that pure love and that belief. It was as though he said, "Here it is. I want to give this. If you take it, that's wonderful. But if you don't, that's all right, too, because it's just here, on the table. I found my joy in the giving. Maybe you'll take this next week, next month, next year, or maybe never. But there it is, and I give it freely."

I think part of the "magic" of Daddy's work was that way he opened himself to another person. If the other person subsequently opened himself or herself, then there was even more of the process of connecting. It is within this process that change occurs. He created an atmosphere in which it felt okay, really all right for you to open to him, to change, to give more of yourself and become more of the human being you wanted to be. When that occurs, both participants find joy with each other and with the process. This is a very appealing course of action to continue.

Various people have interpreted this interaction in different ways in their analyses of his work. It's been called "entering the patient's world," "meeting the patient at his level," "using the patient's world as the vehicle or mechanism for change," "utilization," and many more expressions. I think it's more basic. He offered a moment of true human connection and love, laying it on the table with absolutely no restrictions, no strings attached, no prerequisite conditions. The opportunity was simply there. He helped people feel comfortable, confident, and safe on a very deep level.

Certainly I am not discounting other parts of his work. I have no idea of how he created so much of what he did with people. He was simply a genius and could do amazing clinical work with all sorts of people. But that's not all of it.

He had an unsurpassed ability to say words that were so meaning-ful to the individual listener that they were never forgotten, and he did that on a regular basis. I don't know how he did it—I don't think anyone has figured that out. Almost everyone I know who had personal contact with Daddy has told me, at one time or another, "Your father said this to me and it changed my life. One sentence changed my life!" More than two decades after his death, total strangers are still stopping me and telling me, "Your father changed my life. He said, '…'" and then they quote what they remember, sometimes with tears in their eyes.

When something becomes that much a part of you, it has entered on a different level than most words, different than most therapeutic interactions. That's a quality I've never seen in anyone else. Occasionally, of course, any good therapist does it. But Dad did it with such incredi-ble regularity, accuracy, and incisiveness that it qualifies him to be considered a profound healer as well as an excellent psychiatrist.

He would never fully explain what he did. Maybe he didn't know how to put that part of him into words. He would always fully answer any questions I had about hypnosis. He may have felt that was his responsibility. He knew I had learned a great deal about hypnosis just by being with him and so he wanted to be sure I had the intel-lectual underpinnings as well.

But he didn't explain how he could communicate on such a very deep level. I can still feel the power he had in that kind of communi-cation. Once, while he was still walking with a cane, I was visiting and sitting on the arm of the chair by the front door with my toddler David, on my lap. Dad paused during our casual conversation, looked at me intently and said, "Keep David away from the next patient."

I asked why, and he replied impatiently, "Because I said so."

I thought to myself, "Well, I'm David's mother and he is so adorable there is no reason why he should be kept away from anybody in my family's own house." So I asked again, "Why?"

He was standing about 10 feet away from me, supporting himself with his cane. He did not move. I am absolutely certain he did not even shift his weight. He just looked at me. I immediately felt some power hit me and I instinctively clutched my son to my heart and bent over him protectively. "That's why," Dad said.

I was stunned—I still am. This was my father who walked with a cane. He was 10 feet from me and I was right by the front door. Yet, without moving, he made me feel such fear that I instantly shielded my child from some sensed threat. "How did you do that?" I asked in astonishment. He just stood there. I asked again, "Daddy, how did you do that?" He replied, "If you have to ask, I can't explain it." Clearly he knew what I was talking about because he didn't say, "Do what?"

Today my son is a grown man. I think of that particular event at least every six months. I am still trying to figure out what Daddy did. I have asked countless people whose insights and abilities I respect and never received an answer that fits. My father made me feel deep fear for my child, apparently without doing anything I could recognize consciously.

Clearly, he wanted to convey a message. "This patient is dangerous. Keep your child away from him." He wasn't going to debate and he wasn't going to give details about a patient. As a sidelight, I looked at the patient when he arrived, with my son safely in another room. I saw nothing that made me feel the least bit uncomfortable.

Dad was able to understand and convey enormous amounts of information on many different levels. Gregory Bateson once called him "the Mozart of human communication." He truly was an orchestra of communicative information. From teen-age years on, I would ask him about things I didn't understand, saving up questions about things that somehow didn't seem quite right. Sometimes he would give direct answers and sometimes he would answer metaphorically to let me create my own answers, and sometimes he would give information that I didn't particularly believe. I would always put that information in the back of my mind and wait to see.

Once, I was sitting on the bed where he was resting, talking to him. My oldest son was still a baby and my girlfriend had a son exactly that same age. I told him that my friend and I, in the way of new mothers, were looking at our sons and saying, "Isn't it amazing how much we love them?" I went on to say, "I would fling myself in front of a train if I knew it would give him a happy, a good life." My girlfriend replied, "I think I would too," and we continued talking. Something about that had puzzled me but I didn't know what, so I asked Dad what he thought. He replied instantly, "If she has to think, she won't," and he said that I'd known that without knowing how I had known.

This expanded my whole way of thinking about people on many levels. There are situations where, if you have to think about doing something, you won't do it, which, of course, is both good and bad. Dad didn't bother to explain; he just offered the idea. It was then up to me to make sense of it or not, to believe it or not. He often taught like this—the offering alone.

My mother doesn't think like him. My second son had colic as a baby and cried a great deal. When he began teething he cried even more. I used to stick my finger in gin and rub his gums. The alcohol numbed the pain in his gums and stopped the colic as well. I was a bit uncomfortable about giving my baby even a hint of alcohol and asked Dad about it. "He's probably getting five or six drops of gin a night," I said.

Dad told me that when he was a medical intern, there were no antibiotics. If babies caught pneumonia, they usually died. The most effective treatment was to give them enough alcohol so that they would fall into a deep sleep. I was very interested and imagined giving a baby enough alcohol to make it pass out. Then we went on to talk about other things.

My mother stopped him. "Milton, you didn't answer her question." Daddy looked at me questioningly and then responded, he had. And he had. He provided information, in an interesting way, but I had to draw my own conclusions.

He taught so much and in so many different ways. When he was a young man, there was a boiler factory close to where he was living. It worked around the clock and created a tremendous amount of noise. Dad wanted to continue to teach himself that extraneous circumstances really shouldn't matter. Nothing should interfere if you are determined to accomplish something. This mind-set was certainly illustrated by his canoe trip and the way he crawled across the fields to strengthen his upper body muscles.

He asked the owner of the boiler factory if he could sleep there. Then, he taught himself to sleep in the midst of the clanging and banging of the boiler factory. He had also gained a wonderful story to tell each of us kids if any of us were foolish enough to complain the house was too noisy to fall asleep in! When I married an Air Force pilot and we lived right next to the runway, I remember thinking, "Hey, Daddy, if you can sleep through the noise of a boiler factory, I can sure sleep through the noise of jet planes taking off." My children benefited as well, because the roar of the planes was a natural background to a good night's sleep.

He was able to incorporate a huge amount of the larger situation in his thinking and would then be able to come up with answers almost magical in their simplicity and truth. My husband and I had a pet mouse and one night I had a bizarre and terrible dream about Mouse. The nightmare was so vivid that I woke my husband and we got out of bed to check on her. To my surprise, we found her very sick, lying on her side in her cage, just panting. My husband, who had grown up on a farm, instantly recognized colic. "She's eaten too much," he said, "like a horse that eats too many oats." We spent the next few hours making Mouse walk around until she felt better—the same as he'd done with his horses when they'd had a bellyache.

Later I asked Dad how I "knew" Mouse was in danger, why I had wakened and felt compelled to check on her. Dad asked only a couple of questions. We'd fed Mouse pancakes the night before—her favorite food, and yes, she usually spent the night running in her wheel. The small squeak of her wheel turning as she ran was part of my normal sleep, he said. The absence of that sound was enough to wake me and tell me she was in trouble. I also knew she'd overeaten on pancakes and syrup which isn't a good thing for a little mouse.

Dad did the same in his clinical work: The largest landscape gave ideas and thoughts that could be connected with something else. That, in turn, gave a different perspective to other things. Then people could discover all or part of the picture and utilize their own resources to figure out better ways for themselves. He drew healing and understanding from within a person, by offering a broader perspective, by adding information and allowing them to figure out and change themselves, to heal themselves. He used the person's own unconscious abilities.

He spent a lot of time learning about the power of the unconscious mind. As a college student, he wrote editorials for the university news-paper. He gave himself the task of waking during the night, writing the editorial, returning to sleep, and having amnesia about the entire event. He would then turn the editorial in without reading it. When he saw it in print, he would try to remember writing it. He would use his conscious mind to discover what was familiar to his unconscious mind. He did this exercise for a long time.

Dad always took full advantage of circumstances. In Colorado, he worked at a prison and did some sort of study with prisoners as a part of his job assignment. He also placed a detailed overview about the prisoners on the warden's desk each Monday morning. Naturally, the warden came to rely on that.

When the project was completed, he did not compile his usual report and made himself available when the warden came out of his office. "Erickson," said the warden, "where is my report?"

Dad had been waiting with his reply. "I didn't do it." The warden demanded an explanation. The situation was now set up so Daddy could say, "I'm not paid to do that. My job was the research study and that's completed." That is how he got a job in the prison, which was a great opportunity to learn more about people.

He used the same strategy years later when the family housekeeper's son began working as a restaurant dishwasher. Dad told the young man, "Ask the cook what you can do to help. Stay late, without pay, just to help him." The cook, of course, became interested in helping the young man who was so interested and obliging. Eventually, the young man was so practiced and experienced a cook that he was able to create a career.

Dad used different strategies, but the theme was always that people grew from within and from their own abilities. In the mid-1960s, when I was living in Phoenix, my friend Carolyn's four-year-old daughter had significant problems. The size and shape of Patti's head were clearly not normal and, although she could understand, she made no verbalizations. She made no sounds at all except crying or laughing noises. A neurologist performed many tests and Carolyn returned from her last appointment, sobbing hysterically. The neurologist had said that Patti would be severely retarded her whole life, never learn to speak or live independently. He recommended institutionalization.

Carolyn had one session with my father that lasted about two hours. When she came out of his office, she was quiet and did not speak as I drove her home. I never asked what had happened and she never told me. We continued our neighborly friendship until I moved and we lost track of each other.

When Dad died in 1980, Carolyn called me in Phoenix. She said, "I want to tell you what happened during my session with your father and tell you about Patti today. Your father listened as I cried and cried about Patti's situation. He kept asking more and more questions and wanted to know exactly what the other doctor said. I just cried harder as I told him.

"Then your father looked at me, right in my eyes and said, very very strongly, 'Carolyn, nobody knows the future!' When he said that, it was like a big weight lifted off me. At that moment, I knew Patti could have a life, and I didn't have to put her in an institution.

"Now she is in her 20s. She still can't speak. She raises prize-winning rabbits. I help her with the breeding charts and manage the money she earns. She does everything else and the rabbits don't care that she can't talk.

"There are a lot of people who raise rabbits. We go to State Fairs and shows all over the country. Patti has a whole wall of trophies and has a whole lot of respect from the other breeders. She raises really fine rabbits.

"This is all due to your father. I wanted to tell you and I wanted to thank you for taking me to see him. He changed Patti's life."

The connection Dad made with Patti's mother changed both their lives. No one does know the future and, unspoken in that communication, was the idea that we impact our own futures. Carolyn and Patti could create their own lives, working toward the future. I don't know why they chose rabbits rather than cats or chickens or pigeons. I see the many levels of Daddy in their choice, though. Carolyn was right; the rabbits don't care that Patti can't talk. Rabbits don't make many sounds either.

Carolyn didn't call me to discuss how all this came about. She called to let me know how much healing had occurred, how deeply changed she and her daughter were because of Dad's short involvement.

My mother was a true partner with my father. He was able to expand his own thinking in ways that, without her, he couldn't have imagined. Mom thinks differently than Dad did and Dad learned from her. Mom saw her major jobs as wife and mother and as support for Dad in his professional activities, and she did them all superlatively. Evidence of Mom's importance to Dad's professional life is found in the large number of his students who dedicated books to her. When you worked with Dad, you understood that Mom was a central feature of his and the family's life.

The story of their courtship always amazed me. The middle child of an attorney father and a mother who had worked as a teacher of the deaf, Mom had gone to a meeting at Wayne State University while she was still an undergraduate psychology student. Dad had seen her walking up the sidewalk before she entered the building and remarked to a friend, "That's who I'm going to marry." Dad told me later he knew she was the one for him because of her smile. He asked his friend to introduce him and the three sat together at lunch.

Over 30 years later, I was teaching school in Addis Ababa, Ethiopia and I mentioned to another teacher that I had lived in a mental hospital in Michigan. My friend said her uncle had been a psychologist at Eloise Hospital in Michigan. As we talked, it was clear her uncle had worked there while our family was there. I immediately wrote Mom and Dad to ask if they remembered Luther Babcock, and "wasn't it a small world!"

Mom wrote back, "Small world, indeed! He was the only mutual acquaintance your father and I had and he introduced us."

Dad had a small grant for a research project and hired my mother. She spent the summer living at Eloise working on the project. Dad was divorced from his first wife and had custody of his three small children. He had many little social events at his apartment in "I" Building and Mom, who lived in "D" Building, was always invited. They gradually began dating and although they had decided to marry, they agreed it was important for Mom to finish college. They saw each other about once a month for the next year and eloped on her graduation day.

Love certainly triumphed in this marriage. Mom became an instant mother to two boys, seven and five years old, and a little girl who was not yet three. Mom had literally never cooked a meal! She had nothing with her except the clothes on her back, so she wore her college graduation dress for three days until she went back to her house and took the things she'd sorted out to take with her to her new home.

All this still seems unbelievable to me. Dad was divorced, almost

15 years older, and had sole custody of three small children. On paper, this sure doesn't look like a marriage that would last very happily for over 40 years!

Daddy told me that on their very first date, the restaurant had a little orange-colored cream pitcher on the table. They decided that would be a nice souvenir. So Mom picked it up, Dad paid for it, and it now sits on my mantle.

Mom was primary caregiver, the parent most involved time-wise certainly, as I grew up. Dad always worked very long hours. When I hear my own clients complaining about how their parents didn't attend each game they played in, I recognize that is not the issue. It is really what you felt from your parents, if you felt they cared and were involved. For example, I don't think my dad attended my eighth grade or even my high school graduation, and certainly not my college graduation.

I worked for the curator of the Heard Museum when I was in high school, on a 36-week show on the educational television channel. I was the young girl who asked questions ordinary people were interested in. Daddy never saw a single show. Mom saw them all even though we didn't have a television set. She would go to a neighbor's house or even to the television studio. I could remember this as though I had been neglected, but I never felt Dad was not interested in the shows or in my accomplishment being on them. Dad was always intensely interested in me and, like my children, I heard praise from him. I heard his interest as praise, satisfaction, or whatever else I wanted to hear from him. Additionally, Mom made him a real part of our daily life by including him in the conversation—"Let's remember to tell Dad" and "What do you suppose Dad would say?" kind of things. This was a contribution to our family that can't be overestimated.

Dad grew up on a farm and believed in the adage "waste not, want not." He was also more far-seeing in his vision than anyone knew. When I was a child, Mom saved and froze the bones from our dinner meat. When she accumulated a large amount, she put them in a huge professional-type pressure cooker and cooked them for hours. The bones would turn chalky and she then ground them up in a food grinder and mixed them with the broth. The horrible result was euphemistically called "bone gravy." It looked like cement, had the texture of cement, felt like cement in your mouth and in your stomach, and gritted your teeth like cement. Mom made bone gravy for us children on a regular basis in Michigan.

Dad insisted we eat a helping every day, which was probably about two-thirds of a cup. Mom tried everything to make this really awful concoction palatable. She heated it, mixed it with vegetables, with oatmeal, with everything she could think of. She even tried freezing it and making bone gravy Popsicles, evidently with the desperate thought that if it was frozen it might freeze our taste buds. The least worst way to consume this stuff is warmed slightly and on a slice of bread.

The younger children didn't get bone gravy because when we moved to Arizona, Mom packed up the house alone. I am sure she disposed of the gigantic pressure cooker at the first opportunity. But, all the older children have very good teeth and nice dense bones. Who knows if Dad really knew what he was doing when he made us eat all that calcium and mineral-rich gravy. I would like to think he did.

Mom also was a mellowing influence on Dad, I think. People who knew Daddy when he was older weren't able to really appreciate how strong and dynamic he actually was. Once in my early 30s, he was reading the newspaper when I said to him, "Daddy, if you're such a hot-shot psychiatrist, how come you don't give me a diet that will make me lose weight?" He lowered the newspaper very slowly, fixed on my eyes with his, and replied, "Do you REALLY want a diet that will make you lose weight?"

I said, "No, Daddy."

He said, "All right, then," and raised the newspaper back up. I felt for the first time what so many patients felt—he was really fierce. I asked him later why he had answered like that and he said he knew I wasn't serious. But when I was, he always helped me.

Sometimes he helped me the same way he helped his patients and students. I was quite fearful of the dentist[1], even for a check-up although I had good teeth, thanks to the bone gravy. When my children became old enough to be influenced, I wanted to conquer that fear.

1. This is also discussed in Short, Erickson & Klein (2005).

I spent several days asking Dad over and over again to help me. He kept telling me things like the children's father wasn't afraid of dentist and maybe they would take after him. He wondered why I'd decided to change. My answer was always the same—I didn't want my children to learn this fear from me.

Finally he told me, "All right, I will teach you. In just one day, you'll never be afraid of the dentist again." I could hardly wait. "I will call the dentist's office," he continued, "and get permission for you to sit there all day wearing a homemade sign that says, 'I faint at the dentist's office.' If you faint, I will instruct the receptionist to tell the other patients to leave you alone. When you come back to consciousness, get up and sit back down with your sign around your neck. At the end of the day, you will no longer be afraid of the dentist."

I was horrified. "I won't do it."

He responded, "All right."

I pleaded with him. "Daddy, I want you to help me learn not to be afraid of the dentist for my children's sake."

He looked directly at me and said firmly, "I have given you a way to help your children and you turned it down." Then he turned his back and walked away.

On a superficial level, it looks as though he was not helping me. But if you examine it more closely, he was quite masterful. First, he got a serious commitment from me by delaying his answer. He made certain my motives—setting a good example for my children—were strong. He absolutely knew I wouldn't do what he suggested. So there I was: I could do something I wouldn't do—wearing a sign—or I could be stuck with something I really didn't want—being a poor role model for my children. Or there was a third option—fix the problem myself.

Later, I asked him why he had done what he did. He offered,

"You're not my patient. You don't need psychotherapy. And I knew you would figure out a way."

Years later, my family was camping without an outfitter. We had hiked to the bottom of the Grand Canyon, and my son, who was then about 10, ripped the toenail right off his big toe. He was in agony. We were leaving the next morning and I said, "David, you must walk out. I will not hire a helicopter for a ripped-off toenail and you're too big to carry. You must get rid of your pain so you can hike out."

That entire evening, he sat alone, away from the campfire. Several times throughout the evening, he came over to me and asked, "What am I supposed to do?"

Each time I replied, "You must get rid of your pain until we are at the top of the Canyon. I will not hire a helicopter for a toenail and you're too big to carry."

He would continue. "What am I supposed to do?"

My reply was steady. "Get rid of the pain."

He would ask, "How am I supposed to do that?" and I would respond, "I don't know, but you must." The "you must" was double layered—he must get rid of the pain and I clearly was confident that he knew how to do it. The next morning he hiked along quite cheerfully, even carrying his own pack, although we offered to carry it. It's 14 miles out of the Canyon, not an easy hike with or without a hurt foot. When we finally got to the top, he began complaining about his toe, about how badly it hurt. He complained and moaned throughout that night, but he had accomplished his task and was sort of "entitled" to the pain.

When I reported this to Daddy, he said, "Do you want to know how you could have done it better? You should have taken him to the edge of the canyon, looked at him and said, 'Now we're at the top. Don't you want to leave the pain in the bottom of the Canyon where it really belongs?'" That would have been better—and would have saved David from pain that night.

This is healing: It doesn't matter how you get well. It is the end result that is important. Somehow, you must do this and I don't know how you will, and you don't have to know how you'll do it, but you know you will. This is really what healing is, even physically. We don't know exactly how broken bones knit, how infections are vanquished. We know the process. We can follow and track and understand what is happening. But we still don't know exactly how we do it.

Dad understood that this trust—this faith that the other person knows how, perhaps without even knowing that he or she knows—was part of the communicational structure for activating a person's own inner healing processes.

In July 1961, Dad held a seminar for professional health-care workers in San Diego and gave an example of how he had worked with a cancer patient who had great pain. He had asked me to meet his patient and to go into a trance for her. This is what he told the audience:

I have a 23-year-old daughter who is a school teacher. She is also a good hypnotic subject. She teaches English. She doesn't know very much about anatomy or physiology at all except by virtue of her own life experiences. I took her out to see a cancer patient last night. The patient was troubled with nausea and vomiting and had been rather difficult to handle in that regard because she does not have much belief in herself. So I asked my daughter to go into a trance and then I explained to my daughter for the first time: "This lady has cancer. She suffers from nausea and vomiting. I would like to have your advice about what suggestions I should give this lady." Here is a 23-year-old girl who teaches English being asked to be a medical consultant in that sort of a case. And so my daughter, in a very profound trance—because I had her in a trance when I put that question to her—said, "Let me think."

She thought a while and said, "I can answer." I asked her how she could answer and she said, "I made myself sick. First I got nauseous and then I felt all the muscles in my stomach as they started to heave. And then I cut it off. I produced a cut-off right through here and lost that feeling of nausea. I cut off the contractions of the muscles." I asked her where she felt the nausea and she said, "I felt it first right here (pointing to her ears) and down here (pointing to her abdomen) and then I felt it back here (pointing to her throat)." Immediately her mother spoke up and said, "The semi-circular canals are so often involved in nausea and vomiting." So I asked, "What do you do about this feeling there?" (pointing at the ears). "You cut it off." "What do you mean by that?" "You produce an anesthesia. You direct attention elsewhere. You change the way you're thinking."

I use this as an example because it's so awfully important for you to realize that when you ask patients to do things, you have to depend upon them to do it in their own way of doing it. I didn't know what my daughter was going to do. I knew my patient could lie in the bed there and watch my daughter, listen to my daughter and become tremendously impressed. And then that would give her the feeling that she could go ahead and perhaps work out her own way of handling it.

I remember that time very clearly. I recall being in the trance and making the nausea and feeling it in my ears first which was a surprise to me. I changed the experience of nausea in the same way you can change the way you look at a waterfall. You can look one way and see all the water cascading down. Then you can "click" your eyes and change your view, now seeing individual parts of the waterfall falling down in front of you. Most people can easily do this with a waterfall—they can even use water coming out of a faucet. To change the feeling of nausea, you have to change what is happening in your inner ears the same way that you change the way you look at the falling water.

I still remember the lady listening to me and watching her go into such a nice trance at the same time I was talking to her. I think Daddy used me to talk to her because I was different than her doctors. I was no more "an authority" than she was. So she had to listen to me differently than she listened to her doctors. Let's go back to what he said about the case:

The patient was lying curled up on her right side. She'd been fed so much morphine and Demerol® that the drugs were inactive. She'd had deep X-ray therapy for metastases from breast carcinoma, metastases to the hips and throughout her abdomen and lungs. She was lying curled up there and in absolute pain. She'd been referred to me with the idea that hypnosis might help her resolve the pain. Certainly morphine and Demerol® didn't and deep X-ray therapy didn't. When I walked in, she said, "Don't hurt me. Don't hurt me. Don't hurt me. Don't hurt me. Don't hurt me. Don't hurt me." She gave a continuous monotonous recitation. Now and then she'd intersperse, "Don't scare me. Don't scare me. Don't hurt me. Don't hurt me."

To get her attention was very very difficult except I did it in this particular way. "But I am going to hurt you. I really am going to hurt you. I am going to hurt you quite a bit. I will hurt you more than you're hurting right now. And I'm going to scare you too. I'm going to scare you but not too much, but I'm definitely going to scare you."

She paused in her monotonous verbalizations and said, "Please don't hurt me, please don't hurt me." I told her, "But I must hurt you. I must scare you. And the thing we've got to find out is how much I've got to hurt you and how much I have to scare you and in what way I am going to scare you and why I'm going to scare you." I finally had her attention. I pointed out that the hurt would be less. I wanted her to think of turning over in bed and of all the pain that she would have if she turned over and bent because the X-ray showed metastases in the neck. I got her to think that over and she said she didn't even want to remember how to turn over. So I told her, "You either think that or go to sleep." So I asked her to "go to sleep, sound asleep." But in doing so, she was keeping her mind wide awake. Her body was to go to sleep, just her body. Her mind was to stay wide awake.

She finally agreed. Her body was sound asleep. And I told her, "Now there are certain things I want you to do. You don't have to think of turning over in bed. That would really hurt. But I want you to develop a horrible, a horrible, a very horrible and terrible itch on the sole of your right foot and really develop it there and make it horrible, terrible." The patient said, "Why? I've got enough pain." I said, "Yes, and you know what pain is. I want to use your knowledge of pain so you can develop a horrible itch."

I told her she would not know why, but that she ought to do it. She finally agreed to do it. She tried hard, but all she could do was develop a numb feeling on the back of her foot. I let her apologize for it and I let her point out that she couldn't help it. She tried very hard to get an itch, but instead that numb feeling developed and she couldn't help it. Then she told me (again) that she couldn't help it. I was very glad to have her tell me she couldn't help it, because then I could agree with her that she couldn't help it, that she couldn't help that numb feeling spreading and spreading and spreading all over her body. This woman had pain throughout her entire body, terminal cancer pain. And so I taught her to have pain through a numb feeling throughout her body. Within three hours that day, the patient was pain-free. And she has remained pain-free.

You need to say something to a patient so the patient will make the patient's own response. You can have your own ideas. You offer the ideas to the patient in such a way that patients have an opportunity to interpret what you said in their own way. Whatever the patient produces, you accept. With respect to getting that itch on her foot, I knew I'd better talk about something horrible, terrible, disgusting. That patient was oriented entirely to something horrible and disgusting. Why should I talk about pleasant things? Against the background of her experience and her expectations, I'd be doing wrong to talk about pleasant things. Therefore, I could talk about a horrible itch. She wouldn't want to add a horrible itch; she would want to add a numb feeling. I would have the totality of her desires bringing about a numb feeling rather than a horrible itch. That's what I wanted, but I didn't have to tell the patient that. I merely presented ideas in such a way that the patient could buy them, accept them and develop them.

This is such a good example of how Daddy worked with so many people. He listened to them. He was there. He really heard what they were saying. By the time he began discussing the situation, the person's unconscious would be saying, "I already know what your point is." He didn't take behaviors away from people; he expanded and broadened their options. He didn't teach people to get rid of pain, to eliminate it.

Pain is usually a warning and needs to be recognized. It also can be useful. Dad used to say, "You never want a woman not to be able to have a headache. Headaches can be useful. 'Not tonight, honey, I have a headache' is a cliché. What people need is the ability to have a headache or pain whenever it is a symptom or warning or when they want it." He was in the forefront of working with people in this way. This way goes back to his fundamental belief that people will generally do the right things for themselves if they have options.

Sometimes symptoms occur for a particular psychotherapeutic purpose but become habitual. A child may become a thumb-sucker because that provides nighttime comfort. At age 12, that type of comfort has been outgrown but thumb-sucking has become a habit. Many symptoms have nothing to do with the current problem.

Many have tried to break down, to analyze the different ways Dad worked with his patients. There is talk about techniques—joining the reality, reframing, even inserting curiosity. All these are useful and appropriate in good psychotherapy. I see what he did from a different angle. He was interested and curious and joyous in what a person had the ability to do, and he offered what they could do back to them. That is different than "reframing" or "inserting curiosity." It's more a giving patients something about themselves that, in turn, gives them the ability to join Dad in a new world of their own making rather than Dad joining them where they are. I acknowledge that it's possible and even fruitful to ascribe techniques to his approach. However, those partial views shouldn't obscure the broader view that he worked with.

I remember a patient he had when I was in high school. This man was afraid to drive and would faint whenever he tried to navigate a vehicle past a certain distance from his starting point. Dad gave him a letter on letterhead stationery saying that this young man was following "doctor's orders" and if there were questions, to please call for further information. Then the man got in the car with his letter. He drove the "safe" 400 or so feet that he'd previously measured. Then he got out of the car and followed the instructions to lie down on the side of the road. It was all right to lie on the side of the road because he was following "doctor's orders." It would also be all right if he fainted because he was already lying down. It was also all right if he didn't faint. After a very short distance, the man decided to give up this symptom which was so debilitating to building a productive life.

Some might see this as ordeal therapy but that misses the more important view my father had. He accepted people. He let you know it was all right, it was fine, to be who you are, but you can also have a broader range of action and understanding should you choose to accept this expansion of your situation. Dad usually worked with symptoms. He saw them as guiding the course of therapy and knew that if one small part of a complex changed, the rest of the situation must change too.

A lot of Dad's patients and students have told me, "Your father accepted me." That doesn't mean he accepted dysfunctional or inappropriate or even non-productive behaviors. He felt that everyone needed to reach legitimate personal goals in the most wholesome way possible. It is certainly not a legitimate personal goal, productive and wholesome, to faint when you drive. Patients knew Dad accepted the basic essence of the person.

He aimed at an inherent practical wisdom that all people could understand. Although it may seem simple, this wisdom is not. His type of wisdom was like working with a computer. Word processing on a computer is infinitely more powerful than working with a pencil and paper, even though pencil and paper can accomplish your goal. Each level of learning on a computer makes the learner a more effective computer operator; each layer of wisdom, makes the learner a wiser person and human being with all that wisdom entails. Wisdom is always wrapped in goodness. Manipulation misses the context of wisdom—manipulation is the tool of the con artist or the rote performer of repetitive tricks.

Gregory Bateson understood the complexity of this "simple" wisdom. Each person earns his or her own wisdom, one step at a time, one layer at a time. You may not be the world's best healer, but each piece of learning you acquire can make you a better healer and a better and wiser human being. This outlook is implicit in Dad's work.

As he opened himself to others, he created an invitation for students and patients to join or tap into the wisdom of their own lives. Patients and students contributed to the vastness and the depths of Dad's own ever-evolving wisdom. When they joined him tapping into his wisdom, they also tapped their own life wisdom. You can't just watch someone opening into his or her own life wisdom without gaining something in return. The healing, or therapy, becomes a back and forth flow.

Dad was an absolute genius at understanding this and taking what people had to offer and then making it work even better, even more productively, and, in a way, more wisely for them. One of his patients was a woman who had frequent psychotic episodes in which she saw little green naked men following her. This was certainly harmful to her daily life. Daddy opened her eyes to the possibility of putting the little men into his locked closet where they would be very safe, resting and waiting for her. Whenever she wanted, she could come to his office and they could unlock the closet door, let the little men out, talk to them, and then place them back in the closet where they would safely and happily wait for her next visit.

Sometimes when Dad was out of town, this lady would come over to the house, go in the office and lock the door. We could hear her in there, talking away to whom or what, we did not know. When she was done, she would come out having gained sustenance for yet another week of work. Dad let her have what she needed at that time in her life, managed her very serious symptom in a way that did not negatively impact her life or the lives of the people around her. He opened her eyes to a way in which she could have a manageable life.

I admire that way of healing people. They have their lives, their dignity, their autonomy and yet they learn how to make their lives better for themselves. Dad had another very interesting patient named Ben who had been diagnosed as schizophrenic. His only goal was to live independently on his rather modest income and to stay out of a mental hospital.

After some time with Dad, Ben got an apartment close by and he and my mother went to the dog pound to get a dog, subsequently kept at our house. Rescuing the dog from the pound was a very important metaphor for this intervention. Ben named the dog Duke and Duke was his responsibility. Ben then had a reason to manage his life in a way that made psychotic episodes very unwelcome. The psychotic episodes had to be managed because Duke was counting on Ben. Ben had a reason to get up every morning—Duke needed him. Ben couldn't resent this reason—Duke loved him and was a safe and accepting haven for his love. Our family had a dog as well and Dad was adamant that Duke was Ben's dog. In fact, sometimes he was even called "Ben's dog."

Duke was the perfect dog for Ben. He loved Ben dearly but it was as though he hated to show it. That reserve made him even safer for a schizophrenic. He would wait at the back gate for Ben to arrive and as soon as he heard Ben approach, he would walk away and be "surprised" when Ben called his name. We finally had to take a series of pictures (see photo page 194) to convince Ben that Duke waited for him every morning.

My two sisters and I sent Ben a "baked-good-of-the-month" as a Christmas present for several years. We started taking turns sending him a baked item each month and he, of course, would have to write a thank you note. Twelve times a year, he had interactions that, on one level, were unnecessary. But again, he liked us and we liked him so he had to accept and grow from this involvement. In addition, he had tasty food that he could bring over to the house and share with Mom and Dad. This evolved over the years into us giving Ben a list of items we were willing to bake so he then had to write and specify what he wanted that month. He couldn't refuse because his request to us was part of the Christmas gift, and history had already been established. This created an extra interaction each month.

I watched as his signatures to me changed over the years. First notes were signed "Duke and Ben," then "Ben and Duke." Then he added "Affectionately." Finally, he signed his notes, "Love, Ben."

Almost everything Dad did had multiple layers of meaning and import. I once asked him about the baked-good-of-the-month. "All right, I understand what Ben gets out of this—good and nourishing food, he gets to share, to interact, the whole scenario works. But what am I getting out of this?" Dad replied instantly. "Four times a year, you get to thank God you are not like Ben." Without disrespect, he completely answered my question—I got to thank God I was healthy.

This doesn't even address that we all loved Ben and the whole of this expanded interaction was right. The legacy has continued with Ben. To this day, every trip I take, no matter where it is, I send a post-card to Ben and bring back some sort of present for him.

Dad gave Ben a life on his terms—a wholesome and productive life—which is the most respectful way of healing people, of treating them and of interacting with them.

There was another patient, Tom, a talented but literally starving artist. He never finished anything or even wanted to sell it because, typical of some artists, each piece he created was not "good enough." He wanted to continue working on it to make it better. Not only that, if he did sell a piece, he felt as though he'd lost a part of himself, a part of his creative expression.

Tom's regular job was as a carpenter and, in the course of that, he had an accident and cut off three fingers of his right hand. His wife called to tell Dad and his response was immediate. "Tell Tom I will teach him how to shake hands so no one will know he's lost any fingers." That was an incredible piece of communication. He didn't say he'd help Tom adjust. He did say that Tom would be normal again without actually saying those words which Tom wouldn't have heard or believed.

It was such a startling thing to say—who would think of the problems of shaking hands if you're an artist and have just lost three fingers on your dominant hand? That element of surprise caught Tom's attention, just as the "I'm going to hurt you" caught the cancer patient's attention. Then Tom could hear the real message—that he would heal, different than adjusting or even getting better. He would heal.

Sure enough, Daddy actually did teach him how to shake hands so that the other person would not notice Tom had lost fingers on his right hand.

Tom didn't have any money. This was in the '50s when "barter" was accepted like the country doctor accepting eggs for his fee. Dad had Tom work on our backyard with the assistance of my two younger brothers and me. We weeded and seeded and mulched; we worked and slaved at the direction of Tom who worked right along with us. As I've said, Dad believed in the intrinsic value of hard work and this work had a real purpose. Tom got to be the instructor—he was chosen by the doctor to be the instructor of the doctor's children. He had to be brave and work hard; he was our role model. We all listened and learned from him. Everyone received a benefit from this work.

The work took a long time. I remember Allan and I finally became tired—no matter how much we did, Tom wanted more. Finally we simply announced it was done, it was finished. There is no doubt in my mind that Dad knew this moment was coming because he said nothing about our uncharacteristic rebellion. But from that moment forward, our backyard was called "Tom's backyard."

For as long as we lived in that house, it was Tom's backyard. For many years, he would periodically come over and say, "Let's go check the backyard." Tom would walk around and tell us what we needed to do and we'd listen. I don't remember actually doing the work he suggested, but he always had many ideas of what needed to be done. This was such a wonderful and loving lesson for Tom. The work was done but Tom still "owned" it. His ownership was recognized and respected by the "real" owners—they even named it as his. Even years and years later, when we were not living in the house, it was Tom's backyard. Mom and I had driven over there one day to look at it. Someone else was living there but kindly invited us in. As we entered the backyard, I turned to Mom and said spontaneously, "See how good Tom's backyard looks!"

This is such an elegant example of Dad's healing work—Tom was put in a situation where he could heal himself in ways he couldn't have imagined. Eventually, Tom achieved great success as an artist, had pieces displayed in important locations through out the United States and earned a living with his talent.

Yet another example is shown by Mr. Woodley, a very thin young man who lived with his mother. According to Mr. Woodley, who was not at all hesitant in talking to me as he waited for his appointment, he had a very delicate constitution and stomach. He had spent many years bent over, "protecting his stomach," and his backbone had finally frozen in that position. His physician had sent him to Dad with the goal of Mr. Woodley gaining enough strength so that the surgeon could operate and straighten his spine.

Mr. Woodley was very friendly and spent many hours in our living room before and after his appointments. His mother was frequently with him. I remember Dad openly praising her for the fine care she'd taken of her son and for devoting her whole life to cooking special foods for him. She would beam as Dad asked her questions about her careful food preparation.

Dad always loved trivia and I found out later that he had many interesting conversations with Mr. Woodley and his mother about babies: Baby whales gain about 200 pounds a day. A human baby only triples its weight its first year but that is an amazingly fast rate. Baby food has to be extremely nutritious because babies are small and delicate.

These conversations, of course, took more time and were far more indirect than I am reporting.

Finally Dad and Mrs. Woodley literally cooked up a wonderful idea to help her son. He would be given baby food to help him grow strong quickly for his operation. Of course, Mr. Woodley was soon begging to eat "real" food. Strained squash and strained liver don't taste so good even though they're highly nutritious and easy to digest. I remember Mr. Woodley being so excited when he finally got to eat a tiny portion of mashed potatoes. He continued to beg for more "real" food, gained weight, had his operation, and continued to see Dad. I remember him taking long walks on our block; sometimes one of us kids would walk with him because he was a very nice man.

Dad allowed him and his mother to keep their dignity; he didn't tell them anything they didn't already know, but he allowed them to use their own ways, the ways they had already developed, to make themselves healthier. I don't know what happened to Mr. Woodley, but I wouldn't be surprised if, with his new-found health, and his mother's involvement in his behaving more normally, he began to develop his own life separate from her.

Many patients came in and out of treatment quickly. Mr. Olson was a wonderful man who'd been raised in an orphanage. He'd been married multiple times and this was the 1950s when divorce wasn't so commonplace. He was one of my mother's favorite patients. When Dad told him that the woman he'd chosen to become his seventh wife, was a good choice and would make almost as good a wife as Mr. Olson would make husband, he was overjoyed. He picked up one of the balls on the floor in the front room, and threw it in the air, exclaiming, "Hooray!" The ball hit the ceiling and broke a tile and all he could do was laugh with joy. My mother simply couldn't tell him, "Yes, but you broke my ceiling." As long as we lived in that house, there was that broken ceiling tile and every time we looked at it, we thought of him and his happiness.

Mr. Beckard was another patient I remember clearly. He had experienced a terrible cancer and half his pelvis had been removed—he wanted Dad to help him with phantom limb pain so that he could eliminate the pain medication on which he was dependent. When I first met him, my children were about two, three, and four years old.

Once when we were visiting, Mr. Beckard stood with his canes and his pants leg folded up, to walk into the office. My four-year-old yelled, "Michael, Kim, come look! Hurry!" David was actually lying on the floor looking up to see where Mr. Beckard had put his leg. Mr. Beckard, thank goodness, recognized that they were children, certainly rude children, but still just children.

Afterward I asked Dad, "Why are my children so awful and what should I do next time?" He pointed out that my children had spent their whole lives on military bases. They had never seen a physically imperfect person except for Dad, who didn't count because he was their grandfather. "Distract them," he said. "Drop your purse, ask them to pick it up." Shortly afterward, my family went to the circus; a midget and the fat lady, obviously part of the circus, were walking in front of us. David opened his mouth and I immediately threw my purse on the ground calling, "David, Mom needs her purse. Please pick it up for me." As he reached for the purse, he called, "Michael, Kim, get over here and see this!" Later, I told Dad what had happened and he just shrugged and said, "Well, you can't win them all. They'll grow out of it."

Family members knew nothing about the patients other than what they chose to tell us as they waited in the front room for their appointments—or, sometimes, what was obvious in their presentation. There were many who didn't share anything about themselves and that was all right. We could often garner something about them, but we really didn't know or, in fact, care. There were so many who contributed to our lives, as we did to theirs, that it was easy to ignore the ones who were more reserved.

Dad rarely spoke about his patients in any way. Once there was a young man whom Dad had worked with for quite some time. He was also a friend and was standing in our kitchen, eating. Food was going everywhere, on the floor, in his beard, on his shirt. It was awful. I went to where Dad was relaxing, and told him, "Daddy, you need to work on this man's table manners. They're disgusting." Dad looked thoughtfully at me for a moment and replied, "When the foundation is cracked, you don't worry about the color of the shingles."

I remember a young man who got up every morning during an Arizona summer, walked over 10 miles to our home and was waiting on our front porch when we got up in the morning. He would then come into the house and sit on a chair and read all day. He brought his lunch and got up only to use the bathroom. Then he walked home every night. He did this for one entire summer. He rarely spoke; he just sat and read. I've never seen mention of him in the literature and still have no idea what was going on with him.

I often asked Dad, "Why do people do all these difficult things you tell them to do?" He would always answer, "Because they know it will give them what they want, that it will make them better people."

I also remember a young man who had hitchhiked from Los Angeles to see Daddy unannounced. He just appeared at the door, hoping there was an appointment. He spent two days, waiting for times that were available, sitting in our front room. He had had an operation for some sort of cancer in his throat that had left a terrible, bright red scar almost encircling his neck. He had felt a lump on his back and he was afraid it was a metastasis, and in truth, it probably was. That was why he wanted to see Dad.

This young man sat in our living room, waiting, weeping almost steadily. Every once in a while, one of us would come up to him and ask, "Do you want a drink of water? An aspirin?" He would look up, say politely, "No, thank you," and go back to weeping. It was so distressing that I finally went and asked Dad what was happening. Dad asked what I knew and I told him that I knew the man had been operated on for cancer, felt a lump on his back and felt it was a recurrence.

Dad said, "What are his choices? If it is cancer, he can do nothing and die. Or he can do what the doctors advise, which won't be easy or pleasant, and will give him only a small hope of life." Then he talked about how hard these choices are for anyone—to come to terms with uncertainties, with ambiguities, and with desperate choices. The young man's task was to come to terms with, to choose between seemingly equally awful choices. Dad taught me on a very deep level, never to be afraid of symptoms or facts and that hope arises from our seeing that we have more choices than we previously assumed.

There is another case that I remember for many reasons—it was one of the few times I saw Dad truly upset over a patient. Steve Jones was an American child who had been born in the Philippine Islands at the outbreak of World War II. He was only about two when the guerrillas overran the area in which he was living and he witnessed the murders of both his parents. He spent the next several years living in the jungle with the people who had escaped the massacre. He was taught to do nothing except to be silent, to be still, and to hide. The lives of everyone depended upon remaining hidden.

After the war was over and the people returned to safety, Steve's one remaining family member was traced. His much older brother didn't even know he'd survived. He brought Steve to the United States for care and Dad became his psychiatrist.

I remember Daddy coming from the residential facility where Steve was living. It was about the fifth or sixth hospital he'd been in. He was a difficult patient because no one knew what to do for him and it was clear the boy was severely emotionally damaged as well as still suffering the lingering effects of near starvation. Dad rarely initiated any remarks about his patients, but this time as he walked in the house, he looked at me with great sadness and announced, "I just left a little boy who's 12 years old and he was holding a ball. I asked him what he was doing and he looked at me and said, 'I'm trying to learn how to play.'" I will never forget how really shaken Daddy was at the poignancy of that scene.

Dad found Steve a really good foster home that he monitored; he helped the foster mother learn to parent a child who had such deficits, and continued to serve as his psychiatrist for many years. Although he had been very damaged as a child, Steve grew up, became employed, and he lived his life.

He became a mail carrier. In this career, he was completely grounded and he knew his routine. He earned his living by knowing exactly where he was, every moment, and where he was to go next. Like Patti and her rabbits, he found a job where he could excel. His limitations became acceptable and even assets. I don't know how much Dad influenced Steve's choice of work, but my hunch is that his connection with Steve helped Steve understand what he needed so he could continue to heal himself every day.

Recently I watched a video of a 20-year follow-up to one of Dad's cases involving a paraplegic 17-year-old girl presented at one of his teaching sessions. She'd suffered a broken back and was in a great deal of pain as well as being deeply depressed over her paralysis. Dad asked her, "What do you want?" She replied, "For you to make me walk." Daddy went on. "And if I can't do that, what do you want?" She answered, "Please stop the pain," which was clearly more than just physical pain.

Dad began by saying, "You don't use your muscles enough." This surprising opening statement—like those that caught the attention of Tom and the cancer patient—opened the door to his continuing. "You have un-exercised dimple muscles."

On hearing that truth, which had many levels of meaning, she smiled. Twenty years later, when she was reviewing her interactions with Dad, she commented that she wanted to get well. Her therapist wanted to give her peace. Dr. Erickson had told her a story about how the Native American Indians used to hunt. They would go into the forest and look for a trail that rabbits used. Then they waited. They didn't know if a fox was going to come, if another rabbit would come along, a bird, a deer, or if anything at all would use that trail while they were waiting. They just waited to see what would come by. "Dr. Erickson gave me patience," she said.

I am still in awe of that magnificent work. He didn't tell her that no one knew the future in a blunt way, as he did Patti's mother. He let this girl understand, in her own way and time, that we never know the future and that sometimes the result is not what we want. Native American Indians could starve to death if nothing came along the trail. But they were patient and, having done all they could do, waited. To me, that understanding is healing—she was able to make peace and happiness within, from her own abilities that Dad helped her to see.

Dad taught that we are what we have in our heads and hearts. Everything, except for physical limitations, which we don't fully know, is in our minds. In the 1940s, he had a woman patient with unpleasant issues from her childhood. Under hypnosis, he created an imaginary history for her that included a loving "February Man" with that name chosen because the woman's birthday was in February. He helped her create new internal experiences, which changed her perceptions of her childhood. As she changed experientially, she changed the way she dealt with the world and she healed.

Instead of focusing on overcoming her particular fears, he enhanced her own good memories and created more for her by trances that were like dreams. In essence, the woman re-dreamed the make-up of her own self to be more of what she really wanted to be in her life.

Dad was a very wise human being and a completely ethical person. He didn't recreate a person's experiential past indiscriminately. There was a psychologist who worked with him in the early 1960's. As a child, she'd survived a Nazi death camp, and she told me, very bitterly, that Dad had created a new childhood with the February Man, but he'd refused to do it for her. I think he had refused, in her case, because the entirety of her childhood was a tragedy. The other woman had only pieces that were bad. You can re-arrange pieces and make a new picture from the puzzle, but you can't take a long-term, life-encompassing calamity and change it to another event.

Dad did tell me about a case he'd investigated years previously. Two little girls had come home from elementary school and seen their mother stuffed in the furnace, burning up. They had been able to tell the police about it, and the murderer—their father—had been arrested, but six or seven months later when Dad interviewed them, they had no memories of what they'd seen. The police wanted Dad to hypnotize the girls and make them retrieve these memories for the trial. Dad refused. Seeing their mother being burned in a furnace was too horrendous an event for those two little girls to handle. He wisely accepted that some memories need to be repressed and kept in the unconscious; that there are some things you don't need to remember or re-experience.

But he never missed an opportunity to give people something to remember to enhance their lives. He rarely, if ever, merely signed his name when he autographed books for people. He would write something that was meaningful for each person. Many years later people have said to me, "Your father autographed this book to me, saying something that I didn't even know was true about me then." That's the connection he had—he was able to see within them and pull out the best for them to use. To me, that's healing in the highest sense.

His basic philosophy was that life is joyous even though it is hard, unfair, filled with pain, and that every choice has both cost and benefit. Each of us is in charge of how we use what's in our minds and hearts. He simply did not believe in a victim mentality, although he certainly recognized that people can be victimized. He was compassionate, but simply did not support a victim stance. I remember him telling me never to let my children suffer unnecessary pain, but to accept they will suffer pain because that's part of life.

Over the years people have often asked me what was the most valuable learning I received from Dad. Over the years, my answer has changed. At this point, I believe it is the belief that the only immediately renewable, life-long pleasure is learning. Therefore when I, or anyone, make a mistake or do something wrong, I get to learn something new and that can be a great pleasure. Anyone who pounds that notion into his or her mind cannot be a victim because we are each responsible for our own learning and we can find pleasure in all learning. To be a victim says you are choosing not to learn. Certainly he knew what he was talking about. He walked with a cane his whole adult life, had been paralyzed and heard his doctor tell his mother that he would die before morning. He spent years of his life in a wheelchair with the dependency that entails, he had learning disabilities as a youngster, was tone-deaf and color-blind his whole life. Yet he was never a victim.

He believed that people don't have to understand in order to handle situations—some things are totally "un-understandable" but that doesn't excuse not dealing with them. Railing against unfortunate, unfair, or cruel circumstances is futile. If you take responsibility for the unique life you have, you can never be a victim and you will always be striving for achievable bettering of yourself. Dad never stopped advocating complete self-responsibility.

Most of all, he believed in living without compromising personal integrity. Integrity that has been compromised creates an existential emptiness, a hollow spot within the self, the heart, the soul.

The words "too hard" or "too scary" were not part of the thinking he espoused. It might be too hard, or cost too much, when the full cost and ramifications are considered, but nothing was ever "too scary." When he used hypnosis, I never heard him talk about "going to a safe place"—he knew that any place to which we would voluntarily go was safe and if the subject discovered something painful, it was time to heal.

He always said there were only two kinds of fear in the world. One is the fear of a tiger. If a tiger walks into the room, swishing his tail, licking his chops, with his hungry yellow eyes looking right at you, that's real fear! All other fears come from your mind. Even though the fear created by your mind is often more powerful than real fear, it comes from your mind.

He used that premise when he helped my brother Allan. As a toddler, Allan got the idea that he had to hold onto something as he walked. He would brush his hand against the wall, while he walked to a chair or table that he could grab. He had to plot his course as he moved from one point to another so he always had one hand touching a physical object. Although limiting, his strategy was effective.

It's difficult to fight this type of belief directly—even children passionately defend their beliefs. Allan remembers that Dad rolled up pages of newspaper until he had a sturdy tube. He showed Allan just how strong that rolled-up paper tube was. Then he gradually took out sheets of paper until Allan was holding only a single sheet of rolled newspaper. Next he handed Allan a piece of string to hold, but dropped the other end. Allan remembers walking across the room happily grasping the string as the other end trailed behind him.

There were several people in the room and Allan remembers all but Dad were laughing. He says he still remembers looking at Dad and knowing that Dad didn't think anything was funny—that he and Allan both knew everything was just as it should be.

Allan was just a little boy, but Dad empowered him, and then stepped aside so Allan could learn more of what he could really accomplish. Dad used the wisdom of the totem, an amulet, a "whistle a cheerful tune in the dark forest," to help Allan become more of what he wanted—to be more independent.

Dad made it easy for people to make decisions that helped them be more of who they wanted to be from an independent stance. He could connect in such a way that they did it from within—he didn't do it "to" them—he healed rather than treated. Simply telling me that I would be happy looking back on a difficult task, rather than telling me that I should or needed to do something because it was good for me, fostered independence, and allowed me to nurture myself from within. That is still how I approach challenges—because I want to have done them.

I have heard there are highly recognized and revered spiritual teachers, including Mother Teresa, who say all circumstances, including those that bring confusion and suffering, whether brutal assault, financial calamity, or serious illnesses, are gifts of life. All the terrible things that can happen are, at the highest level of meaning, gifts and perhaps the perfect learning for each person at that time. This is very similar to Daddy's wisdom. Jeffrey Zeig has a quotation from Dad in the front of many of his books: "Into each life some confusion should come... also some enlightenment." Misery simply happens. Saying "Deal with it" shortchanges what it has to offer. When challenging things occur, you "get to learn," you become enlightened.

My son David was once tentatively diagnosed with a terminal disease. As the physicians tried to finalize the diagnosis, they went through long lists of possible diseases, one more horrendous, painful, and deadly than the other. After extensive tests, and still without a clear diagnosis, David remarked, "The doctors have a long list of things I do not have, so on one level, I am healthier than most people."

As I worried over him, David said to me, "Mom, the tea's been drunk and the leaves have settled. All we're doing is waiting is for someone to read the tea leaves." I heard his grandfather in that wisdom.

When all was completed and a probable treatable diagnosis was given, I told him he had changed. He replied, "Mom, when a doctor says three little words to you, your life changes forevermore, and in an instant. The three little words are not 'I love you.' They are 'fatal,' 'incurable,' and your name." Those are very wise words from a man still in his thirties and that wisdom was most likely derived from the time he spent with his grandfather. Daddy's life-threatening, life-changing polio was a part of all our lives, and it taught David, as it taught others, that bad things happen, so learn from them.

Of my three children, David spent the most time with his grandfather. He learned things from him that I didn't know he learned. He is able to use hypnosis for anesthesia better than most people can. Not only did he use it for his ripped toenail, but he has used it for extensive dental work needed from a mouth injury. When he got his first root canal on his front teeth, he took a comic book into the dentist's office. When asked if he wanted Novocain, David said he didn't care, but he did want to read his comic book.

He sat reading his comic book while the dentist worked. When they came out of the treatment room, the dentist had a puzzled look. He told me, "When I said your son could get out of the chair, he asked if I was already finished." David did not learn that from me.

Dad often expressed that he'd learned a great deal from his bout with polio. He told me he used to lie in bed and listen to the people in the house. He would try to figure out what they wanted to ask or what they were really saying before they got to the point they actually wanted to communicate. He learned that a great deal of conversation entailed circling around that point with the implicit hope that the other people would make the leap into what was really intended.

Dad did those types of things his whole life. As a very young boy, he used to get up very early on snowy mornings to walk to school and create a path through the fresh snow. He would make parts of the miles-long path straight and parts very circuitous. Then, after his morning chores, he would hide among the trees and watch his friends and schoolmates follow his path. He would see just how winding and twisting he could make the path before they would leave his trail and make their own through the untouched snow.

As an adult he liked to read the last chapter of a book first and then figure out how the book got there. Conversely, after reading the first chapter, he would figure out what the last chapter was going to be and then see how correct he was. This was not just curiosity and intellectual stimulation. It was a genuine desire to understand people, to become a part of the way others thought.

It was the same when he learned to walk by watching his baby sister learn and breaking down that complex task into individual units. In 1920, when he did this, educational theory did not understand that learning is enhanced by breaking complexities into manageable discrete units. Dad desired understanding on the deepest level, to become part of the world at large and of each person's smaller world.

He observed desired outcomes and conceptually broke them down for deeper connections and understandings. He told me the best way to walk on ice is to forget you're actually walking on ice. Your body will automatically make the necessary adjustments. We walk differently on cement than we do on grass, and differently on gravel than we do on sand, yet we never think about how to adjust and compensate when we change our path from grass to gravel. We just get out of our own way and our body's wisdom does it automatically.

Dad spent so much time exercising his own mind. It was not his way to work with a patient, a student, or in his own life, trusting that an unfertilized and barren unconscious would produce valid or respectful results. Hard work and discipline were deemed necessary for effective results, for unconscious processes to produce wisdom in life, in teaching, and in the therapy room. I remember how he used to write out an induction for a patient. He would reduce 20 pages to one single page, spending enormous effort to get it exactly as he wanted. The hardest writing is done in the fewest words, but it is well worth the effort because each word then becomes significant.

What Dad did with himself, his students, and his patients can also be characterized as successfully distracting the conscious mind in order to keep it from interfering with its natural growing and healing processes. He mentioned that in the script of his work with the woman with cancer. He did that with himself as he practiced writing editorials for his university newspaper while in a deep trance. Healers must help patients get out of their own way so each person's healthiness can be activated and each can heal himself or herself. Dad did this over and over. He would occupy the conscious mind with some related task and this would teach independence even as the unconscious healed the person.

This is the wisdom of a healer as opposed to expertise in the technical craft of psychotherapy. Gregory Bateson used to say the best way to heal a forest is to leave it alone. It has its own self-corrective processes that restore the ecosystem. People are the same.

Of course, sometimes, obviously, we need medical or psychological interventions. There are times when people need treatment in order to move on productively. Dad was also an expert at knowing when these moments occurred.

It is important to say that his general advice to "trust your unconscious," which has turned into a mantra for many, is only true if you have spent a great deal of time pouring relevant experiences and well-developed thoughts into your unconscious. Dad spent a huge amount of time thinking and structuring and filling his unconscious mind.

Like all highly talented people, and because he was a maverick, Dad did attract professional animosity. Some people even disliked him because they could not understand that money was not his most important goal. He was doing what he wanted to do, what he liked, and what he was good at.

Over the years, many people have asked how much Dad charged for his work. I really don't know what he charged his patients but I am certain that he saw some people for virtually nothing. He often would barter—lawn work for therapy was a favorite.

He could have charged his students almost anything especially towards the end of his life when so many were lined up waiting for a place in his seminars. He told his groups of students, "My standard charge is $40 an hour." They would ask, "$40 per person?" and he would repeat, "My standard charge is $40 an hour." They would ask again and he would repeat the same words. Sometimes they would tell him that there were 10 people and that meant each would pay only four dollars. Dad would repeat, "My standard charge is $40 an hour." That was his charge per hour and he was happy with it.

Daddy believed that knowledge and caring should be shared freely. He didn't hesitate to share his and instilled that belief in those around him. Once I told him about one of my students at an alternative high school. The 16-year-old had a lengthy and varied police record and was tired of that life. For over two years, I had spent many hours working with him outside of school, and Nathan had spent even more long, hard hours bringing his schoolwork up to grade level and learning acceptable behavior. When he triumphantly transferred to "regular" school, we hugged each other and cried. We were so happy but so sad to leave each other.

I told Daddy that Nathan had said he wanted to thank me but he didn't know how and I had replied not to forget me. Dad said, "Next time, tell him to pass on what you gave him, to give it to someone else who needs it. That way, he will remember all the good things you both created."

The way Dad lived his life, with our small home, one automobile, which was rarely a new one, our modest way of living made some people uncomfortable. Those people he simply ignored.

We lived a thrifty life. My orthodontic braces were the first purchase, including the house, my parents made without paying cash. In our home on Cypress Street in Phoenix, we had a fireplace. After every storm, we children had to go out with the wagon and bring home branches and limbs that had fallen from neighborhood trees. Sometimes a couple of us would have to go because the wagon would be piled too high for one person to balance and pull. The wood was placed in the side yard and sawed up into neat stacks of firewood for the two or three months every year it was cold enough to permit a fire.

My younger brothers and sisters did most of this work, especially Allan, who still greatly enjoys working with wood. But all of us who lived in that house learned the true satisfaction in taking something considered trash, and by your own sweat, turning it into something useful. To this day, decades later, when I see a fallen branch, I automatically calculate where the cuts would be to make it fit in the wagon and then how much fireplace wood it will produce.

The older children received money only for work; we did not have allowances. I remember being paid for working in the garden in Michigan as well as for other extra work. If we saved the money, Mom and Dad would double it. If we didn't save it, that was all right too. I think we were all raised to respect money and to live within our means. The children and most of the grandchildren respectfully regard money as a tool, a way of purchasing goods and services and that legacy has been very valuable to us.

There were so many ways that we learned important lessons. Dad quoted Chief Seattle of the Suquamish tribe in the American Northwest—"The land does not belong to us; we belong to the land"—over and over. Even though small farms are vanishing, he believed raising a family on a farm taught many values. He held that belief from his youth—his first publication, when he was still in high school, was in the Wisconsin Agriculturist and was titled "Why Young People Leave the Farm." His insistence on a garden wherever we lived and his determination that we children work in that garden was part of that belief in values as well as the other advantages learned from working with plants. Hard work was one obvious benefit. So was growing food. Just as important was learning lessons only the land and nature can teach—there is a time to sow, reap, and harvest, as well as a time to wait for reward and a reverence for the magnificence of the world even in the small arena of a blossoming flower or a bright orange carrot.

If Dad had a cause, he would not tolerate people trying to prevent the right thing from being done. For example, private psychiatric hospitals were first built and financed by psychiatrists who then had a vested interest in referring people for inpatient care. Dad thought that highly unethical and made enemies over his stance.

He always did what he thought was right. For example, for years he was one of the few white members of the National Medical Society, the medical society to which most blacks belonged because at that time, they did not feel readily accepted by the American Medical Society.

He was rarely included in the social gatherings of physicians in Phoenix, perhaps because of his membership in the black society. I'm sure he did not particularly want to be included in many of those social events, but he was clearly isolated by most of the psychotherapeutic and medical communities both locally and nationally. Looking back, I've sometimes wondered if he ever got his feelings hurt or if he was lonely on a day-to-day basis.

There have always been people who believed amazing things about Daddy. Some were true. Some were not. There are lots of stories of people fervently believing amazing things. I think one of the Beatles claimed that a group of people in India levitated two feet off the ground. I don't believe that happened, but I believe that man believes it. What's real to each of us is what's in our minds. Unless a belief harmed the person or another, I don't think Dad felt it was particularly important whether or not it was objectively true.

He did take a stand on certain beliefs: He had patients and even students who believed he could read their minds, but he couldn't and he never had hesitation about saying he couldn't read minds. He also had patients who believed he could "make" them do things they didn't want to do. He couldn't—in fact, he spent a great deal of time supporting the tenet of hypnosis that says hypnosis cannot "make" people do something they ordinarily wouldn't do. He didn't "make" people do anything. He just presented things in ways that when they knew they could and that they should, they would.

Mostly he enjoyed exercising his and other people's minds. When I was a little girl he told me he would give me five dollars if I could find a book with page 99 on the left side and page 100 facing it. I looked for many long hours for a book like that but they simply aren't published that way. I kept the challenge in the back of my mind and told my children how Grandpa had made this offer but I had never found such a book. My son David actually found a book, printed in English by the Ethiopian Air Force that had page 99 facing page 100. He mailed the book to his grandfather with a letter to collect the money. Dad sent the book back with a note, "Congratulations! And you get 10 dollars because times have changed."

He had lots of these stimulating little queries like the one he asked his students about the 10 cacti at the front door of the office in five rows of four each. He once told David that if he could guess what some particular stones were, he could have one of them. He gave a couple hints: "You have never seen these stones in action, doing what they did. In fact, no man has." David puzzled on this riddle for several weeks before going back to his Grandfather and asking, "Are they the gizzard stones of a dinosaur?" Of course, they were and David received one.

Daddy loved stupid jokes, the cornier the better. He also loved puns and had a wonderful, teasing, and playful sense of humor. He taught us all that humor tops everything. You can learn to laugh, and you should learn because after all, so much of life is quite ridiculous. With humor, much of the pain and tribulations of life is less.

When my brother Allan and I were young teenagers, Daddy took us to Meteor Crater in Arizona. At that time you could walk to the bottom, and Allan and I did. A freezing rain and snow began while we were at the bottom. It was very cold and we weren't even wearing jackets. It was wonderful to be where the meteor hit though and we were inspired to leave some sort of mark that we had been there. We gathered big rocks and laid out our initials on the ground, laughing about how furious we would each be if Dad had told us go walk to the bottom of Meteor Crater and, in a freezing rain and snow storm, gather rocks and lay them down in different places. We finally completed our initials, walked back up, and told Daddy to look through the telescope to see if he could see what we'd done.

On the drive home, I complained about how tired I was, how bruised, how stiff I was going to be the next day. I whined non-stop. Dad simply said, "The physical pain you feel from lugging those rocks around will be gone in a day or so. But the memory will last forever."

That sunk deeply into my psyche as did so many other things he told me that were uniquely meaningful to me. I have built my life on the experiences I had as his child. I am very grateful because when I face the challenges of life, I know that I know how to choose a mountain I am able to climb, a joke that is as ridiculous as the situation I'm in, a gift for someone that is as unique and special as that person is. I know all of us are capable of creating beautiful, wonderful, and great contributions to the world. I have my mother and my father to thank for that.

Best of all, I think, the gifts that were given me have never stopped. I am still learning from Dad, from the memories I have of him, from the knowledge he gave me, and the wisdom he taught.

CHAPTER TWO

ROXANNA ERICKSON KLEIN

MEMORIES OF MY FATHER

The Atmosphere

Inviting patients into the home office set the stage for a relationship of wholeness, integrity, respect, and many more therapeutic possibilities than are allowed by the rigid environment of today's professional settings. There was no concealment about who the doctor was as a man with values, as a part of a family, and as a professional who believed in his work and had the confidence to show all of this to his patients. This full exposure was a statement about Milton Erickson as a man and healer.

The therapeutic atmosphere was further enhanced by the presence and involvement of the entire family, from Mom to the teens and the younger children, to the family dog when it was appropriate. Many times it was integral to a patient's therapy to observe interactions among a healthy and active family, each member with his or her own interests and responsibilities.

I enjoyed interacting with the waiting patients and respected our rule that it was the patients' decision and privilege to choose whether to converse or to sit quietly. Sometimes I would lie on the floor playing with my toys or reading a book, "available for conversation." I remember many patients actually getting down on the floor with me, playing dolls, teaching me origami, asking for cards, or otherwise actively initiating play—I remember those times as wonderful.

No markers other than a simple "32 West Cypress" sign were outside to alert new patients that they had found the office. I once asked why this was and Dad replied, "Our invisible sign works just fine." I suspect it was part of his larger commitment to assist patients to function in normal society, in everyday settings.

We lived in a modest neighborhood in Phoenix, where it was unusual for a physician to live outside the country club areas. Dad

MEMORIES OF MY FATHER | *85*

and Mom spoke openly against that philosophy, stating it was not a service to the children to bring them up with skewed expectations and with the idea they are somehow better than those around them.

We lived on a street that encompassed a variety of styles, from very large beautiful mansions at the corner of Central, to "rooms for rent" farther down the street. People of all walks of life lived side-by-side in a friendly, cooperative, and mutually supportive manner. We knew all of the neighbors, and Dad referred many out-of-town patients to the boarding house next door; many of them would sit on the porch in the warm evenings before air conditioning was so prevalent. In this setting, we could become familiar as neighbors, people, and sometimes friends.

In 1970 my parents purchased the home on East Hayward, and there my parents remained for the rest of my Dad's life; Mom is still there. The home on Hayward had two significant features: a large yard with the most magnificent specimen of Palo Verde tree any of us had ever seen, and a home office. The new residence had similarities to the house on Cypress—both were small homes in large yards; they had modest, homey looks; and they were within diverse residential neighborhoods.

The Office

In both locations the office was part of the home. Patients or students came through the living quarters into the office. The dining table stacked with work in progress provided evidence that the family made accommodations for Dad's professional work.

The office, in both locations, was lined with bookshelves and adorned with a vast and diverse array of artifacts. Some of them were gifts, memorabilia, archeological finds, and works of art. Dad had an aboriginal piece brought from Australia by Betty Alice that he loved to show off. He would start by having the student guess the origin of the unusual and distinctive piece. Guesses were invariably wrong, and then he would begin to throw out clues: the straight lines, subtle colors, and careful details. He would talk about the culture and how the environment influences the artist. Eventually Dad would point to a boomerang with similar markings and give away the puzzle.

He had puzzles for all ages. One was a series of cards with some cowboys, and some bucking broncos. In order to get each cowboy on a horse, the student had to reach outside of normal thinking. The only way to solve the puzzle was to place the cards in a sideways design, match the head of one horse with the tail of another, using the legs of the cowboy as a bridge to complete the visual illusion. The clever gimmick changed the perspective of the whole entirely.

One of Dad's favorite props was a foam rock. With numerous groups of students he went through an elaborate demonstration that often took more than one teaching session. He would start by talking about ironwood, letting students heft certain specimens, such as a carving of an octopus sitting on a rock, so they experienced the surprising density and weight of the wood. Students would admire the collection of specimens, the delicacy, the fineness of detail, and then feel their surprising weight. Either preceding or following the lesson of unexpected density, Dad would add his foam rock to the lesson. Sitting in the wheelchair he would make a silent, slow presentation—leaning over, reaching, struggling in a most tedious manner before the group. He capitalized on his physical frailty to create the illusion that the weight of the stone was great but that some urgency existed in his hefting the stone to his lap, declining all offers of assistance. Once the rock was in his lap he would rest, further creating the illusion that he needed to recover after such a formidable task. This interlude gave students the opportunity to see the magnitude of the small boulder with its realistic shape and texture. Anticipation and curiosity built: What could be so important about a seemingly ordinary rock? Then suddenly, with an unexpected flick of the wrist, Dad would nimbly toss the specimen at a startled student who inevitably leapt out of the way. Finally, a student would bend over to retrieve the specimen and lead the chorus of laughter as the joke was revealed. Having made a serious point that "things aren't always what they seem to be," Dad laughed along with the group.

Community Ties

The Heard Museum was only a block from our home on Cypress Street, and we each individually and also as a family spent considerable time there, knew the curator, and attended most of the special events. Changes that came about were topics of family discussion. When the museum decided to create a membership organization, our family was the very first to sign up. We grieved when building plans meant moving some of the palm trees that inhabited the large lot. We celebrated when the spring Indian fairs were a huge success and drew crowds. We took great interest when a new display was put together, and each of us would slip over to visit, previewing it for Dad, and helping him to come if the display was of particular interest. And even today family members share a sense of pride that we helped the Heard Museum become the gem it is today.

Likewise, Dad cultivated within the family a sense of connection with other community resources. The botanical garden, North and South Mountain Parks, Squaw Peak, Encanto Park, the public library, Boyce Thompson Arboretum, Sunset Point, the Superstitions, stretches of Dreamy Draw Wash, the Salt River bed and the Estrella Mountains were all locations that we became very familiar with. We had experiences and associations with those geographic places that were expanded, reinforced, and cemented within us through our discussions. Whether this process of becoming grounded in the community was happenstance, deliberate planning, or coincidental is uncertain, but regardless, it is an important part of the atmosphere in which Milton H. Erickson raised his family and treated his patients.

Innumerable students and patients were directed to one or more of these public places, sometimes given specific directives to look for a particular feature such as the Boojum tree at the botanical gardens, or the scientist sculpture at Encanto Park. When they returned from their assignments, the experiences provided a platform from which further experiences and learnings could take place. When a ship leaves a dock, the view of the port ties the crew together for a journey. The experiences of one enrich the others. The view changes each moment, and the forward movement eventually overcomes the looking back, but the sweet memories of choice moments sustain many conversations as the journey progresses.

Countless students were directed to Squaw Peak. And countless came back to comment that the experience was life changing—the effort necessitated by the journey, the presence of life in the harsh environment, the changing perspective, the clear view of the valley, and the extraordinary within the ordinary.

After Dad died, we decided it would be fitting to scatter his ashes on the mountain. A group of us went up at midnight on the night of a full moon. Dad had never been all the way to the top, although one group of students had valiantly carried him in the wheelchair nearly to the summit. That night he made it. Then we convened at the chosen site, part way up and overlooking the west, to return his ashes to the soil.

Life Together

Dad and Mom worked as a team. Dad was able to be as productive and creative as he was because Mom was behind him supporting him in every way—physically, emotionally, intellectually, in all practical matters, and professionally. He returned love, appreciation, and respect for her in a multitude of ways that went far beyond the special gifts he chose for birthdays or holidays. In fact, even in celebration he was able to convey that it was not the occasion itself that was important; the occasion was merely an excuse to appreciate the celebrant.

My own birthday happened to fall the week of the annual American Society of Clinical Hypnosis meeting. That meant that, for all practical purposes, Dad was out of town on my birthday during my formative years. This was not ignored, but rather dealt with directly, proactively, and cooperatively. Months in advance, Dad initiated a discussion: "Looking at the calendar I see I'll be gone on your birthday again. What would you like to do to make your birthday special?" He would participate actively while I planned a menu, decided whether I wanted to go on some special outing, or selected a date that he was available to join in. It gave me a basis for anticipating conflict, and for heading it off well before its inception. It is a skill that has spilled over into other areas of my life, from relationships to household maintenance to health care.

The respect that was so effectively modeled by Dad and Mom and extended to the family involved a style of daily living. Dad always encouraged Mom to explore her passions in the same way he expected support for the interests he had. He helped her to plan family vacations and to visit sights that she was particularly interested in, regardless of whether it was something he was interested in. And when interests overlapped, he sought opportunities for each family member to enhance the others.

When Mom would take us on a family trip, Dad was always eagerly awaiting our return, and we all rushed into the office to give him the details of our adventure. I remember one occasion when we had been up to Rainbow Bridge, and our recounting of the trip went on for hours as Dad gleaned from us the sensations of the grit on our skin and in our hair and mouths, the beauty of the sky and the majesty of the canyon. I had been timid about some of the climbing, and so he quizzed me about the internal sensations that I felt as I saw Allan and Kristi walking sure-footedly on the slick rock trails. My brother was enthusiastic about drinking water that required you sieve out tadpoles with your teeth. Mom expressed her discomfort with some of the homemade ladders we explored, which leaned against the canyon walls. I loved the night sky with the billions of stars and Milky Way so clear it felt like you could touch it. Dad came outside to admire the thick red dust that remained on the car, in our clothes, and in our baggage. Allan even got out the small folding shovel and pushed it into the ground to demonstrate the depth to which the car had been trapped in the sand, and we marveled over the lucky appearance of the Indian boy who had worked with Allan to free us. Rainbow Bridge was only one of a series of remote and isolated spots that we visited. Thinking back, I realize how courageous my mother was, to undertake these trips with young kids and not a lot of emergency resources. Fortunately, things rarely went wrong, and Dad always praised the effective resolution of unexpected problems. We all absorbed our experiences and adventures as events that Dad shared with us. We would not have, and could not have done this without his active participation in the planning, the preparation, and the enjoyment of the journeys. Although he was not able to accompany us physically, he was there moment by moment in spirit, and we took care in remembering the details so that we could relate them all to him and let him share in the elements that he most enjoyed—the telling of the story.

As long as I can remember, there had been students, arriving individually or in bunches, who were committed to studying the works, the techniques, the words, and the person of Milton Erickson. Fascination with the professional work reached over into curiosity about the home and family. Dad truly loved it when students came and he gave generously of his time and his wisdom. Students' interest in Dad's unique approaches and successes definitely pushed his own work forward. He loved to present his cases, to stimulate questioning, and to be the center of inquiry and intrigue. The epitome of his pleasure was when he could roll his clinical prowess, his teaching abilities, and his family relationships all into one grand scenario where everything was happening at the same time. So Dad would create intersections for his students and family whenever it was possible. For me, this provided ongoing experiences of learning hypnotic techniques, and ongoing contact with the students. I would sit in the office during discussions, I would prepare lemonade for the groups, and I would show them various features in the landscape of the home or yard. And sometimes I would go out in the evenings with them when their lessons for the day were concluded.

Dad taught me in a very dramatic way what it is to be in a group of professionals who are passionate about their studies. I met people of all ages and stages in their careers. The students had often gone to great lengths to seek my father's guidance and knowledge—sometimes they had a thinly concealed personal problem they sought to resolve, and other times they had a commitment to improve professional skills.

Dad was able to connect with each person in the group in a way that made them think his words and stories were specifically targeted to them, and yet they were presented in a way to preserve dignity. In my view, the stories were general, universal, often repeated with tailoring and modifications for emphasis. Dad was uniquely effective in connecting with people through nonverbal nuances—pauses, eye contact, shifting closer, leaning to one side or another, speaking to one ear and then the other, manipulating his voice and, most important, giving the knowing smile. It was fascinating to listen to the students at the end of a day express wonder at the ways that Dad responded to their specific questions (often never expressed) and anxieties—as if they each were the only student in the room and others were merely bystanders to a lesson specifically targeted to them. Dad knew how to create a generative atmosphere, where the enthusiasm of one student had positive effects on another, and this created a circle of reinforcement and ongoing desire to learn more, to seek further, and to enhance oneself and others.

Family Life

Dad was a disciplinarian and established firm standards early: Each member of the household participated in maintenance of the home and family activities. Our jobs were not equitable and neither were our strengths, abilities, or talents, but our efforts to work as a team were something we all worked hard at. And we all enjoyed the benefits.

We all did extensive yard work, some of which was arduous. As with our vacation experiences, Dad remained an integral part of the team by taking an active interest in the smallest details of the experiences. He would participate in the planning, the decision making, reviewing, and extracting from each of us the minutiae of the sensory experiences. Finally, as a team, we would appreciate the success of the work, and comment on all of our contributions.

Maintaining the woodpile was hard work that often needed attention and supportive effort from several kids. As we walked about the neighborhood we scouted for recently trimmed trees. Then we hauled them home in a wagon that Allan built, and sawed them into lengths that would fit into the fireplace. The logs were long and heavy and often required two of us to lift them onto a sawhorse. We used a two-man saw that necessitated adaptation to the rhythm and the strength of one's sawing partner. Since we were different ages with individual attributes, the differences were marked. Each time we worked, we learned a lesson about adapting to a partner and the benefits of working at a steady pace.

Tending the woodpile opened the door to the next level of cooperative interactions. It was a skill to build the fire and the privilege to learn that skill had to be earned. In our evenings around the fire innumerable questions were raised and discussed: How cold was it? Did we want a fire for just a few hours, or did we want one that would continue to warm the house most of the night? Was the log dry? Was the log an unusual shape that would need special banking? Did it have a lot of sap that would send sparks flying?

After I had nagged about wanting my own chance to build the fire, I remember Dad giving me a "test" to see whether I was ready. Allan brought in the large log for the evening and the rationale for the choice was carefully explained to me. My task was to select the remainder of the wood in appropriate proportions. It was explained that if I had watched closely on previous evenings, I would have an idea of the proper proportions. Dad established that if I did not know this step, I had more to learn before I was "ready" to share the privileges of stacking the wood and striking the match.

Smaller logs and kindling are valuable resources and not to be wasted. Each piece had its special position in the making and in the maintenance of the fire. If one does not conserve the resources and use them in appropriate proportions, then more foraging will be needed to get through the cold season. A good balance mimics the proportions seen in nature. Of course I failed my first test, and later my second and third, but eventually I learned to make a fire in the rain with a single match. I am proud of this skill and am grateful that Dad enforced the long interval of learning needed. The lesson has served as a foundation in many aspects of life.

Dad never hesitated to model the enjoyment of life as well as hard work. We had a homemade bird feeder outside of the breakfast nook windows. When we were in the kitchen, Dad would sometimes turn his gaze towards the bird feeder and comment on the "visitors." We kept a list of bird species spotted on the feeder on the homemade bulletin board. As the list neared 100, we consulted a field guide to verify new visitors. Out in the yard was an array of birdhouses, including one made of a log that had been brought from Michigan. Our interest in nature taught us a great deal about finding opportunities everywhere, being unobtrusive, taking inventory of positive experiences, using resources, and relishing the beauty that surrounds us.

For everyone, daily life is replete with occasions for learning. What makes a lesson significant and memorable is not so clear, but Dad had a way of seizing opportunities to make a point in a way that would be remembered. He has been lauded for his exquisite sense of timing, and that is surely part of it.

One such lesson remains with me half a century after the event took place. It was common for Dad to lie down for a short nap, and Kristi and I were permitted to lie down with him, read, play on the bed, talk, or do whatever we chose. Sometimes Dad would tell us a story, and sometimes we would read comics together. When Dad was ready to get up again, it was our job to help him put on his shoes. He wore a standard style of brown leather dress shoes, which were kept highly polished. Dad was lying down and telling us a story. The story was a very long one, so we were putting on his shoes as he talked. We had a lot of trouble that day, struggling for quite a long time. Finally the shoes were on, the story concluded, and Dad sat on the edge of the bed with his feet on the floor. He said quietly and firmly, "Now, look at your work."

We must have been very young, because we didn't immediately recognize that we had put his shoes on the wrong feet. Dismay set in as we recognized the need to begin our work anew, and we asked him to lie down again so that we could re-do the job. It was much easier to put the shoes on correctly the second time.

For years I pondered this story, wondered how many times Dad may have tried indirectly to notify us of the error in progress. And I also thought about his discomfort as we pushed, jammed, and shoved his tender feet into those stiff shoes. I even tried on my own shoes in reverse to evaluate the experience from "his point of view," assessing that it was impossible that he was so engrossed in the story as to not have noticed. I went back to him some time later to ask, "Why didn't you just tell us?" I remember his reply: "You needed to learn to look at your work."

His willingness to endure discomfort, his patience in watching his children err so that they could learn to evaluate their own work, has stuck with me and given me guidance as a parent, as well as in my own life.

Emphasis on Formal Education

When I was in first or second grade, Dad bought necklaces from an Indian trader. They were made by Leekya, a well-known master Zuni artist who specialized in fetishes. Dad showed the necklaces to Kristi and me, who were quite young at the time, and we got to wear them for a little while. Then he announced they were our "College Graduation presents." They stayed in the safety deposit box for many years. Finally, with great ceremony, Dad presented a necklace to each of us on graduation. There was never any doubt that he communicated to us that formal education is an asset. Although he did little to influence our choice of a career, he consistently reinforced sufficient and proper education to get there.

My parents were hopeful that each of us would go to college, and most of us have graduate degrees. At the same time, Dad emphasized that we should know the limits of our education so that we would not reach beyond our own reservoir of knowledge. When I would come to him with a comment about a patient, he would sometimes ask, "Where did you get your medical degree?"—a harsh reminder that my observations needed credentials before they had credibility. Simultaneously though, he also taught us that we could learn in many ways, from anyone, and that wisdom and education were not synonymous. More importantly, that respect is not reserved for those with the highest credentials, but rather is earned by those who have the wisdom to use their unique knowledge with dignity. Whether a man's knowledge comes from a trade, hobby, special interest, life experience, or highly trained profession is of little importance—it is the earned knowledge and its application that are admirable.

White Tummy Stories

When we were youngsters, Dad used to entertain us with stories that he made up as he went along. Frequently he used a central character called White Tummy. The stories often started with the same rhythmic beginning: "Once upon a time there lived a frog who had a green back and a white tummy. For that reason, he was known as White Tummy. White Tummy lived in a pond in the woods and he liked to spend his afternoons sunning and eating flies." This would be followed by a colorful description of the multi-hued flies, including the great big purple juicy ones, and White Tummy's habit of snapping out his long tongue to capture a fly and draw it into his mouth. Sandwiched between the trance-inducing litany, which invoked every sense and lulled the listener into a quiet expectation, was a tale of adventure. Sometimes the tales were mere enjoyable moments in the life of a frog, and sometimes they contained lessons about coping with troubles or events that one of the children was facing. If the child had a recent injury, it would not be unusual for White Tummy to have a similar impediment that turned into an unexpected asset. If the child had a bad day, White Tummy was likely to discover that muddy turbulent water in his pond led to an unexpected discovery.

When the family felt a sense of loss and grief over the death of a beloved dog, Roger, Dad began writing letters in the voice of Roger from the Great Boneyard Up Yonder to White Tummy. The letters turned into a series that eventually omitted the frog and were addressed directly to family members. Whereas stories were told to those of us who were handy, the letters were sent to a wider group. Dad, as Roger, started scratching out stories with the same proliferation as the more serious articles he wrote. Our secretary (always ours even though she never did anyone's but Dad's work) would transcribe his barely legible notes, then Dad would proofread to assure they were correctly done. Then she would type as many copies as were possible with onion skin paper and carbons, sending them out to a variety of lucky family members. For me, the letters eased my transition of moving out of the home, giving me continuity and warmth of familiar day-to-day interactions even though I lived on my own.

Purple

Dad's wearing purple was one of the ways that I recognized that our family life was unique and different. Dad enjoyed the color purple and he liked the association that people made between the color and him. Over a long period of time he had adopted the color purple as kind of a trademark, and people always looked for purple shirts, socks, ties, and so forth to give him as gifts, which he wore enthusiastically.

When I was in high school, Dad had an interval of poor health in which he wore clean purple pajamas every day, not feeling up to dressing in the light woolen slacks and nice shirts that he usually wore. As he did not want to receive people in his pajamas, he spent several weeks consulting with patients on the telephone.

It struck me that if I could sew a suit as comfortable as pajamas, that looked as respectable as street clothes, it would give him a chance to see some of the patients who were asking for appointments. I found a dignified purple cotton blend, clearly a day-wear fabric, and I modified a pajama pattern to look more like a suit. The outfit delighted him. In fact, he was so happy with it he rarely went back to his "old look." From that time on he wore purple suits.

Dad was meticulous in grooming, always wanting his hair neatly cut and combed, his eyebrows and mustache trimmed, and the details of his clothing in order. He topped off his outfits with bold jewelry, wearing silver collar points on special occasions. He consistently wore neckties, either a standard or a bolo, from his large collection, which included many purple ones. One had a swirled design on it and he called it his "hypnotic tie." In his later years Dad always wore bolo ties—ones that he had especially selected or that were meaningful gifts. One of the ones he had made was a silver rendition of his favorite portrait of Mom. When I was a young child, he bought a batch of Kachina bolo ties, which were very dramatic. He had each of the girls choose one for their "future husband," and each of the boys chose one for themselves. Then he kept a couple for himself, and gave a couple to special friends. The ties were handmade and individually designed. Despite their regional acceptance, they were bold, even gaudy, and made a statement. I remember once overhearing someone "complain" about talking to "someone who had a damn doll hanging around his neck!" It puzzled me enough to wait until Dad came out of the office so I could check it out myself. It was only the Kachina bolo, something that looked perfectly normal to me.

Spirit of Adventure

Exploration, discovery, travel, and self-expansion are family values that Dad emphasized and reinforced. In everyday life the experiences that could have become routine and repetitive were welcomed opportunities for expansion. He modeled flexibility and interest. Special attention was given to tasks that occurred many times so that they never became routine, but required active involvement and choice making.

Kenilworth Elementary School was a mile from our home. It was two long blocks to the west and about ten to the south. I remember frequent discussions initiated by Dad about which route I would take to get there. He would ask, "Have you walked up Central and then turned west on Palm Lane, or have you gone up Third Avenue and turned on Granada?" In reviewing the route I had taken, he called attention to the fact that there were at least 20 possible "correct" paths, all of which led to Kenilworth. Dad would query me in a way that made me wonder whether I had missed an interesting landmark on one of the streets, or even in an alley. I would randomly choose my path as I walked and be very attentive to the appearances of the homes and plants on each street in my anticipation of Dad's eager interest. He even expanded my routes by asking whether I had ever considered going up Seventh Avenue or all the way over to Roosevelt to come down to Central. Although I did do this occasionally, it added more distance to what already seemed to be a long route.

As I think back on those conversations, I can see how Dad was honing my own abilities to find a goal and to stick with it, not to wander too far astray, to look and listen and learn as I went along, and, most of all, to enjoy the experience of being in the moment. As a parent, he was also gathering a lot of information about how I was spending my time, who I was with, and what I expected of myself. Further, he was using my eyes and ears to extend his own joy of day-to-day living.

Learning Hypnosis

Work with hypnosis was considered an everyday matter in our household. Each member of the family was required to learn some basic factual information about the topic and to be able to identify common misconceptions, but we were not required to study or explore hypnosis unless we had a personal interest in doing so.

Dad was able see my own genuine interest in hypnosis, and supported me by offering circumstances and occasions for practice. I was only about 10 years old when he taught me the basics of trance. In his initial work with patients he would offer them the option of watching me enter trance before experiencing their own. As my interest and knowledge grew, he began to include me regularly with his groups of students. He even brought me to the American Society of Clinical Hypnosis meetings and to lectures he gave, using me as a subject in those settings.

With practice, I developed the skill of drifting rapidly into a trance. I learned to explore the sensory variations that I found to be particularly intriguing, but there were other tasks like automatic writing that I never learned to be particularly good at.

Working with Dad hypnotically was always approached collegially, as if he could learn as much from me as I could learn from him. He expressed deep interest in my experiences and encouraged me to tell him the tiniest details. He had a way of raising questions about how far I had gone and why had I stopped there—did I think it was possible or reasonable to explore a little further? Initially he taught me using a standard formal trance induction, going on to hand levitation, crystal ball gazing, counting, the elevator, and several other techniques. The fastest and easiest technique for me was the confusion technique. I remember a long interval when he worked with me exploring the process of drifting in and out of trance, up and down with the deepening, and with memory. He found a lot of opportunities to show me the power of memory work and made arrangements so I could sit in with the Los Angeles Police Department students who were learning how to interrogate witnesses. He seemed to have a very precise feel for the place where memory ends and imagination begins.

Patience with Patients

There were many times that Dad facilitated an opportunity for me to work with patients, doing hypnosis and in other capacities. Sometimes I was part of the therapeutic constellation, and other times it was circumstantial, since the patients were in our home. I remember many wonderful relationships and a multitude of lessons that came out of that contact.

One patient with whom I spent quite a bit of time looked and behaved in what I perceived as a very well-adapted way. Although we were not permitted to inquire as to the nature of the patients' concerns, I did comment to Dad that I couldn't understand why anyone as well-adjusted as she seemed to be would require his services. He was very assertive in his reply, "Don't be fooled by what you don't know." The woman was a master of disguise.

One patient with whom I have maintained a long friendship is James. He worked with my father over many years. He had come to see Dad when he was still a young man who had been diagnosed with a severe progressive neuromuscular disorder, and faced a future of ongoing and increasing debility accompanied by pain. James talked to me about how Dad helped him with acceptance of and adaptation to his condition, and he also talked about the unusual elements of his relationship with my father—different from what he encountered with other medical resources.

James explained it this way: "I initially saw Dr. Erickson very frequently, sometimes every day for about a year. While I was at the office I would visit with the family and with other patients, and kind of make myself at home. I would say that the major groundwork was laid then. Dr. Erickson would check with me to see that I was really doing what I said I would do. I think he worked with me so intensively at that time because he didn't want to pass up the opportunity to strike while the iron was hot. Also, he knew that when I went away to college it would be a lot harder for me to get in to see him, and he needed to implant as many suggestions as he could, when he could."

After that initial interval of treatment, James described the relationship with Dad as being one "just like father and son. I would come over and just shoot the breeze or whatever was going on, unless of course I had something I needed to consult about."

Over the long course of James' treatment with Dad, the disease progressed, and James learned techniques of making ongoing adjustments to anticipated and real losses of functioning. Most importantly, he learned to maximize his life. These pivotal and central skills involved a long, incremental process of life lessons: skills of caring for oneself, taking responsibility for living independently, budgeting resources of all kinds, socializing, and participating in healthful recreational activities. James also learned to create an awareness of the physical changes his disease brought. Dad did take on James in a fatherly way, and the family members who lived at home accepted James and began to think of him as a close and valued friend—a relationship that persists today.

James erred in his self care repeatedly in the beginning, once even badly burning his feet on the hot pavement in Phoenix because he chose to walk barefoot like all the local youth. The consequences for this and other errors in judgment were severe, but handled as an opportunity to learn more, to avoid even more serious errors. After his feet finally healed, James adapted by wearing moccasins, a local style that offered both comfort and protection.

So many people credit Dad with the ability to magically arrest disease or to change the course of disease. It is impossible to know to what extent he was able to influence a progressive condition like James', but it is indisputable that James has adjusted philosophically to live each day for what it is and to make the most of it. He strives to be the best person he is able to be and he participates in life in such a manner as to be an inspiration to all.

James readily speaks of the concurrent struggles of increasing physical debility accompanied by inevitable pain of ongoing muscle deterioration, and is honest about his troubles as well as his successes. He describes Dad as an inspiration and role model as well as a guide for the challenges that he had not yet imagined at the time. James explains that Dad taught him at once to become more sensitive to protecting his body, and to learn to put the unpleasant sensations into a perspective of background noise.

When I asked James, years later, about the ways in which Dad had taught him to cope with his pain, James explained that he would "… drop a comment into the conversation. It may superficially sound ordinary, but something about it doesn't fit into the rest of the conversation. It may have been a socially appropriate thing to say, but it was not really logically appropriate. It would start a thinking process that I would come back to again and again. Although these comments would 'fit' conversationally, they would have a more far-reaching level for me. His comments turned out to be suggestions for me, just like a ball rolling down a chute—my obsession would define the parameters of where those comments could go."

James gave me an example of one of those seemingly small

comments that had a long lasting effect. "Once I had a little tiff with Roxanna, where I had done something she didn't think was funny. I don't remember what it was. Then Erickson commented that I have a great sense of humor. I have continued to think about the essence of humor for the last 30 years!" James does make use of good humor and finds it to be a quality that helps to sustain both him and others.

James explained my father's influence on him: "He helped me like a weaver creating a rug: A strand of warp and a strand of woof, one at a time, plotting out the journey of acceptance and adaptation over a long period of time. These included regular interactions with family members, being invited to spend special occasions with the family, and even the simple events of staying for dinner, or sharing a joke. Erickson accepted it when I felt bad, but he didn't accept that a bad feeling should be the 'end of the story.' So little by little, experiences built up that I could feel good about, experiences that fit into values that I already had and wanted to keep."

James has never been able to completely eliminate his physical pain. Instead, it is more of an acceptance and adaptation, part of the fabric of life we rest upon. The key is to not become trapped, ensnared, or lost in the negative net of pain and sorrow, but to keep moving along in the experience, and to seek a balance where the pain is tolerable and provides the least amount of distraction to living. The desirable experiences of life are also drifting by, and it is a human choice to grasp and retain those elements that best define ourselves. The focus of who we are and where we reach comes from within the self, and all people must adapt to limitations of one sort or another.

Another patient with whom I shared meaningful contact was Mr. Jones, who suffered from the loss of his right arm followed by phantom limb pain. Phantom limb is a condition in an amputated stump when the residual nerve continues to send sensations. The signals may give the person the feeling that the missing limb is twisted, cramped, or in an uncomfortable position. This condition can be agonizing and is often resistant to most forms of treatment.

I only was in the office with Mr. Jones and Dad one time, but on that occasion he recounted in extreme and excruciating detail the sensations associated with a tangled, twisted, knotted nerve of his amputated arm in an unnatural position. He told of the irresistible impulse to reposition, and the repeated horror of looking over and not seeing the absent limb. During the session, with us both in deep trance, we had a back and forth conversation reviewing the physical sensations associated with positioning of the arm and of moving the arm. It was a combination of my positioning, feeling the sensations, amplifying those sensations, and describing them. Starting off with arm levitation (a technique in which one's arm seems to lift sponta-neously) and going forward with trance catalepsy (frozen body posture), it was a natural progression.

In the appointments that followed that occasion, Mr. Jones greeted me in the living room in a warm way, but never further discussed his pain—it remained in the office.

Later he brought gifts that he had made: A set of cutting boards from blocks of hardwood, or a large bag of beautiful halved walnuts that he had removed from the shells intact. The art and craftsmanship that he was able to achieve after the loss of his dominant arm was testimony to adaptation. The gifts he brought were appreciated and treasured—the walnuts were used to adorn my wedding cake!

Our obligation as family members was to be polite and responsive to patients in our living room. One particular patient, John Doe, was challenging to socialize with due to his unexpected verbal outbursts and other unpleasant behaviors, including leaving a trail of chewed paper bits torn from the pages of our magazines. Although I remember John with a great deal of sympathy, at the time I was uncomfortable and complained to Dad that every day John Doe was waiting for me as I came in from school, lurking with an expectant look on his face. I didn't have a chance to relax or even go to the bathroom before John called me over and grilled me about my day. He asked about every class, every assignment, every teacher, every lesson, every kid in my class, all the while inserting paper or removing spit wads from his mouth and depositing them in the chairs, between pages of magazines or other inappropriate locations. John was there so early that it tied me up for almost an hour every day before he was called in for his appointment. I asked to be excused from the duty of being responsive to this patient who waited for me.

Dad responded by giving me an educational lesson about the notion of "shell shock." He talked about the tragedy of lives lost in battle, and the difficulties faced by soldiers who survived the combat and miseries of war. He talked about the irony of soldiers escaping with their lives but losing themselves. He lamented the burdens on families who remember the young, healthy, strong men leaving home and the jubilance of their return, transforming into tragedy as impairment and damage gradually revealed itself. He talked about the glory of our nation, of the tremendous cost of freedom.

I left the office with a deep sense of pride for our history and of shame for my own impatience. I regarded John Doe as an unsung hero to whom I personally owed my freedom. Over the next few weeks even the spit-wad problem evolved into a humorous competition among my siblings and me to see who could discover the most wads, as if it was some sort of an Easter egg hunt.

The lesson Dad gave me was to re-examine my own stance. He gave me enough information to show me that I had missed knowing the true strength of this tragic man, and I came away with a deep understanding that the lack of ability to present oneself well does not negate the treasures of individuality within each of us. I trusted that Dad would not ask me to participate in an activity that was not both safe and beneficial for me.

Another patient with whom I developed a close relationship was Jane Doe. She was an obviously quite disturbed teenage patient relocated to Phoenix for long-term treatment by Dad. It was obvious to all that Jane struggled with hallucinations and that her independent living in an apartment was an alternative to inpatient care. It was also clear that the relationship she had with her mother was a loving one and that separation from her family was a sacrifice.

As a teenager myself, I supposed that Dad did not appreciate the central importance of style, and my suggestions to "get her to dress more appropriately" were dismissed, although he did encourage me to spend as much time with Jane as I wished.

Sometimes Jane would bring baked goods that she had made, and sometimes she and I would bake a batch of cookies together in our kitchen. The treats were good and we had a lot of conversations on how baking provided such an easy common ground to make new friends—a tool Jane used extensively.

Jane got around on an old bicycle, keeping a tattered purse perched in the basket as she rode. I remember her tearful arrival at an unscheduled time, crying because someone had snatched her purse. The police were summoned and handled the report with extreme seriousness. I was confused by her sorrow—she stated the purse was of no value and the contents were only old Kleenex. I was as puzzled that a thief would target such an unlikely subject as her as I was by her despondency over the loss.

Jane was inconsolable and required much time with Dad that afternoon, but by the next day she was laughing. "Imagine the thief's surprise at finding only crumpled Kleenex," she told me gleefully. As she reveled in this image of discovery of the paltry booty, she declared that she was going to begin carrying much more worthless items in her new purse, and that she would "be prepared" to really enjoy the next thief to come along. Her sorrow had given way to enthusiasm and future planning. The underlying element of "being ready for the next thief" provided a change of stance, reducing the probability of her responding with despondency again.

When I visited her years later, I was pleased to note how she had grown. The details of her appearance, her ways of interacting and her general presentation were the same and yet spoke of transformation; a few details of interest added to her casual clothing replaced the look of neglect. Her haircut, while still bushy, was tied with a ribbon that kept it out of her face and prevented it from looking unruly or unkempt. She was carrying a respectable handbag. The minimal differences transformed her appearance in such a way that it would no longer be a detriment to her social acceptance.

In her work with Dad, there was a small and quiet tilt to the trajectory that her life took. The tilt dramatically influenced her ability to grow in a positive way. Each mannerism, every detail of her looks, every comment she expressed gave testimony to the positive being she became.

Mr. Frank was another phantom limb patient. He had cancer of the leg and had experienced a hemipelvectomy years before. He was a very remarkable man who was smart, courageous, and humble. He dressed in dignified suits with the pant legs rolled up, and he walked with a set of aluminum canes. He was friendly and inviting, calling me to sit and talk with him when I came through the room. His conversations were captivating and enjoyable.

On our first encounter, he was forthcoming that the reason he had come was to overcome bouts of pain that recurred in the absent leg, robbing him of his hope for a future. He actively solicited my opinion as to whether Dad would be successful in the management of such pain. I responded that Dad forbade us from talking about a patient's problems outside of the office, but that he seemed to be able to help just about all of the patients he saw. Then Mr. Frank began to treat me in a concerned grandfatherly way, focusing in on my future and my interests.

After Dad had begun to talk with Mr. Frank, I was asked to come into the office. I expected the usual brief trance demonstration, but instead the experience was much more extensive. After Dad had asked me to show Mr. Frank a simple trance, he asked me to consider the ways that I feel my body, and to consider feeling those same sensations in a new and different way. Dad's trance work was always replete with comfort, and always involved some drifting and some transformation of the senses, always involved an appreciation for inner strengths and the pleasure of new discoveries.

For a long time that afternoon in the office, Dad guided me in trance, exploring a multitude of alterations of senses, discovering one sensation and having it blend, or move into another, taking control of the find, and transforming it into another sensory value. There seemed to be endless possibilities of modifying and changing the information as it came in—time, intensity, wave pattern, adding color or sound, covering with imaginary blankets, remembering the sensations of touch and massage or temperature, modifying the sensations into another media. For the entire session Mr. Frank just watched me. I wasn't sure whether he was in trance or not, but he was genuinely interested in the long exploration of possibilities.

Then before I was excused, Dad gave me my reminder and "pep talk" that some day I might find these discoveries to be useful. I had, after all, talked about becoming a nurse, and in that line of work I would surely come across people who had difficult pain that needed attention. And pain, when properly treated, always required a full battery of diagnostics before any change of sensation would be appropriate or effective. I could take my new discoveries and new skills, and keep them secure until I found the right time to put those skills to use.

Mr. Frank continued to come in and always spoke freely to me about his progress, as if I was "part" of the medical team. He expressed hope that he could reduce or eliminate the use of painkillers because he knew he could better manage the pain than he had been able to before. He explained that a hemipelvectomy was a far bigger adjustment that a mere leg amputation, and that as a "future nurse" I needed to understand the magnitude of the adjustment that a patient like him has already successfully achieved. He was outspoken about the initial post-operative pain, and the complications of various tasks such as using the toilet. He also talked about the natural fading of the initial pain coupled with the insidious creeping-in of the phantom pain, and how intractable the latter had been. He said with confidence that this, too, would fade away, and he would be free to enjoy life with his family, and he expressed hope that some day I would be able to visit him at his own home. But he also said, in a remorseful way, that if the cancer returned, he didn't know whether he could tolerate it.

A year or two later, after a visit with Dad, Mr. Frank called me and arranged that I come visit him in his home. We spent an enthralling day in a nearby national park—a special gift to me. Not long after that, I learned that the cancer had returned and Mr. Frank had chosen to end his life.

I knew without doubt that his decision was not a hasty or a reckless one, but thought out with his own well-being and that of his family considered. I felt a great sense of loss, regret, sorrow, and frustration—feelings I discussed with Dad on the phone, and which he also felt. But I learned from that event that some problems cannot be resolved and that the end of life comes. More importantly, what is done is done, and the only useful direction is forward. I left my conversations with Dad with a resolve to enjoy every minute and every moment with a friend as if it may be the last.

Plants

Active participation in nature is an important part of the teachings that Dad promoted. Noticing, nourishing, and interacting with plants was part of our daily life as well as our growth over the years. Every side of our home had a collection of interesting plants. Some beautiful plants had distasteful elements when you got to know them better with the nose. Others had irritating qualities—the roses were hard to weed, the lantana prickled when it was trimmed, the pepper tree made you sneeze if you tried to climb it, and the pyracantha concealed thorns. All of their maintenance took place under Dad's watchful eye. Several of us planted our own Palo Verde trees in the ditch on either side of the house. Dad would generate great interest in the growth, particularly as to whether it was actions we had taken that encouraged rapid growth, or whether the plant was nourished by circumstance. His interest included not only the events of planting a new tree, but a genuine interest in daily watering activities.

Over the years, a series of extensive yard projects were undertaken. Though the backyard was dominated by two large and productive pecan trees, there was ample room for improvements. Like every other aspect of our lives and recreation, Dad was active in the planning, the creation, and the enjoyment of these projects. Bert built a fishpond in the northwest corner of the backyard, stacking a mound of dirt behind it to make a hill for a cactus garden. In addition to the fishpond, a picnic table was constructed by Allan and Bert, and also a barbecue pit that we used for family picnics or birthday gatherings. Literally every corner of the yard was regarded as fertile territory for cultivation of familiar or unfamiliar species. Each brought joys and changes on a daily basis.

After the move to Hayward Street, interest in new plants and trees continued. With Dad's support, I brought in a new element. In Phoenix, there are few rainstorms, but the few that come are deluges. The skies open up like a water faucet and the ground is saturated quickly causing flooding. The water force would often rip full-grown cacti right out of the sand, and float them downstream far from their origin. Ocotillo and barrel cactus would lie helplessly on their sides with the roots exposed and drying in the warm air. Unless they came to rest in a spot that was particularly receptive to the growth of new roots, they would dry up and die, a casualty of a short storm that no one had noticed. I found this particularly fascinating because the ocotillo is the plant that most boldly announces the extra drink of water. It gets little green leaves on its long bare spiny arms, and puts out bright torches of red flowers at the highest points. Now those leaves and flowers took on a new meaning to me—they were not merely flags of celebration for a long awaited drink, but they were wreathes of mourning for comrades that had been washed away in the brief flood.

Upon returning home after such a flood and consulting with Dad (who always queried me in detail about my walks, and the season, and the plants and wildlife I had encountered), I was encouraged to return, to salvage what I could and give the casualties another chance for life in our own yard.

I waited eagerly for the rains and searched for survivors with a passion. Timing was critical—the rains were rare, and there was only a short interval before the life would dry and no longer regenerate. I was unable to handle the task alone, and found myself recruiting my brother Robert, friends, school acquaintances, and even students who were attending Dad's seminars. When we would arrive home with our finds, Dad would stop whatever he was doing to come out and examine the specimen still in the car. The work was hard, exhaustive, and inevitably resulted in cuts, bruises, and needles under the skin. But by the end of the day we had the reward of a magnificent new specimen in the yard.

Ernest Rossi, now a renowned author and psychotherapist, helped me one week with a whole stand of barrel cactus planted near the alley. Once Robert and I planted a particularly large ocotillo in the yard of the office, and within two weeks it put out leaves and bloomed the most gorgeous set of blossoms I have ever seen. Another time a friend came across a saguaro arm lying in an unlikely place for growth, blown down by violent winds. He single-handedly rescued it, bringing it proudly to our doorstep.

Each occasion, Dad rushed out and supervised the positioning of our new specimens. They were welcomed into our yard with the revelry of being reunited with long lost friends. Dad instilled in us a pride in our cacti, most of which still thrive. Some have grown magnificently, taking over large sections of the yard.

Humor
Telling jokes, listening to puzzles, reading cartoons and cartoon books, looking for funny events around us—these are parts of life that were carefully cultivated. Dad's favorite comics were Pogo, Little

Lulu, and Peanuts, although he also read Tubby, Donald Duck and Mickey Mouse, as well as Nancy & Sluggo and Blondie. We would often read in tandem in the evenings around the fire. It was fairly common, when one began laughing, to pass the humorous selection over to one another so that we could laugh together.

Dad loved to keep people guessing what the things in his office were. One unusual item was a dried skate fish that had been marginally modified to look like a dead devil. Another item was a carving of a person in mid-transition into a werewolf. There was an old clock in the back area, which ticked loudly, positioned so that you could not see the source but only hear the tick-tock.

More than anything else, Dad loved to create elaborate and unexpected scenarios that would amuse others in a good-natured way. He would sometimes spend months in preparation for a good laugh, enjoying each of the elaborate steps along the way.

When he wanted Grandma and Grandpa to visit, but felt they were too proud to just accept the tickets, he created a puzzle that resulted in the fare being sent to them. His limericks were another way that he would call humorous attention to qualities within himself or others—often referring to himself as "the Old Codger."

Dad was the only member of the family who noticed my fascination with becoming familiar with all of the floorboards in the home on Cypress Street. In the office there were a few centrally located loose floorboards. Dad acquired a piece of driftwood, shaped vaguely like a shark, which was positioned atop a bookcase. He called me into the office and instructed me to, "Make it talk!" With a little practice I was able to discreetly step on the loose boards and make the driftwood rub against the wall. Shifting my weight, I was able to produce an eerie, dramatic sound that seemed to come directly from the "shark." He would call me into his office in the middle of sessions with students, doctors, or even patients and say, "Roxie, isn't it true that the shark can talk!" And I would obediently follow through with the joke that he had initiated.

One of the more elaborate jokes that he pulled on me was when my husband and I took a prolonged journey and sent our beloved dog Earnest to live with Dad and Mom. Earnest got in a fight with Betty Alice's dog Tom, and ended up with a temporary eye injury, which Mom reported in detail in a letter that never arrived. Some time later Mom wrote only, "Earnest is completely recovered," along with a photograph that displayed extensive bandages. I studied that photo for hours and hours trying to discern whether this was a setup for a joke that Dad was cooking up.

Dad was cooking up a joke all right, but not that one. My husband feels particularly strongly that a dog's first duty is to "greet his masters." When we returned home after our long journey, Dad waited until Earnest was in the midst of his emotional welcome, and then shouted, "Dad's dog!" Earnest instantaneously abandoned us to sit next to my father. Then as Dad slowly wheeled himself into the next room, Earnest was at his side with rapt attention, totally ignoring us. For our long visit Earnest remained single-minded in his devotion while Dad grinned, chuckled, and literally roared with laughter at our dismay. For the rest of the Earnest's life, my husband and I would frequently call him "Dad's dog" as we honored the great practical joke.

Ironwood Collection

Beginning in the early seventies, Dad became acquainted with anthropologist Jim Hills, who had done quite a bit of work with the Seri Indians of Mexico. Hills had taken a special interest in the native craft of carving ironwood. Hills made periodic "buying" trips down to the Seri region, followed by "selling" trips to Arizona, where Dad would be one of his first stops. Dad was fascinated with many aspects of this art. He and Mom both had a love for Indians as well as Native art. The harsh conditions of the environment where the Seris lived and their adaptation to sparse resources added to the intrigue of the beauty they created.

Whenever Hills came, he would spread his new acquisitions all over the living room, and talk at length about each piece. Hills knew all of the artists personally and took great pride in encouraging their refinement of skills. All of the pieces would be carefully wrapped and handled gingerly. The conversations between Hills and my father would go on for hours, sometimes days. There was discussion of each artist's individual talents, an examination of the knife marks, marveling over the smooth surfaces and the shine, admiration of the fine work, mourning over cracks in the brittle wood, and evaluation of repairs. The rendition of animals was considered, whether they showed movement, and whether the beasts were actually present locally. Signatures would be examined and Hills would express his hopes for the future development of each artist's talent. He would compare current works with earlier ones by the same artist in Dad's extensive collection. Each piece was regarded as an element of the persona of the carver, as a sign of the craftsman's learning and maturity. Sometimes innovations were shown: A collection of miniatures was made from the splinters of larger works, a moon, a musical instrument, and a pair of people. Hills would speculate on how these innovations would impact other carvers, and together they would speculate on how the array of wares would change before the next buying and selling journeys.

Finally Dad would make his choices for purchase. The new acquisitions would be ceremoniously positioned for immediately catching the eye. Then family members would come in to admire the new arrangement and the array as a whole. Hills' final comments, always the same, would be that Dad's contribution to the economy of this tribe was important. And Dad would respond that he took pride in owning "what is surely the most extensive ironwood collection in existence."

Every evening Dad would sit and admire the carvings. Every day he would invite new people to come in and look at the marvelous collection. He never tired of explaining the inherent qualities of the wood: It is a desert wood that is exceptionally hard, so carving it is a tremendous challenge. He let the collection communicate his admiration for a people who survived in harsh conditions, who found beauty all around them, and who found the inner resources to express that beauty in a way that could be shared with others.

Planning and Writing

Dad was an early riser and would get up in the quiet morning hours even after staying up late. He didn't seem to need as much sleep as the rest of us, and would often pick himself up with a short afternoon nap.

He arranged his office and his desk in the manner that allowed him to reach for a piece of paper to record his ideas and notes whenever they came to him, keeping a box of "scratch" paper that had only one side used. A special box a patient had given him held the stubs from pencils other people had "used up." He encouraged us to bring home all of the pencil stubs from school, and the children competed to bring the most or the smallest pencil stubs that could still fit into the brass pencil holder he always wrote with.

It was as if his mind was always full of ideas that he could scarcely find the opportunity to get down on paper, or to refine and re-write in a more effective way. During every spare moment, he would drift to his desk and begin to capture those ideas on paper. But the ideas seemed to come faster than his ability to record them, and he could never catch up to the practical matter of getting all of them into articles for publication.

He was able to keep his patient records in his head and never needed extensive note keeping. He approached each encounter with the information of previous visits right in his mind, and only scribbled sparse records of vital statistics or other pending issues.

When he drafted a professional article, he would often call Mom into the office to develop the ideas a step further. She would usually stand, or lean over his shoulder, as opposed to most everyone else, who, when called into the office, immediately sat in the patient/student chair.

Canoe Trip

Dad never talked about his canoe trip unless you asked him. And if you did, he told only little bits of the adventure that shaped him. It was a personal time for him. But Bert has a real knack for seizing meaningful moments and planting little seeds for further conversation. I remember so many occasions when Bert would point to a photograph or a feature in nature, and make a remark like, "I like this picture because there were sycamores along the river bank when Dad made his canoe trip." Then I was left with asking for more information, or letting that piece of the story just soak into my background frame of reference.

I grew to understand that Dad's canoe trip did much to strengthen him physically. It also gave him the opportunity to regain his independence after the assault by polio. It was almost impossibly difficult to imagine that he could have the fortitude to embark alone. But he understood his own needs, and in the journey overcame a multitude of handicaps. The journey is a quiet backdrop for our family, which has tolerated, even encouraged, adventuresome travel among the young adults.

Creative Maintenance

Although Dad did not physically participate in the household maintenance tasks, he cultivated the energy in the children who had a tendency to want to do those chores. Some of the home improvement tasks were extremely large and successful. Bert worked with Allan and Robert to extend the garage complete with a bomb-shelter-quality doghouse (bomb-shelters were popular in the fifties) and a small greenhouse. It also had a large composting area where we recycled all our organic garbage. The new garage had room for the washing machine (we never had a clothes dryer) and enough room for a workbench in front of the car. The older structure was a narrow board design, but they managed to seam the concrete slab foundation flawlessly, and to join the two structures with remarkable professionalism.

The gravel driveway was replaced with a concrete one that Allan (who was deeply involved in the labor and has a talent for math) informs me, was 10 feet by 137 feet, and each bucket of cement was mixed in a small home mixer. The labor was hard, but as with the other projects that Dad supervised, he was there praising and admiring the work as it progressed. The end result was a very well-built structure, a monument to cooperative labor.

Dad was involved in every step of the planning, and his time and physical limitations were accepted as part of the configuration. I remember feeling how lucky we were to have Bert and Allan who were so willing and enthusiastic about doing this manual labor, and I even recognized how they had special and unique talents. What I now realize is that the encouragement that Dad provided and the collaborative effort were also special and unique elements that were exceptional.

The Question of Death

When I was in the fifth grade, I witnessed a baseball accident in which a friend died. I was quite troubled. The unwitting actions of another friend, the third baseman, had contributed to the accident, and the sudden finality raised all of the typical questions regarding the nature of life and what happens to one's being once life is extinguished.

We did not belong to a church, and Dad rejected the notion that accidents and crises such as this were part of God's plan. He was comforting in response to my questions, emphasizing that we cannot know or even imagine beyond the experiences we know of life. What exists before and after is so far beyond the scope of what our minds are able to grasp, that it is really counter productive for us to waste our time imagining and attempting to define the un-definable. Rather, it is our task, even our duty and responsibility to attend to the life in front of us, to make the best of it in every moment, especially with the understanding that it is a finite, unique, and fragile gift. This is where we need to focus our energy, our attention, our questions, and our direction.

Dad guided me towards an inner exploration that would lead to more accurate discovery than debate and discussion with others. "Search your self, your history, your own origin—the story is all told in there," I remember him telling me. "Anything that you hear from others has already been distorted by their own need to explain what cannot be explained. The truth, the answers, the information, the secrets are all within you. What is God? You can never know from asking another man, you have to look within your own self." Between those curtains of darkness before birth and after death, we do have a short time, but the question of eternity lingers in my thinking and in my choices.

While in high school, I visited a vast number of churches and once found myself in a position where a teacher suggested I would make a better grade in class if I would continue to attend his church. I was torn by the ethical dilemma and sought Dad's advice.

Dad explained that what I had witnessed was an example of the fallibility of organized religion. He encouraged me to hang in there, to learn all that I could about the ways that so-called religious people bend the rules in the name of religion. He told me to explore what this experience really taught me about the nature of God and man. It was my responsibility, he stressed, to re-examine my own values and to recognize just standards.

The most important lesson that I learned was that one need not depend on any outside definitions of good and bad, or morality or justice, but that we can find these directions within—and the compass that inner guidance provides is powerfully strong.

The Long Line of Students

Dad had cultivated interest in his work from the time he was a boy. Some of my aunts told me about occasions when he would demonstrate hypnosis to his siblings, or do experiments that he would later be thrilled to explain to anyone who would listen.

The trail of students coming to our doorstep continued throughout Dad's life, and each serious student was enthusiastically welcomed. It was a phenomenon that was enriching to the family and advanced Dad's work in ways that reached beyond what he was able to do alone. This is the true value of teaching—that good can be spread so much further.

The great work that was extended by students was not lost on Dad or on our family. I personally have developed a sense of duty and an obligation to share knowledge that can help people in many ways. It is not always possible to foresee how small acts of courtesy or kindness can impact people later, sometimes in very profound ways. I recognize that my own influence may positively affect untold numbers of nursing students and the patients in their practice. In conclusion, I have tried to live a philosophy of life that I learned from my father: Recognize your own unique situation and do the best you can with it.

CHAPTER THREE

ALLAN ERICKSON

FURTHER REMEMBRANCES

My favorite story about my father took place very late in his career when a clinician asked him how long it took him to be able to understand and effectively use hypnosis. My father turned to him and said, "Well, I think I'm just beginning to get the knack of it." That was not the response that the inquirer wanted. He desired a simpler answer. What my father was saying, which is something that has impacted me a lot, is that if you don't learn, you wither. You need to learn until the day you die. You've got to learn all the time. I used to think about this when I was working, before I retired. About once a year, I'd say to myself, "I have to take a class! I don't care if it's relevant; I need to sign up for a class. I must learn something, or else I may deteriorate."

My second story involves something that happened to me when I was about 12 years old. I can clearly recall the context in which it happened. This was the first time that I realized my father treated me differently than the way my friends' and acquaintances' fathers treated them. I also realized that my father's way of parenting me was a lot better:

I'm in the backyard of a friend's house during a Boy Scout meeting. I'm about 12 years old at the time. We are standing in a circle and the adult leader is in the center. For reasons known only to him, the leader points to the opposite side of the circle from me and asks a kid, "What does your father want you to be when you grow up?" The kid thinks for a few seconds and gives him an answer. I'm standing there thinking, "Pretty soon he's going to ask me that. What am I going to say?" He goes to the next kid and again I hear, "What does your father want you to be when you grow up?" It progresses nearer to me, and I begin to panic because my father hasn't ever told me what he wants me to be when I grow up! I'm getting more apprehensive because I don't know what on earth I'm going to say. When one of my friends replies, "My father wants me to be a rabbi," I immediately think, "He wants to be a rabbi as much I do, and I am not even Jewish. He doesn't want to be a rabbi when he grows up. I know my answer now!" When the scout leader comes to me, he points his finger and asks, "What does your father want you to be when you grow up?" I reply, "My father has never told me what he wants me to be when I grow up."

The scout leader didn't like that answer, but I thought at the time, "I'm right! Every one of these boys and their fathers are wrong. They're not living for the right person." I had a very good feeling, and to this day I happily remember this story.

Now I have a third story. Perhaps it has something to do with my father's genetics. His talent must have skipped a generation and gone into my daughter. My daughter is very good at implanting ideas into other people in an unexplainable way. I was traveling with her and know her well enough that I sometimes can anticipate the occasions when she is going to implant an idea. I once sat back and said, "I'm going to watch how Nicole is going to implant an idea in that person that we just met." Exactly what the idea was, I do not remember, and it is not important. Perhaps it was something as simple as getting the person to join us for dinner. What I do remember is that I could see that Nicole was getting ready to implant an idea into this person's mind! The next thing I remember is he was going to join us for dinner, and I had no idea how she got that idea across to him. I watched carefully and tried to discern what she did. However, after Nicole implanted her idea, I had no more knowledge of what she had done than I had before. Once when Nicole did this in front of me, I asked her afterwards, "How on earth do you do that?" And Nicole's answer to me was, "I don't know. I know I'm doing it, but I don't know how it is done."

I can figure out what she doesn't do. She doesn't make promises, she doesn't flirt, she doesn't ask, but suddenly the person is suggesting

122

exactly that which was Nicole's idea in the first place. Dad had this same sort of ability. He could get his patients to do things that he wanted them to do with outcomes that were good for them. I think he knew that people are naturally resistant to people asking them to do something. Furthermore if something was "their" idea, my dad could, without all of those logical steps of persuasion, get his patients to do beneficial things. It's a mystery that I have never been able to figure it out, even though I tried to carefully observe occasions when I knew it was being done by both my father and my daughter.

I'm now older, with many years of observation, and I have developed more, but by no means do I have a complete, understanding of my dad's manner of persuasion. I also have listened to and read several explanations by the so-called experts on these matters, and, to be frank, some of them don't know what they're talking about. What's been written about my father's manner doesn't, for the most part, reflect what he did. These explanations miss the most essential aspect of what goes on in my father's kind of indirect influence.

If someone writes down the words my father said in a clinical session and then reads them like an actor reading a script, using all the same vocal inflections, it will not be the same. A certain form of intimacy is required, which is conveyed through body language as well as tone. There's no seduction in any way, shape, or form. That's what makes this so mysterious. Something fascinating and essential is going on at the nonverbal level.

Clearly there is a heightened connection with the other person, and an aim to positively influence them.

My father's resourceful way of influencing others also required saying the right words. He didn't say things that got the person inappropriately diverted, and while he was using words, he carefully took notice of the other's responses. My observations of my father reveal that when he was trying to positively influence or to implant ideas, the person doing the persuasion is very carefully focused on the person.

My sister Betty Alice and I were in the far reaches of the world with this workshop leader who was telling a bunch of stories about my father. I was sitting there, kind of over in a corner, groaning. What the leader said was not the way it happened. It was not reality. He essentially argued that if my father wanted "Happy Birthday" sung to somebody, he would start breathing in rhythm to the song and pretty soon other people would pick it up. I was thinking, "Wait a minute. There's a little more to it than that. You've missed the bigger point." I said to him, "You only have about 10 percent of what's going on, and you're attributing the whole behavior to this 10 percent, but there is a lot more than that going on."

I know enough about how my dad influenced patients to know that others have not adequately figured it out. I talked to quite a few of his patients, and some became my friends. I could tell that they were being influenced to behave in their best interests, but they did not know how they started behaving the way they did. Sometimes you see this same manner of influence exhibited by outstanding politicians. John F. Kennedy had, I believe, this charismatic influence that could get people to go along with his ideas without any direct suggestion.

Again, the ability to carefully observe the other person while interacting with them is definitely a part of this influential process. Nicole traveled the world by herself for about 18 months. She was able, while walking down the street, to say to herself, "Watch out. That guy is dangerous." The average person is not able to pick out this person as one with evil intent and that person as perfectly fine, while going down the street. Yet in spite of this kind of gift, Nicole is not, and my father was not, 100 percent accurate. He'd occasionally get it wrong, and there were patients he could not help.

In my opinion, one mark of a good therapist is being able to say, "I can't help that person. He or she is beyond my ability to do anything positive with." My dad once told me about a sociopath who he hoped would be locked up and the key thrown away. He had killed, for no apparent reason, five people. Dad had no hope for the man.

He also recognized when the patient needed to be given additional help that he was not qualified to give. Sometimes he would say to a patient, "Go get a complete physical, and then come back and tell me about it." Once he got the physical problems out of the way, he could deal with the psychological aspects of the situation in a more productive way. "You only need me for part of your problem," he'd say.

My father was very careful to help keep people from wallowing in their weaknesses. He believed people should build on their strengths. He wouldn't be happy with today's proliferation of treatments that underscore the role of victim. A story that my wife recently told me nicely illustrates his outlook. She teaches developmental reading at our community college, where she hears a lot of excuses for "why I can't read." Recently, a person came up to her and said, "I'm having trouble because I'm dyslexic." She immediately retorted, "Well, so is half of my family! That's not an excuse!" My father was dyslexic. It took me 40 or 50 years to learn how dyslexic I am. It became apparent to me while reading an article about dyslexia, and I said, "Hey, I have that symptom! No wonder I have trouble with that. I didn't know I was dyslexic. How about that!"

My father was very good at "working with what's on the plate that's brought to you." He used the strengths a person has to overcome their weaknesses. He didn't obsess about where you were coming from or the traumas or limitations of your past. All he wanted to do was solve the present issue that you were worrying about.

There was a woman who came to my dad and was videotaped in a clinical session. Her problem had to do with low self-esteem. My father, through age regression, took her back to her childhood. What he constantly emphasized, in his roundabout indirect way, was, "You are unique. You are different from everybody else. Let's use your uniqueness to help make you feel good."

When my daughter, Nicole, badly sprained her leg and developed difficulties with it, my wife, Luanne, and I went to every doctor we could find to check out what was going on. They all miss-diagnosed her condition. They tried to place it into a diagnostic cubbyhole that just didn't fit. Then we met a doctor who stood Nicole up and tapped her leg until she said, "That hurts." He went farther and up and down her leg, noting each time where it hurt and where it did not. Soon he could outline the muscle that was sprained. After that, he pulled out his anatomy book and said, "Looks like that muscle, doesn't it? That's what is often called 'the monkey muscle.'" Now that doctor was not a genius at diagnosis. He was very interested in not being distracted by cubby-holes. My father was also reluctant to put a name on a patient's illness.

My Dad had one patient who was what would be called bipolar nowadays, but there were no drugs back then to alleviate the symptoms of bipolarism, so he had no choice but to work with other means. Instead of pills, he emphasized giving people tasks. There were always hidden messages within the tasks. Sometimes the patients wouldn't finish the tasks, but that didn't matter. This particular bipolar patient became a very good friend of mine, and helped me through high school Spanish and taught me how to play chess. Dad gave him the task of building a chess set. I could see that he would never complete it, and so I told my father, "Hey, he's never going to finish that chess set." My father simply replied, "I know that. Stay out of it. It has nothing to do with you." The patient never finished the chess set, but his life moved forward in a very positive way.

Most of the tasks that my father gave to people carried a hidden purpose. The person would have this task, which they often didn't really want to do, but they would do it or partially do it, and it would result in a desired outcome. I would occasionally discuss this with my father when I was older, and he'd say something along the lines of, "Hey, you're missing the point." He suggested that the task was only there to divert in a useful way.

My father had great respect for the subconscious (or unconscious). He wanted your subconscious to solve your problems. I visually conceive of my subconscious as a sack I have over my back. I throw problems into this sack and then, when I need to, I stop and pull out the results I want. I believe my father utilized the idea that we can put things, to use my analogy, in the sack and let them distill. And then when appropriate, we stop, set the sack down, reach in and pull out an outcome where everything is nicely connected. Dad greatly admired the subconscious mind and its natural ability to solve all sorts of problems. What he also did was indirectly take the patients' strengths and uniqueness and set up situations where they could move past their difficulties.

The subconscious, by definition, can't really be explained, articulated, defined, concretized, photographed, or measured. Perhaps, in some way, it is equivalent to what other cultures in the world, that don't have the word "subconscious," would just call "great mystery" or even "spirit." It is outside the purpose of our directed thinking. When you play jazz piano, you can't think of where you're putting your fingers. It's your subconscious that directs them. When I was young, I had contests with myself to see how fast I could run down long flights of stairs. I found that I had to think about something else while I was doing it, because as soon as I thought about what I was doing, I'd trip. When you watch people who knit with great skill, they're watching television or focusing on other things, while they're carrying the pattern in the back of their mind.

As I travel around the world, one of the things I love to watch is the weaving of carpets, and I often ask many questions about it. When I start inquiring how the weavers are doing their weaving, they can't answer me. They don't know because they're not doing it; their subconscious is doing it. They can make an extremely complicated pattern while chattering away with their friends. As they swiftly weave away, I may go over and request, "Please slow down your work so I can watch your fingers." When they do slow down, they often make little mistakes because now they're thinking about it. After I watch them for a while and get a general idea of what is going on, I say, "Thank you, now go back to normal." Then, once again, I have no idea of what they're doing.

I'm convinced I could teach myself knitting if it was important enough to me. It's not that hard a task. I would have to do some kind of ritual to distract my conscious mind in order to let my unconscious take over. I might try some nonsense behavior like walking, spinning around five times, and then walking backwards. That's one way of getting my conscious mind out of the way so the real worker can get on with it.

I've watched various people conduct hypnosis, and it's pretty easy for me to tell the masters from the people who just don't know what they are doing. The way you tell is that the person doing the trance is intensely looking at the patient, looking for feedback. As soon as the patient is the slightest bit resistant to the way that the practitioner is pointing, the master adjusts, retreating, to go forward again. Whether in hypnosis or therapy, the masters pay attention to the feedback, knowing that each person is unique.

When I go to the dentist, I say to him, "Don't bother me. I'm going on a hypnotic trip. I'm going to my backwoods and walk around among the trees while you do your work on my teeth. But don't call me back here. You can ask for my cooperation, but do not call me back." Unfortunately, many dentists do not understand what is going on, so they do call me back—again and again. They do so by asking, "Are you all right?" "Hey, I was down under the oak tree, and you just brought me back to this dumb dentist's office. Of course I'm all right! I would have told you if I wasn't." Now I have found a dentist who pays attention to me and lets me go out under the oak tree.

Perhaps for people to heal, the therapist must divert, not "heal." And to do so, you must act in the patients' vested interest. You divert their unsuccessful maneuvers, getting them out of the way so people can use their own creative resources to solve their problems to the best of their ability. At the same time, you never push anyone beyond his or her limits. I'm never going to be a Russian linguist and some others are never going to be mathematicians. We have to learn to embrace and utilize our strengths, while being amused by our shortcomings.

I remember a patient who came to my Dad because he wanted to lose weight. Metracal had just come out at the time—it was essentially a drink for losing weight, you drank meals of only Metracal and it gave you a balanced diet and you would lose weight. This man had been on it for a very long time, but he wasn't losing weight. When my dad cross-examined him, the awful truth came out. Metracal tastes quite bad, so to make it taste good, he had put two heaping scoops of ice cream in it! Once Dad knew that, he could move forward with a plan to help his patient lose weight. He was a master at finding out what was going on in a patient's life, so he could use the data to constantly readjust his interaction.

My father and I enjoyed humor and practical jokes, and we would go out of our way to play them on each other. Once I was able to pull one off on him—the only one where I had real success. He used to edit a journal on hypnosis and I used to read it, especially if there was an article by him, because all the kids wanted to see if their names were mentioned. We'd glance through it real fast to see. One particular article was on mirror-writing. He talked about a woman who mirror-wrote under a trance, mirror wrote left to right and right to left. I was confused as to how one can mirror write left to right!

I wrote him a letter, saying, "I think your article on mirror-writing is really confusing, particularly when you mention frontwards and backwards. No wonder your subject was having trouble with some of your instructions, you gave her confusing directions and there's no way that she could have done that." I signed the letter, H. A. Noskcire, which is Erickson spelled backwards. I was really surprised, because within a day or two, I got an answer back, and he very carefully cleared up my misunderstandings. I sent him another letter, saying, "Thank you very much for your letter. You absolutely cleared up everything. It was a wonderful letter." My last sentence was, "Perhaps you noticed the mirror-like qualities of my name." When he read that he went to Mom and asked, "Betty, what's this guy talking about?" That's probably the only time I pulled one off on him.

In my adolescence, I was exceedingly shy with girls, but isn't every

15-year-old or 16-year-old boy exceedingly shy with girls? They absolutely covet girls, but they don't even know how to talk with them—which is a big problem. During this time in my life, I received a phone call from an extraordinarily nice-sounding girl. No matter what subject we discussed, she always knew the answer. There actually were two girls who would call me like that. They'd get on the phone and talk with me, and when I'd ask them something like my dog's middle name, they'd know it! I never figured out what was going on until my father woke me out of bed late one night, and introduced me to these absolutely stunningly beautiful girls—the girls he'd had call me. He was doing this not just as a practical joke, but as a way to help me be able to interact in appropriate ways with girls. I was astonished and amazed. I am sure it was a win–win situation. That's how he worked. I don't know how it was a win for them, but I'm sure it was. And everybody won in it and everybody had a good time.

These days, I frequently e-mail my sister, Betty Alice. We do what we call "reality checks," that is, we check out our memories to verify past stories. We remember that there were a lot of elaborate practical jokes in our family, but they were fun and did not have a mean cast to them. We continue learning to appreciate and respect both the absurdity of our own lives and the people who came to see our father for help.

OPPOSITE PAGE:
MHE with Bert and Lillian's son Albert, with Betty Alice's son David Elliott, with Roxanna's daughter Laurel, with Allan's daughter Juliette.

CHAPTER FOUR

GRANDPA'S LETTERS

ALLAN ERICKSON:

Years ago, I played a practical joke on my dad. I had been married once before, but it didn't last for various reasons, mainly because (as my first wife said) she was not suited for me. I finally met Luanne, and she and I got along very well from the beginning. I could tell that there was great potential in developing our relationship. We met at a time when I had a number of old cars. I decided to send my dad a picture of my '61 Cadillac, an eight-year-old vehicle. I positioned Luanne on the hood of the car in a very nice pose and then had her sign the photograph, "With love, Luanne." I didn't want to tell my dad anything, so I just put the photograph in an envelope and added a simple note, "Here's a picture of my 'new' car." He wrote back, defeated, saying, "All right, what's her name?" I sent my father her name and address, with no other comment.

LUANNE ERICKSON:

Then Allan's dad wrote me a letter and, although I lived in Maryland, I hadn't grown up there, so I'd never heard of the use of "Miss" with a first name like "Miss Mary" or "Miss Lynn." He addressed his letter to "Miss Luanne." I don't remember anything of the content of the letter, other that it was addressed to "Miss Luanne." I wrote him back a letter, saying, "My name is Miss Crozier or Luanne." I addressed it to "Dr. Milton." From then on, I always called him Dr. Milton, and he always called me Miss Luanne. We had a correspondence before Allan and I were married. Then it turned into a correspondence with the children and the dogs and everything else. It went on for 11 years, with our exchanging initially about two to three letters a month.

The correspondence became more intense after our first child was born. Dr. Milton complained that he wasn't hearing enough from our baby daughter. That's when the letter writing increased. Often I wrote daily; sometimes I wrote two a day. I wrote in the mind-frame of our daughter, from the perspective of how she experienced her life. He would always write back saying that the child was doing her job very well and that she was effectively teaching her parents. "Keep doing what you're doing. You're doing a good job." The letters were never about our relationship. They were only about our relationship to the children.

It started out in fun, but we learned that you are successfully able to hypothesize a child's thought patterns if you pay attention to their behavior. For example, when Juliette was 18 months old, she was walking in a garden. She found a bush that was just the height for a small child to think it was a chair. She walked up, sat down on it, and smashed it! She was surprised that it went down, and I was horrified that she'd ruined a bush in this garden. We wrote a letter saying, "Dear Grandpa," and "this is what I did; this is what I thought; and this is how Mom reacted." He wrote back his comments. Sometimes he'd just send a cartoon with a comment like, "This was your father when he was a child."

It was a lot of fun exchanging these letters and it provided us with great entertainment. We all had a good time doing it, and there were a lot of messages and wisdom in what he wrote.

He had a patient who had a dog, and before long that dog started writing to our dogs. Our dogs would write back. The correspondence was only between the dogs. They would tell dog adventure stories written from the dog's perspective. I am sure he had a reason why that patient, out of all the dog-owning patients he had, started this. But it turned into a lot of fun for us all.

BETTY ALICE ERICKSON:
Dad was a prodigious letter writer, and wrote to no one more than he did to Allan and Luanne and their first child, Juliette, who was born July 14, 1972.

The first of June, 1969, Dad wrote Luanne:

Concerning my views about dreams, I can state quite simply that they are the substance that pave the way to goals of achievement. Such goals are reached more rapidly if a dreamboat is available… Not being a psychoanalyst, I do not draw obvious inferences about slips of word/mind unconsciously the self, often with only a slight disguise.… Miss Luanne, you write you would like to look through my 200-year-old Encyclopedia Britannica. *Miss Luanne, the darn thing is opaque. You just can't look through it.*

He continued writing to her, continuing conversations and answering questions. In October 7, 1977:

Auto-hypnosis once learned is always learned. However you should plan to use it for this and that, now and then, without deciding specifically what it is to be.

Remember that spontaneous unexpected trance you reported. Well, have more such unexpected trances. They pay big profits.

But most of his letters were to Juliette. He wrote directly to her, asking plaintively why he hadn't heard more from her parents, whom he knew "were very busy with a new family." Luanne, caught up in observing the amazing development of her first child, decided to respond from Juliette's perspective. Dad would then respond to "Juliette with the 2 e's and the 2 t's." Later, he addressed Juliette's sister Nicole as "Knee-coal," giving both girls a special and silly variation of their name from Grandpa. He wrote to both Juliette and Nicole, and to their younger sister Jill, until just a few weeks before his death.

They wrote about everything—Juliette's adventures, her thoughts about her place in the world, the birth of her two sisters, and often about her problems with her parents as she was trying to teach them just how individualistic she was. His responses created a world that Juliette could cherish when she grew up and that her parents could appreciate both then and later. Some of his letters were about his philosophy of life; some were in praise of Juliette's behaviors, naughtiness as well as milestones. They included cartoons and jokes, questions, and information about events and even the yard—sometimes in a child's phrases, "My eggplant has four eggs on it now." Some were just playful stories.

One of the very first letters was from September 16, 1972:

My Dear Sweet Juliette: (with 2 e's and 2 t's) ...I want you to start life in a state of delightful sweet innocence, but to learn as rapidly as possible that every rose has its thorns and there are roses of many different names, shapes and sizes. Practically everything in life has its imperfections.

You are quite right. I have imperfections. But none serious enough to prevent me from living on borrowed time even behind three score and ten, and I have every intention of continuing to live. I have succeeded in wearing out one wheelchair and the second is beginning to show signs of wear and tear. My beautiful black hair is thin and has faded to a silver color. That handsome face that captured Betty, your grandmother, is no more. In fact, there have been many changes, and many losses of virtues, valors, and values once highly esteemed, but sufficient remain to give your grandmother some small bit of happiness. However one of the greatest values that remains unimpaired is a sense of humor. It is outrageous at times, but as the years pass, it is remembered with tolerant amusements....

By the time you have reached your late teens, you will find yourself in an unbelieving frame of mind that your father can be that poorly formed, maladjusted, limited, and restricted, but at the present time, enjoy him and do not dread your progressive uncovering of the many things you will uncover as the years go by and wish could be different. There is also a possibility that the time will come when you will express doubts about your mother. But as the decades go by, you will reach a stage at which you will be pleased that your parents managed to survive despite their many deficiencies and their failures to achieve actual possibilities of achievement.

One other thing you should know at the present time is that there is coming to you in the relatively near future, a realization that your parents do not fully appreciate you, that they lack the subtleties of understanding necessary to satisfy your wants, and they may even take exception to the things that are possible to do, and they will confront you with problems similar to ones that your father encountered very young, which caused him to ask his mother this question, "Mama, how can I get so dirty just standing still?"

To summarize, life is full of all manner of things, ranking from the very best to the very worst. But the good things have got the bad things beat all the way to hell and gone.

Your very understanding paternal Grandfather

PS, I do have a riddle for you. Your father always had difficulty getting people to spell his name correctly, and he made sure you would have that same difficulty. What should puzzle you is why he didn't put two l's in your name? Your amazed paternal grandfather, the grandfather you have always wanted.

He continued writing. When she was a year old, one of his letters said:

Juliette, …you can handle the impossible with the greatest of ease.

Another:

[Your grandmother is] sending you a dress specially designed to pick up dirt, stains, etc., …all of which is a universal practice for the intelligentsia of your age.

In a letter about Allan, Juliette's father:

…your father was all that a man should be, a man of character, keeping his word, doing a good job, …[from] your one and only, wondrously wise and good and great paternal grandfather who thinks the learning of self-discipline adds greatly to the joys of life, especially if you have a beautiful wife and a charming daughter….

The letters continued on September 7, 1973, to Luanne:

...It is best to leave the specific wording [of hypnotic suggestions] to your unconscious mind. People could do things much better if they relied upon their unconscious, experiential learnings.

September 10, 1973

To be philosophical, perhaps it is well that you learn early that parents are a source of handicaps and embarrassments to their offspring for what seems to be an interminable, unendurable length of time, and then they become a source of joy and inspiration to their grandchildren.

October 12, 1973 to a 15-month-old Juliette:

That snapshot, of you pushing your stroller, was charming, but a word of advice. That pleasure is decidedly transient, so get all the joy you can from it because it will soon be a thing of the past.

November 17, 1972, he wrote to 4-month-old Juliette:

Regardless of what others think, an individual's learning should be accomplished in his own way. For example, some of the neighbors thought I was mentally retarded and my mother emotionally defensive because I was not talking at the age of four, while my sister, two years younger, had been talking incessantly since the age of one. My mother's defense of my silence was accurate, "The boy is too busy doing other things. When he gets around to it, he'll talk."

Isn't it outrageous how some people, even parents, will repeatedly ask a normally bright child, "Show me your hair, (eyes, nose, mouth, chin, ears)" and do this time after time, week after week, and wait with baited breath for the child to comply. Do they think the child should monotonously demonstrate that there has been no forgetting? Or is it that the parents have forgotten? Or do they think the child should keep in practiced readiness to inform strangers who may not know these simple things.

Hence do not get bugged by adults who are very likely to have weird things of what and when and where and why and how you should learn. Stick to your patterns; your inherited genes are all that you need.

On January 18, 1974, he wrote to 18-month-old Juliette:
I have taught a lot of people the importance of knowing that battles can be lost and from lost battles comes knowledge of how to win more important battles.

Some of the letters were jokes constructed especially for a little child. Consider the one written on February 12, 1976:
Juliette, I am in terrible trouble and very sad. I just hope I don't cry. I got into trouble when I opened the letter you sent me. I took the letter out of the envelope and unfolded it, but when I tried to read it, the letter was upside down and I never learned how to read upside down. I feel so bad. Can you tell me what to do?

Juliette's little sister Nicole was born February 3, 1975. "Wise and Wonderful Paternal Grandfather," who often signed his letters with those initials, continued to write Juliette "with the 2 t's and 2 e's," but began to include Nicole in some of the letters, as well as writing some to Nicole herself.

April 11, 1976 after a visit, he wrote to 3-year-old Juliette:
A wonderful trip home. I am so glad you could make things really exciting in the airport. Why do parents think that the only way to change planes in the airport is to walk straight ahead as fast as you can without looking at anything, and never seeing all the things and other places and other places that are so good to see and go to.... Of course, your sister is still a baby, even if she can walk, so she missed all the special fun you had. Did your Mama tell you that it was your help that it made it possible for your baby sister to walk? You showed her how to walk.

There are a lot of things you will have to teach her because your Mama and Daddy don't know how to teach your baby sister as good as you can.

April 12, 1976, to Juliette:

I know your Mama and Daddy are busy and sometimes forgetful. I bet they forgot to tell you it is Spring. So will you please tell your baby sister that it is Spring and explain what Spring means? It's nice that baby sister has a great big sister who can help baby sister, who teaches lots of things to the baby.

May 31, 1976, to Juliette, who was almost 4 years old:

Lots of times, parents answer philosophically when a simple answer would do as well... A simple question, and they will bore you with a long-winded explanation having no bearing upon your question—when all you want is a simple how or why or what or when or who. Want to have some fun with your parents? Ask them separately how come they picked out a sister for you instead of a brother. They will go into an elaborate explanation, and I think their explanations will vary greatly.

In my next letter, I will give the simple and understandable answer that neither of your parents could think of.

June 1, 1976, explaining to Juliette why her parents had chosen a baby sister rather than a baby brother:

The simple answer I promised is this. Everybody knows there are only two kinds of babies—girl babies and boy babies.

Well, when your mother decided she wanted another baby, she wasn't thinking boy or girl. She was just thinking "baby." She took the first one she felt, and she fell in love with it before she knew whether it was a boy or girl.

August 2, 1976, when four-year-old Juliette had cut her hair herself:

Now I know you are a big four year old girl. There is one thing every big girl has to do, and she really should do it as soon as possible when she reaches the advanced age of four years. Some girls are so silly that they wait until they are almost five years old before they cut their hair. Your mother cut her hair, and so did both of your grandmothers and all of your aunts, but only those that were trying hard to be five years old. …I am very glad that you are all through with that four year old hair cutting. Now you can settle down to the long hard job of becoming a good, strong, smart five year old girl.

August 28, 1976, when Juliette had taken care of Nicole:

I am very glad that you are such a good big sister to Nicole. Little kids don't know a lot of things and really need help. Little kids don't always know the right thing, but you showed you did. Having to help look after a little kid like Nicole is a lot of work, but it will help you to grow up and be a Big Five Year Old Girl and learn the things you need to know to be like your mother, but not so old.

September 3, 1976, to Luanne about a decision Juliette had made:

…don't be misled by the simplicity and quietude of Juliette's discovery.

November 28, 1976:

…in the process of growing up, many difficult choices have to be made and you might as well start learning as early as possible. In making those choices, the obligation is yours and you must not make false choices. Now your mother has lots in her favor and there may be some things that can be said for your father. But the day is coming when you will have to replace him with someone younger and more handsome. But your mother's virtues are long-lived.

1977, to Luanne when Luanne wrote how she had handled Nicole's attempted manipulation of her:

I hesitate to give advice and I'm glad you beat me to it by having Nicole weep at your request. Also…when she demanded to wear no mittens, you demanded that she wear no coat. Always let the child get away with something that doesn't count—the train ride was important to you, the ticket to her.

In rearing children, the best advice is: Suffer now, enjoy later. Also bear in mind that kids, in their efforts to find the right way to do things, first explore all the wrong ways. It educates them better if they have lived through it.

June 3, 1977, to 2-year-old Nicole:
One of the sad facts of life is that grown-ups always take advantage of their superior strength and size. But, that is also their weakness since they get accustomed to depend upon that.... Well, educating your parents will be your duty for some time and you have the talent for that.

June 13, 1977, after 2-year-old Nicole had followed Allan on her little riding toy. Allan often took Nicole as he walked the dogs but on this occasion, he told her to stay at home. Nicole was disappointed so she waited until her father was far enough ahead of her that he probably wouldn't see her when she set out to follow. Several hundred yards from the house, she caught up with him, much to his astonishment.
...I am, indeed, very pleased and proud of you for your long adventurous riding toy trip. Of particular merit is the fact that you followed behind your Daddy. That was an example of true wisdom in making adventurous trips. That is something your Daddy lacked when he was young.

July 22, 1977, to Nicole:
But don't you think you are big enough and old enough to scrap the whining and crying techniques? Your mother is getting wise to it. Why not try the techniques of innocence and deafness so much used by adults. It gives you an opportunity to get a lot done even before your mother realizes that you are "deaf" and comes charging over to you, much to your frustration.

September 12, 1977, 2½-year-old Nicole wrote her grandfather about a battle she was having with her parents over her potty-training and signed her letter, "Stubbornly, Nicole":

I fully believe in… conniving. Frustrating Mother is far more fun than wearing pretty big-girl panties ever could be.

At about this same time, her parents also received a letter:

To Luanne and Allan,

Nicole's latest letter is beautiful and so promising. She is telling you and herself that she is the master of her fate, the captain of her soul.

This means a good future. She will never be forced to join the "In Group." She will never have to smoke pot, take drugs, do alcohol or be promiscuous, "like all the others."

Nicole is Nicole and belongs to Nicole and she intends to find out, for herself, all the possibles and all the impossibles, and there are fewer impossibles for her than for others.

At her present age, Nicole knows very little and she has to try all the variables. She is secure in herself and her likes in her future. She likes diapers, puddles, and frustrating you. She has to find more likes so that she can make comparisons and judgments.

Instead of being frustrated by Nicole, why not frustrate her? That will be a wonderful learning for her. Too bad the puddle is so small, too bad the puddle wasn't over there, over here, too bad that she didn't have on her prettiest panties, too bad she didn't get her old panties wetter. Is there no way she can frustrate you? Come to think of it, maybe if no puddles and the pottie being used will frustrate you, but no, you just don't believe it.

You can look hopefully for puddles and wet panties. She has to know how to frustrate you, but she is also discovering the joys of dry panties and moves on with new learnings, comparisons and judgments.

April 25, 1974, to 21-month-old Juliette:

Parental bullying is one of the hazards of life. But don't worry about it since you have the stuff to come out the winner.

A truly amazing phenomenon of life is the skewed attributes of human intelligence resting in the youngest and the oldest generations, with barely a trace left for the older generation.

April 21, 1977, to 4-and-a-half-year-old Juliette:

I tell you it's not an easy thing to understand the funny way grown-ups act and talk.

July 8, 1974, to nearly 2-year-old Juliette:

... keep busy, keep your parents in a state of alertness, be unexpected and be acutely aware that the obvious is usually the unexpected by parents. Among the most worn and frayed statements in all languages is, "But my child could...."

August 25, 1975 to 3-year-old Juliette who was complaining that her father asked her why she asked "Why?" so much:

Why don't you follow your father's noble example so much and demand to know why you say why, and then explain that you say why because you want to know why you ask why, and why don't you already know why you say why and why is it necessary to keep saying why and why isn't there some other way of saying why, and why did why ever become the only way of saying why and why can't there be other ways of saying why, and why doesn't your mother like to answer your whys when why is the only way to learn why, and why does your mother think you have a bad case of the whys when she doesn't even know the whys of Nicole will cause a new rash of whys from you, and why did your mother ever get herself on the answering end of why, when she had already had the frustrations of the asking end of why, and why are there so many whys, and why isn't why something other than why, and why aren't some whys whats and why aren't some whats why? Tell me, please, why.

February 28, 1978, to Jill who had been born the previous day:

My dearest youngest granddaughter, I welcome your arrival....

October 7, 1975, to Luanne and Allan:

Children are born ignorant [and] learn slowly at first. It slowly increases to an arithmetical progression at about one year as opposed to a unit at a time and, between age one and three, you might compare it with a glass with an amoeba which divides into two every minute. How long will it take when the glass is half full to become entirely full? The answer is one minute.

Well, at the age of two years, 364 days, there comes the 3–5-year-old state and that small glass of knowledge becomes full. It's like shifting from a single-shot target rifle to a modern automatic machine gun and every bullet hits a target—there were misses with the target rifle.

A bright three year old becomes overwhelmingly aware of so many many things, each of which offers a multitude of opportunities.

Knowledge brings power and a tremendous need to exercise that power. But how? That's the question! At age three, the child doesn't know many ways and the few they know, the parents are always taking away. For example, "Don't throw food on the floor, don't throw your dishes down, don't spill your milk, don't, don't, don't." Parents complain about the terrible "no" stage of the child. Try to guess how sick and tired the poor kid gets from all those "don'ts" from pa and ma, and ma and pa get fed up with "whys."

But the kid gets fed up with the inadequacy of pa and ma's inadequate explanations and lack of directions. Parents need to observe and steer that aggressive and active child into aggressive and satisfying action. Remember the old "What's to do and what's to eat?"

February 7, 1980, six weeks before his death, he wrote a little story to all three girls, Juliette, Nicole, and Jill, who would soon be moving to Australia with their parents.

We are your Growing Up Fairies. We have eyes to see everything you do and ears to hear everything you do, because you are like all other children. Each of you has a special Growing Up Fairy.

Nobody can see us and if you did see us, you would be so full of wonder that you wouldn't be able to speak. We Growing Up Fairies have to look after little children and each child has his own special

Growing Up Fairy.

Maybe you would like to know what your Growing Up Fairy looks like. We all look the same. We have eyes on the top of our head, on each side, in front and behind our head and all over our head so we can see everything. We have ears on our cheeks, a big swivel ear for each cheek so we can turn it in all directions and we can hear from every-where. We all have three left front feet and we write with our middle left front foot which has 32 toes on it. That makes it hard for us to know which toe we should put the pencil between, so we always try to find some secretary to type our letters. The outside left front feet we walk with. That makes us two times faster on the left side than on the right side. We have only one right front foot.

We also have a row of ears on each side of our neck, across our shoulders, all down our sides and on both sides of our seven hind feet. We have seven hind feet because we like to go barefoot and it gets awful hot in the summer time, especially in Australia, so sometimes we wear shoes on two feet so that our feet don't get too hot. I walk on two of my right hind feet so I can walk two times as fast with my two left front feet. That way I can go in a straight line and I have a row of ears down my backbone, clear out to the end of my tail. The end of my tail has a great big ear on a swivel joint. It keeps turning every which way and we never miss anything.

Sometime, if you want to come to see me, you will find me in the Third Hole in the Middle of Nowhere and there is nothing around, not even dirt, so it is awful hard to find me. It is very warm and comfort-able there, and if you ever come to visit, you may meet our best friend, the Easter Bunny.

We were talking with him the other day and we said it would be very nice if you sent us each a Valentine card, but don't send any earrings. When we try to wear earrings, they make an awful lot of noise and we like things quiet so we can hear things....

With love from your Growing Up Fairies

CHAPTER FIVE

CANOE DIARY AND PHOTO ALBUM

ARUM, NEVADA

1901, MHE's father, Albert Erickson I, with Mr. Simon Davis, his partner at the silver mine, remembered as the Silver Bell mine. LOWER LEFT: 1901, Mother, Clara Minor Erickson with sister Florence and baby MHE LOWER RIGHT: 1903, MHE in the saddle with Mr Davis, his father's mining partner.

WISCONSIN

1906 – 1919

CLOCKWISE OPPOSITE: 1906 Family portraits after returning to Wisconsin: Albert, Florence, Winnie, MHE and Clara; 1910 MHE, Florence, Winnie; 1915 Clarence, Winnie, Mildred, Florence, MHE, Effie, Bertha, Cecelia, and Edith Carol (added later) with their parents, Clara and Albert (seated left and right).

BOTTOM LEFT: In 1919, MHE was stricken with infantile paralysis and almost completely paralyzed. This picture was taken as he began to recover in 1920, or even 1921, as he was re-learning how to walk.

146

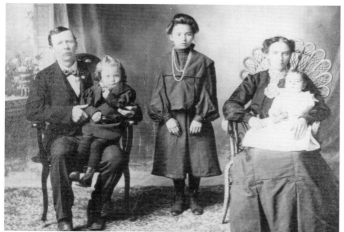

VINTAGE MHE JOKE

An old farmer was asked why he seemed so gloomy as the weekend approached. "Well," he said, "on Saturday we hitch up and go to town. I get my Saturday shave, talk with the boys at the barber shop, Ma shops at the general store and then we listen to the band play in the park. So far, so good. But then I get together with the men and like every other Saturday night we get good and drunk! And, oh, how I dread it!"

1922 – 1924

TOP RIGHT: High school graduation class trip to Standing Rock, Wisconsin. It was the tradition for high school senior boys to jump from one rock to the other. MHE jumped before he became ill.

MHE'S
DIARY OF CANOE TRIP
JUNE 15–AUGUST 27, 1922

In the summer of 1922, three years after being stricken with infantile paralysis, and as part of his recovery, MHE took a canoe trip. He began at Lake Mendota outside Madison, Wisconsin, down through the chain of three adjoining lakes, to the Yabara River then, following various rivers, to the Mississippi. When he started the trip he was unable to portage his canoe without help from others. At the end of his trip, he returned to his starting point, paddling against the current and able to carry his canoe on his shoulder.

He kept a meticulous diary of his trip and later corresponded with many of the people he had met. Erickson's attitude toward hardships, his optimism about the innate goodness of humans, deeper reflections on life, homesickness for his girl, his abiding connection with nature, and his personal evolution are all apparent in the words of this

20-year-old farm youth. Excerpts from that diary follow; some punctuation and words in parentheses have been added.

NIGHT JUNE 14TH. Thump! Thump!—"What the deuce is that?" I asked sleepily, and awakened to stare at a flashlight. "Well, what do you want, Buddy," I asked. T'was only a cop, who merely wanted to know my family history and why I was sleeping in Tenny Park.

JUNE 15TH. Started at 4:00 A.M. Started in rain & wind. Thru (Lake) Monona and half way thru Waubesa. High wind—whitecaps. Had to make for shore—got acquainted with Mr. & Mrs. Whitson—supper and fishing with them. Ardath—how empty life would be without thoughts of her. Studied history and Psychol.

JUNE 16. Started 8:00. High wind. Did not get out of Lake W. until 4:00. Could not find outlet and had to fight wind! T'was wonderful. Caught a bluegill. Ate supper of boiled fish, cocoa, bread. Wrote more in Ardath's letter. A beautiful sunset. Arms, shoulders, forehead sunburned. Wrote Mother.

JUNE 17. Dull, dark, dreary and cold. Stayed here. Supper of perch, boiled beans. Was all discouraged until I ate my nice supper. Read history, studied two German lessons. Dreamed a lot about Ardath. Never an unworthy thought enters my mind when she is in it. And every night her picture, as I wind my watch, is a source of inspiration to me.

JUNE 18. Sunday. Caught 6 fish, went thru L. Kegonsa, broiled fish for dinner, reached Stoughton. Hunted up Rev R. Jones. Ate supper there, went to Epworth League, spoke 10 min. on a "Practical and Reasoning Religion." Got acquainted with Ralph Chipman. God gave me much to be thankful for.

JUNE 19. Chipman and I start out, he to help me pass dams. The Jones gave me $3 to help me out, packed up a lunch and told me sometime to help out somebody else. I surely will. We passed four dams. At Fulton, lost ax in 8 ft water, dived after it, had glorious adventure wading and swimming back and forth in H20 clearing way. We camped on river bank, had supper, wandered up to farm house to sleep in barn. Dreamed all night long about Ardath. Saw some beautiful scenery, shot a lot of rapids, had to go barefooted, wade and pull canoe in places.

JUNE 20. One year ago I sold my first book. (Erickson earned money selling books when he began college.) Reached Rock River at 8:15, beautiful scenery. Chipman left & set out for his home 25 miles away. Hired Ward Bros Transfer Co. to portage canoe $1\frac{1}{2}$ miles around the two dams. When Ralph Chipman left me he gave me $1.65 to help me along. I shall pass that along to someone more needy. Went down river 4 miles. Stopped at Charles Kilmer's farm for canoe had hole in it & needed patching. They are ideal people. Had supper with them & slept in bed.

JUNE 21. Split big pile of kindling, put patch on canoe, left it to dry, wrote to Ardath, Zelma, Mother, Doc, studied German, helped dig foundation trench for sorghum mill, went to Jamesville with folks, milked cows, pumped water, painted canoe, set fish line, studied Psychology. Day by day Ardath grows more lovely and unattainable in my thoughts for what have I done to deserve her.

JUNE 22. Milked cows in morning, packed up, Mrs. Kilmer gave me a nice lunch. Wrote letters to Ardath, Zelma, & Mother. Called at post office, only one letter—from Zelma. Boy helped me portage dam. He speared couple of Buffalo (fish) for me. At Beloit bought sponge $.10.

Yesterday Harry Fox asked me, "Well, Milton, bumming around?" and that word "bumming" hurt my pride. As for these gifts of money, I'm not taking charity, yet to refuse would hurt them, so I'll accept, return it later, and also pass on the gift. I am capable of caring for myself, but people doubt it because of my limp.

JUNE 23. Started at 5:00 A.M. Absolutely discouraged, ready to give up everything. Leg was lame from twisting it last night. Have to worry about my eats, no tent, no money, and afraid that I will get no benefit out of trip. Camped on river bank, read two chapters of history, slept. Dinner of broiled Buffalo. Feeling more cheerful. Studied German lessons. Dreamed great dreams of my future. I wonder how much I will accomplish. Supper—bread, cold meat, cocoa. Started letter to Ardath and Zelma. Am making Ardath's special. No sunset tonight. The sky is my roof.

JUNE 24. Awakened 5:30—fine night's sleep. Determined to enjoy camping. Paddled on, talked to various clammers. Camped on bank of Rock [River]. Got acquainted with Mrs. Jones' hired man. Milked 5 cows, got supper. Got job for next few days watching cows on river bank. I want so much, receive so much, but do so little in this world. If I could only give more.

JUNE 25. Sunday—milked 9 cows by 6:20. After breakfast took cows to pasture, read Tolstoy's "Resurrection." A picture of Russian life showing corruption of government, immorality & ignorance of people. Found that somebody had taken things out of canoe & examined them & had broken cover of box to get inside. Apparently nothing missing, my feeling was an intense desire to get hold of culprit & beat him.

Watching 15 yr. old Ruth Jones and her actions toward her indulgent mother. I am learning to recognize the faults and their causes which I do not want in my children.

An idea for a speech suggested by Tolstoy. Throughout the world we have riches & poverty, luxury & starvation, surfeit & suffering side by side. It is not right. "The poor ye shall have with ye always" does not necessarily mean the poor in worldly goods. But what's the remedy? I know not, save that education paves the way for progress.

When I think over how I used to weigh Ardath and Sara Jones, how I used to think I would not have a girl, how I would feel like forgetting about Ardath, I now believe the only trouble was my uncertainty about myself, whether I was worthy, whether I could have any hope. But now I am determined and I only wish I could show Ardath how much she is to me.

JUNE 26. Milked, watched cows, finished novel, read "American Magazine." Contained articles by successful men telling how they attained their success. According to their formula, I'm well started for I have faith in myself, a definite aim, am willing to work, can utilize my time, and know the reason why I want to do the things I have mapped out. But in this I am no different than other men for they are the same. I am an iron mine. The question is, can I take the ore within me and turn it into delicate finished machinery of service to mankind?

I am writing a serial letter to Ardath, i.e., I am writing a few lines on one page & then continuing a few lines on another, etc. I wonder how she will like it. Every time I think of how Zelma says Ardath is not pretty, it makes me angry. I cannot bear to have anything said against her, yet I have no right to do so. Often, often I wonder what she thinks of me.

JUNE 27. Studied Psych. while waiting breakfast. Wrote letters. Studied German down in pasture while waiting supper & after. The serial letter to Ardath finished. I hope she enjoys reading it.

Darn it all! Every time I think of those money gifts, the madder I get. Yet I had to take 'em in order to avoid wounding their feelings. Better my feelings hurt than those of others. However, I shall merely pass them on. I am able to rustle my way entirely without charity and I aim to produce as much as I consume, more in fact.

I brought out Ardath's picture, the one she pasted in the "Badger" for me. I wonder if she smiled as she pasted that picture in as she is in the picture itself.

JUNE 28. Got acquainted with young fellow. Told me he & his girl intended to take their honeymoon trip in a canoe. A splendid idea.

JUNE 29. Washed out canoe discovered life preserver and bicycle lamp had been stolen. Put initials on paddle. Hated to mar it that way.

Thought this morning about the monotony of farming, the monotony that the farmers permit to arise. They do not seem to know that there is a mental as well as a physical side to life. Their minds are always at rest. They sit, but do not sit & think, they walk without thinking, and they work with their minds at rest. If they are reading a newspaper, and cease, their minds cease functioning. They allow themselves to grow in the habit of not letting their mind function unless they have some definite visible and tangible object upon which to apply it. As a result they become plain and simple in their mental enjoyments. The simplicity of country life is far from being a virtue. It is a vice, for it is a sign of numbed brains.

Tonight milked seven cows in a hurry. Mrs. Jones' hired man is tired and cranky, exceedingly so. But the curious part is that it is infectious. I keep thinking how nice it would be to punch some of it out of him.

Asked Mrs. Jones what she thought I was earning. She said, "Your board." So it stands. Told her I'd leave in the morning, she said, "Why don't you

154

leave tonight (7:30)." I wonder if I can get her to pack up a lunch for me. Well, she has been an interesting study, and I have learned considerable of human nature through her. Am neither cast down nor elated. She merely means nothing to me. It should not be so.

Studied German—dreamed great dreams. May the one greatest of all come true.

JUNE 30. Mrs. Jones, after much hesitation, haggling, etc. finally offered me $.75 to stay 3 more days. Refused. Finally offered me $.50 to stay today accepted. Counted money with me. $8.52. $4.65 given me, $.60 spent, $.50 to be earned, making a total so far of $9.62. Started with $4.97.

Was thinking about this so-called struggle for life—for subsistence. So-called because it is really a struggle to acquire property that must be left behind. To work and slave to acquire a few acres of land means to put your life into senseless dirt. It should not be so. Mrs. Jones is all-together too close as regards board—but the laborer is worthy of his hire, & I eat plenty.

In Well's "Outline of History" came across statement that no political changes or revolution came about without bettering existing conditions. This made me think about Sovietism in Russia. Am well satisfied here for I have produced far more than I have consumed.

When I think of Ardath, I often feel she is too good and pure and holy for me to even speak to her. Yet I want her to love so much.

JULY 1. Summary of stay at Jones. Wasn't good enough for a bed, given a place on floor of porch to sleep. Got up at 4:45 to milk, milked at least 5 cows, usually 6 or 7, drove cows a good 3/4 mile, watched 'em, ate a cold lunch, drove cows up at 3:15, fed 'em grain, milked 8 out of the 16, helped bottle milk, picked cherries and between times I studied. Worked 6 1/2 days, came to settle up. Mrs. Jones informed me I had played a dirty trick for demanding $.50 for my work, carefully insulted me, and then gave me the $.50. The hired man George felt so bad about me being so treated that he was willing to pay me. His sympathy brought tears to my eyes. George is an old man, a grandfather, a man with a big heart.

Left Jones at 8 o'clock. At dam made friends with engineer of power house. He got two friends of his to carry canoe around for me. Had to wade rapids and pull canoe. Had a lot of cheerful kindly questions & greetings thrown at me as I paddled. Ten miles or more down river, camped on bank.

Two men came along in a truck. Looked like rain, so they told me that I must come over to their place on the island. Took down tent and paddled over. They are two bachelors with hearts the size of barns. Had me sit down to supper with them, a dandy; potatoes, bread, milk, eggs. Told 'em about Mrs. Jones, and how they cussed.

The river is getting more and more beautiful. High wooded banks, oak, elm, ash, box elder, willow, hackberry, maple, dogwood, thornapple, & trees I don't know. All along in river are big islands so I never know for sure whether I'm looking at the shore or an island. Camps all along add a human touch. My camp was on the gently sloping river bank in a nice grove. Behind me was a high wooded bluff. The river was wide, smooth, and swiftly gliding. The opposite bank was a high wooded hill with the different shades of green of the leaves making a beautiful picture and everywhere through, 17 year locusts were humming and birds were flitting and singing a beautiful world.

JULY 2. Bill & Marvin are their names. When I awakened, they looked at me smilingly and said, "You talked a lot in your sleep about your girl." I whirled around and faced 'em. "What did I say?" "Don't remember now, 'cept you were writing her a letter."

Had a fine breakfast with them. Visited them, telling them about Aunt Winifred, about my studies and told 'em to use powdered sulphur for chiggers. (They) are two bachelors. Bill is a stock-buyer, Marvin a clammer, about 45 yrs. old & sure all heart. They are greatly worried about my limp & want me to stay rest of summer & rest. A few days ago, Bill picked up a stray little chicken. Now the chicken answers to (the name) of Pete, though whether he, or is it she, is a Peter or a Peteress is not known. This morning, I sat on the porch, Pete climbed up my leg, and after trying to eat my (watch) fob, buttons, fingernails, & teeth, he cuddled down & went to sleep. However, that made the cat jealous, so she did likewise & then Tige the dog asked permission to lie at my feet & wag his tail.

After a while Pete changed his roost to Bill's lap. I saw a big beetle out in garden, went & captured it. Squatted on porch, and waving hand, called, "Hey, Pete." Pete opened his eyes & looked at me. "A moving hand," he thought, "why that must mean something to eat," & jumped down and sailed into the beetle. Quite a scrap & just as Pete killed him, he fell thru hole in floor. Poor Pete! He looked so disconsolate that I said, "Well, never mind, Old Top. Hey Pete, come along with me to garden. Hey Pete, and we'll get some more, Hey Pete." We trotted out, Hey Pete & I. "Hey Pete, come here." Lifted up some boards. "Hey Pete, right here," and Pete valiantly assailed, conquered & devoured about 15 big black bugs. "Well, that ought to fill him up," said Bill, "Hey Pete, come here & go to sleep." And Pete did.

Behind the house is an old turkey gobbler who labors under the impression that he has a beautiful voice & a magnificent strut. Both Bill and Marvin think so too they bought him a few weeks ago, "thought he'd be nice to have around." Bob is "the darndest ornery hog you ever saw." but they like him just the same.

Helped dig potatoes & helped Marvin prepare beet greens. Marvin made dandy biscuits for dinner. Three roughneck friends came over to island bringing liquor and well intoxicated. Pretty soon they were all intoxicated to a maudlin incoherent stage. I soon got away & went to bed. I could not help laughing at the serious manner in which they conversed and the absolute idiocy of their maudlinism, and yet I felt miserable and sorry for such a state of the intelligent human mind. I fell asleep, thinking of what I mean to make greatest in my life.

JULY 3. Everything here scrupulous neat. Went for canoe ride, found a place where current was too swift for me to paddle up. Wrote letters to Zelma, Ardath, Mother. Letter to Zelma contained nothing but the last sentence of my trip-story down here and statement that having written the end of my story, nothing to do but seal envelope and send it. Second letter contained regret for doing so. Third letter contained story.

My wash is dry but it doesn't look like what mother used to do.

JULY 5. Got up at 5:30. Dressed, packed up canoe. Ate breakfast. One (of Bill and Marv's) friend tried to give me a dollar. Persuaded him to keep it so I could write for it if I needed it. Cal (another friend of Bill and Marv) heard the conversation & came & tucked a dollar in my pocket. Nothing to do but accept it. But I can feel truly grateful to Cal. Bill & Marv want me to write and to come back & visit 'em. I certainly like them. Paddled on. All the clammers around knew about me told me to take good care of myself, to get well, not to go too far & on way back to visit 'em all. Friendliness & kindness of human nature. It made me feel happy.

Mailed cards and (letter) no. 2 to Zelma.

A furious wind and killing work paddling. However, zigzagged back & forth hunting for the quiet spots. Stopped on island to eat bread & marmalade. A fellow out canoeing stopped to talk, (name of) Beveridge. Had splendid visit. He decided to help me over the dam. Another man crippled in the hand. "One cripple," said he, "ought to help another." Helped Beveridge portage canoe (and) luggage. Beveridge wanted to come along, said good camping spot on island (a) mile down. He is a wonderful fellow. Talk about being fortunate. All I have is one stroke of good fortune after another. Every piece of bad luck is really good luck & most of it comes dressed up. Had splendid supper, fixed up beds in one of the shacks and we both wrote letters.

JULY 6. Left at ten to ten. A pretty strong wind. Saw Castle Rock and especially beautiful scenery. Talked to clammers. Interested in my trip. Paddled 25 miles. Dixon at 5:30. Pretty tired. Went to Post Office, 5 letters. Read Ardath's first and that was the only one I could keep in my mind. Doc advised me not to go steadily with any one girl. However, Ardath is the only one to convince me of that.

In her letter she reminded me of the fireflies of Vilas Park on the night of the Epworth League party. I was mighty happy that night. Slept in canoe, dreamed everyone was trying to get me to give up Ardath, but I stuck to her.

JULY 9. Arose 8:30 breakfast, shaved, tidied, sat down to study Psy. Passers-by stopped to talk. A scanty dinner of beans. About 1:00, party in car came along, asked me if they could eat there. Said "sure." After they had eaten, one came over and told me I must come over, get acquainted & eat. You bet. So I had a splendid dinner.

After that took Miss Dorothy & another out canoeing. The wind was furious & they were scared. Once I paddled hard for five minutes without making headway against the wind. Finally I got back to shore. A jolly witty bunch out for a good time. Wished me lots of luck & a good time. They all admired my coat of tan.

Went back to studying. As it had looked like rain I had turned tent around & carefully trenched it and fixed up for a rain. It was raining hard & I was in tent day-dreaming & listening to patter of drops. I saw way out in (the) water a whippoorwill went out & rescued it. It was raining all time we were in water. Swam, & floated with water beating down on face & waves washing over.

Fixed up canoe, tipped on side, chest under it quite far up shore. Raining, crawled in tent. Started to wind watch stem broke. However looked at picture and went to sleep. Several times during night I awakened wind blowing hard & raining furiously. A glorious day every minute enjoyed.

JULY 10. Awakened warm & dry. Heard water crawled out to look at canoe & chest. A groan. Water had risen about 30 or more inches, chest half full of water, crackers spoiled, clothes wet, sugar all water, oatmeal wet, a sorry looking sight. Tipped over canoe, washed it out, pulled it up on high bank, unpacked chest & threw things (out). Somehow or other, the calamity was too interesting to feel bad about. Put dry things in chest, took wet clothes up to farm house upon invitation to dry 'em. Trying to dry crackers. Mr. Williams came over to see how I was. Gave me eggs & apples. Mrs. Snyder at farmhouse gave me 3 eggs & some potatoes. Gave Mr. Williams my watch to have it fixed. Took kids out in canoe in afternoon, studied Psy., dug some more potatoes. Got supper of oatmeal with egg beaten in it.

At about 6:00, Williams came watch repair was $.50. I took Virginia in canoe had a philosophical talk with her. She prefers flippancy, thinks me odd because I like to work. Her idea of life is money, good time, no cares. She likes horses & dogs cares nothing for the fireflies, the croaking of frogs, the singing of the tree toads, the quiet of the evening. After we got back, Mrs.

158

Williams left me a 2 qt. can of cherries & a lunch for tomorrow & asked me to write. She is a mighty fine woman and I certainly like her. Fixed up all things for an emergency, went to bed, hoping, dreaming of Ardath.

JULY 11. Rained last night but everything O.K. Got water, breakfast & despite cloudy looks, packed up & started. At first dam, Henry let me thru the locks a kind, friendly-looking man. At second dam, I made my first single-handed portage. Had to lift up a walled bank 4 ft & let it down 5. Chest was hardest. Took me 45 minutes. Paddled a short distance, began to rain furiously. Parked under a bridge between two piles and let it rain. Left the bridge in excellent spirits at 11:00. The sun was shining brightly, soon dried my tent & overalls. Had this morning happened during first week, I would have been heartbroken & utterly discouraged. This morning however I considered it just an interesting little part of the trip. After supper I fixed some apples Mrs. Williams gave me. I wonder what kind of sauce they'll make for I'm boiling 'em now.

This is a beautiful evening. Everything so quiet and peaceful, the river is rushing by so swiftly yet without a sound, the sun is faintly shining, everything getting ready for sleep. Yet the birds are singing, wrens especially. In the distance a Bob White keeps calling. I am sitting in a chair before the camp fire, over which is a camp kettle boiling, the fire is burning brightly, and I am writing this.

All day long have thought of Ardath. My every thought of her draws me closer to her. She is the first person whom I couldn't compel to follow me. She is my equal, has just as strong a will and we have the same ideas and purposes. We think alike, even act alike under similar conditions, yet we have our own individuality and personality with different thoughts and desires & wills.

Just now a beautiful delicate mayfly alighted in my hand to molt—the prettiest little creature I ever saw—the work of God.

JULY 12. Hard rain & furious wind last night. Awakened, raining on me, cold. Put trousers on, draped tent over cot, went to sleep. This morning H$_2$O in canoe. Bailed it out, beans and rice again wet, clothes also. Brought 'em up and dried 'em on stoves. Ate breakfast of apple sauce & crackers. Dinner another qt. & crackers. Studied History, found all of my books had got wet in the brief case. But even that couldn't make me feel discouraged or disheartened. Mastered one German lesson and wrote to Ardath and Zelma.

About 5:10 my morning acquaintance again appeared. He had caught two bullheads of good size and thought I'd like 'em for supper. Man! Wasn't that dandy, for I had boiled plain beans for supper. He paddled downstream & pretty soon returned with a catfish. Wasn't that kind? I hope I can always be as kind to others, as others are to me.

All day two wrens in front of the house and another pair behind have been singing when do they ever find time to eat.

One hears lots about the simple joys of life they must be experienced before appreciated. All day I've run around in B.V.D.'s & trousers without a belt, barefooted and I've enjoyed it immensely. Last night when I found I had a bare cot to sleep in on a porch, I felt ecstatic. In fact I was about tickled to death when I found that I had the dry, board floor of a porch to sleep on. I'm enjoying this trip more & more. Today I cooked my own meals, I studied hard, I wrote letters and I brought pleasure into that man's life (whom I met this morning) as well as received the pleasure he brought into mine.

All day long a remark that Virginia Williams & her chum Miss Harris made keeps haunting me. I was telling 'em some of the things & the work I have done in the past and both said, "My, I'd like to read about the things you will do in the next ten years there'll be a lot of them." Now I wonder what will I have done in the next ten years. I know I will but what.

JULY 13. Left at 9:00. Current very swift river not very pretty. At 3:30 came to summer resort beach. A woman admired my coat of tan audibly & then volunteered to take my picture. Pulled in for her and gave her and another woman a ride. A man Harry Voss came along and when I suggested camping told me I should stay with him. All right. He is with father & mother. He is 35 years old, manager of a dance hall. He is self educated, dead against colleges and I had to listen to him talk. It was his chance to unburden himself to a man of some education & so I filled a long-felt need for him. He showed me a pretty spring, and a hill covered with ferns. I studied German & watched young people at a camp dance at the pavilion. 30 miles today.

At a dance hall to night at a summer cottage place, I am studying German and watching the young folks. What I see fills me with well, I don't know what. For example, the boys & girls, between dances & during the dances, especially the boys, are standing around, doing nothing, not even enjoying themselves, not even thinking. Now and then one will go & buy a bottle of soft drink, sweetened & flavored water, perhaps he's laying down hard-earned money for it, & then goes back to his state of mere existence. Perhaps they can afford it from a financial standpoint, more likely they merely think they can. However, the question is, can they afford it from the point of view that they have a life to use or to lose.

Am I wrong in my utilitarian view of time? Time is my only capital. Is it not of all other youths? When not paddling the canoe, when I am sitting on bank with somebody, and conversation has lagged or ceased or is really amounting to nothing, I feel that I am wasting a part of my life & I would have others feel the same under similar conditions. Yet, I could not have everybody ceaselessly working, but I would never have them act as dumb unthinking animals with a full stomach waiting, waiting for nothing, just letting time pass. Nor would I have everybody study when not working, but I would at least have them keep from allowing their minds to be empty blanks. Not necessarily thinking out great problems, but for example, sitting on river bank at night, at least not merely sit, but sit and notice the fireflies, hear the whip-poor-wills, (think) over a few castles of the intended future. All this requires no effort. It does not fatigue the mind, and moreover it is pleasant.

And another thing, these young folks here tonight, an example of the youth of all the world, are here to enjoy a dance. Therefore they shut their minds to the pleasure of every other thing except a little small talk & that small talk evaporates without a trace as soon as spoken and understood. No, I would not have them discuss matters of state or national importance, but at least somewhere in their conversation let them say something with a real meaning.

Yet, as I look them over, they will undoubtedly achieve in life what they call success. They will be satisfied with what they have done. What right have I to dislike their ideas, or rather, lack of them if I judge correctly.

JULY 14. Left at 10:00. River not pretty but swift. Reached the Mississippi at 5:43. Felt lost on the river. Four miles down I found a camping place. Cooked rice and went to bed. Paddled 34 miles.

JULY 15. That "Old Devil Discouragement" was a-hanging around again. However I took no notice of him. A pretty stiff wind. At 4:00, after 25 miles, it got so bad I camped on a sandy island.

JULY 16. Rained long & hard last night. Had fine sleep but woke up with back tired. A dull cloudy day so will stay here & study history.

There is an old deserted lonely shack near the tent and there is where I'm staying. Have a splendid comfortable seat rigged up, a peach basket cover on legs furnishing the seat, a pasteboard box for a foot-stool. There's not a soul in sight, there's not a sound of a human being, the utter loneliness of this shack, its out of the way location behind the island levee all go to making it attractive & interesting. And yet, in a short time, I will have forgotten it—it has merely come into my life and will pass out again like so many other things. Will it leave any other trace than the thinking I have done under its roof?

Found big brown & black snake curled up beside my tent. Took a heavy club & beat it driving it away for I did not want it as a bed partner. Came back to shack and happened to think that I had undoubtedly injured it, perhaps greatly. Went back to kill it & prevent its suffering, but it had crawled away. How much I regret my thoughtlessness.

JULY 17. 33 miles. I wonder what I will get out of this trip besides health and strength. Will I get self-reliance, an ability to make the most of any and everything, an ability to regard hardships as luxuries, an appreciation of the monotony of woman's work in getting meals, an ability to enjoy the simplest of things and to see much in 'em?

Will it widen any knowledge of human nature? Will it broaden my mind as travel is supposed to do. I did some sewing on a rip in my B.V.D.'s. How I hated to do it and what an endless distance it seemed the needle had to travel. Yet I always rather like to have to do a job like that because I feel the discipline is good for me.

JULY 18. Packed up & left at 7:00. Easy paddling, camped on levee opposite Dallas City. Got acquainted with man, James McCormick, who is batching it there. As he was breaking up housekeeping to go out working he gave me his surplus eats—prunes, sugar, beans, potatoes, bacon, eggs, crackers. Can you beat that for luck? I am getting more and more things every day for which to be thankful. Made 40 miles.

JULY 19. Left 7:30. Said good-bye to McCormick. I put up my jacket for a sail made good time too. At Keokuk, a man (the lockmaster) told me I'd have to wait for a boat and helped me pull canoe up on platform & I went into his office. He was very talkative, discussed Psychology, education, Doctoring & mediums with him. Those locks are wonderful things. When lock is filled with water a foot bridge is sunk to open them. When this is raised again fish are caught on it.

At about 7:00 a passenger steamer with load of passengers with special guide came up to see the Keokuk power house. I put on a shirt & joined. Went down fifty-six feet under water thru various tunnels, wonderful works of engineering. Two boys decided to get off & accompany me in morning! When I get ready to go to bed, the lockmaster, T. J. Harrington, of Keokuk, Iowa, (Tim) told me to sleep in one of the buildings, Last thing he asked me to do was to write to them & to remember that doctoring was a guessing business & that when a man is sick he only has too much money of which the doctor cures him.

JULY 20. Arose 5:00. Another shift of lockmen on but knowing about me, were very friendly. Dressed my fish & they gave me a chunk of ice to keep 'em on. Steamer of night before came at 7:40. The boys, Charles Harris & Fred Kuntz were watching for me.

Had dinner opposite town on island. I was cook & fried fish. Had jelly, bread, honey, prunes a glorious dinner. They told me that I was one of 'em & to share equally with them. We moved on about ten miles and in between islands found a little lagoon, a nice sand bank & a patch of hard ground for the tent. Decided to camp. Cooked supper of fish, eggs, potatoes, bread, honey, butter, I washed dishes. It was a beautiful place, grape vines draped trees, swiftly running water, white sand, quiet lagoon, birds singing. Laughed & talked for a long time.

JULY 21. Left there early, paddled a few miles to Canton, Mo. & there went up & bought two loaves of bread $.15. Everybody rubber (necked) as we walked along they were sure I was either a colored man, or an Indian. A fifteen yr. old boy, J. Wilbur Denniston, took names & addresses & is going to put a write up in the paper about us. Wants us to write to him.

From Canton we paddled across in a strong wind & down stream a short ways and encamped in a nice grove. I cooked beans for supper & studied history. Had a little excitement A bum is living a little ways downstream & boys went there for water & he was unduly curious about our camp & our equipment. Guns were carefully loaded & laid handy. I went to sleep, but the boys were more anxious and stayed awake longer.

JULY 22. Fearfully windy so stayed. Boys anxious to move. Bacon & bread, beans & rice are our supplies; boys afraid of starving, from lack of luxuries. Read History after putting beans on. Also I read Ardath's letter. How much I enjoy it and thoughts of her—they keep me desirous of working. At 5:00 I remarked, "So, Jack, I'm getting tired of staying here." "Hey, Dutch, hear that!"

"Yes, and I'm for moving out to-night." "I'm with you." I said. "So am I," said Jack. "All right, let's pack up." 6:45 we started down the river. During the night, & July 23, we guided our canoes from one river light to another and guarded against dikes by listening. At 11:00 heavy clouds covered the sky & a wind sprang up. Dutch asked, "What'll we do when it starts raining, Pat?" (One of Erickson's school nicknames was 'Pat'—he always had his lessons down 'pat') "Cover up our wettables & keep on moving," I answered.

By 12:00 the sky was clear. About then Jack & Dutch began taking turns sleeping and paddling. I fortunately did not get tired. At 1:00, Jack got some Wiener sandwiches at a saloon. About half past two, as Jack kept falling asleep at the paddle, I tied his canoe to mine & towed them a mile to Hannibal, Mo. There I parked alongside of a launch, and with revolver in my lap, by means of a powerful electric light nearby, I mastered one & a half German lessons during the watch.

At 4:00 Jack awakened, & we got Dutch up, went over to an island, had breakfast & went to sleep. At nine, they went to town for supplies, and I packed up. When they got back, we paddled on, camped on a beautiful knoll in Missouri. They bought a chicken & we had chicken for supper. Also watermelon. We traveled 50 miles in the night.

JULY 24. Left this morning & paddled 10 miles & found out that 'tis 40 miles to Illinois river. As it is mighty hot, we decided to camp & travel by night. After dinner, I took a few tablespoonfuls of cocoa, a lot of sugar, some syrup and some water & made candy. It's cooking now. The boys shot a turtle dove & I'll fry that & have sandwiches for midnight lunch. Wrote a six page letter to Ardath.

Started at 8:00. Nice and cool & quite dark. Dutch and Jack took turns paddling & sleeping. At midnight we had a lunch of bread, turtle dove & some potato chips I made.

JULY 25. We started right on paddling and a few miles down talked to a ferrymen. He told us we had already come 60 miles in the night. We stopped on a big high bluff to eat. The day was horribly hot and we were tired but we traveled slow & at 4:00 we camped. They set up the tent and I put on the chicken—it was mighty fat. At 7:00 we had supper, chicken, rich broth, & bread. As for that fudge I made, it turned out to be splendid taffy about 3 lbs. of it. We all liked it. Then I wound my watch.

JULY 26. Awakened at 9:00 was well rested. I don't know how the day passed.

JULY 27. Dutch called me at 5:00. I got up at 6:00. Packed up canoe, got it in water. Then the boys gave me one of the broad 10-inch paddles to help me up stream a lot of stamps, envelopes, & pencils & thread. I gave 'em corn-meal & lard for their fish to catch. How I hated to say good-bye to them & they to me, but such things must be done. I started up the Mississippi. Found it to be a slow, very slow moving river. A good wind blew against me all the way so I made but 13 miles. Started at 9:00 & quit at four for I found an old uninhabited shack. Will cook on cook stove & sleep on a bed. All day, I have dreamed of Ardath—what will we do when we meet again?

JULY 28. Started at 6:00. Current surprisingly strong. Talked to a sheller who believed & practiced thrift. Gave me a good sound talk on thriftiness. Decided to get home by Sept 1st or thereabouts & help the folks. Fighting the current was hard work & discouraging. At noon decided to camp & eat & sleep till night. Made some fudge too. Dozed only & left at 5:00, paddled on long after dark. At 11:00, I got too tired to continue & paddled up to bank & spread out blankets in canoe & slept to the howling of animals.

JULY 29. Awakened 4:30. Paddled on. At 7:00 finished breakfast of rice. At 8:00 reached the locks, the first in the Illinois (river). There the lock master locked me thru. Discouraging to paddle against the wind & current, for the current is even worse above locks. 6 miles up I stopped and had dinner.

July 30. Sunday. Rained hard last night. Looks that way today. Talked to a great number of men. All the big-hearted sort, all interested in me and wanting to help me. Nelson gave me fish for all day. His father-in-law and I had a good deep serious talk.

Mack is the kind of a man that would go hungry in order to give away his last bite. His wife is like him. He caught a 13 lb. Turtle. Had me over to sleep, eat melons, and eat turtle for breakfast. 'Twas fine—the melons. I can't help but feel unworthy of all the kindnesses showered on me.

July 31. Slept fine. Turtle for breakfast. Delicious. Scot Moore took me over to his place to get a lot of apples. Got 'em & some plums. He told me of his achievements of which he was proud, the gravel road on which we walked was a result of his effort. His wife showed me athletic medals & trophies won by their son. They treated me to pie & cake. I had my first drink at an old-fashioned well with its mossy bucket at their place. If I ever come again I must visit them.

I put a rope on the bell for ferryman at noon & rode over with him. Scott Moore (and) his wife had fixed up a great basket of eats for me. Nelson had brought me 3 loaves of bread. Everybody is afraid I will not get well unless I have bread & other luxuries. They hate the sight of my beans & rice.

A picnic party came up and thought of inviting me. I accepted and had a good supper. I proved my claim to the white race by pulling up my bathing trunks. They too were astonished at my white skin. One of the men, because I'm a cripple traveling for my health, tried to give me $.50.

Studied German all spare moments. Am almost tempted to stay here awhile. Why not? It will give me health and strength and that is what I'm after.

August 1. Still here. Mack wants me, McCann, Nelson, everybody wants me to stay. Didn't feel well when I got up. Studied German. Visited with a lot of folks. Got advice about my limp, what to do for it etc. At noon, Scott Moore brought over a glass of plum jelly for me. Nelson was up river tarring nets so I took charge of the fish market. Went up on R.R. bridge to talk to men up there and look at river from there. While there, a picnic party came & wanted fish. While they were frying fish, I asked if they wanted some melons. I went over to Mack's and got $.50 worth. When I got back, the picnickers said, "Say, boy, you've got to eat with us, 'twill save you cooking." I surely accepted. They treated me like a guest of honor. I ate till I could eat no more. After that I cleaned up the place for 'em and went up to visit the engineers on the bridge. After dark, went up to Mack's, visited with his wife an hour or so & went to bed. Nelson tried to pay me for tending market. Mack tried to for selling the melons.

AUG. 2. Decided to stay until I had finished reading. "Das Edle Blut." [by E. von Wildenbruch and C.A. Eggert, 1908.] Stayed in bed till 7:00. Started to study. Parties came up one man wanted to know if I told fortunes. Nelson's birthday today & his folks came over for a picnic. After I was introduced, I suggested making candy & furnished sugar and cocoa. They were delighted. Chicken dinner. After dinner I took Jewel Knox & Nelson's sister Anna, out in canoe. Took 'em up river a mile. Then was towed by a motorboat a mile or so. Came down stream talking to 'em.

A load of fish came in. Went down & helped Nelson dress and take care of 'em. He left me to clean & lock up and sell in case of buyers. Everybody wants me to stay here a few weeks. I have a half a dozen homes here. Now to feed my vanity, "Old Man Doil," the most popular man around here seemingly, drove up in his car. I met him Sunday. He has told me all about his hunting and fishing trips and a friend of his, sitting and talking here with me, the two started to discuss my grit & pluck in making a trip. They said, "That boy will surely make good in anything." I always give that impression. I'm glad to them, I have to live up to it but can I? If possible.

Talking to Mack, and in case something happens and I have to work this winter, there is a chance of my teaching school down here at good pay.

AUG 3. I hate to leave this place. Finished book, "Das Edle Blut." I was in charge of market. Nelson came back and gave me a dollar for my work, which I considered generous pay. I'd rather done it for nothing. Said "Good-bye."

AUG 4. Breakfast with Mack. Said good bye at 7:30 How we all hated it. Everybody possible there to see me off. Paddled steadily until I reached Bedford, 6 miles (at) 10:30. I went up to see Nelson's folks. Stayed to dinner. They wanted me for supper & night. Decided to stay.

AUG 5. Left at 8:30. About 2 miles up, the shell buyer of Pearl picked me up with his barge. He was towing a sawing-mill engine. The man with the engine from Pearl knew all about me, even knew I am studying to be a doctor. They took the engine to an island & unloaded it, 3 hrs. work. I sat & watched 'em like a kid, a cripple is not a man of brawn. A 12 mile tow. Paddled on after they dropped me for about 8 miles. 10:30 went to sleep on bank of river in canoe.

AUG 6. Started out at 6:45. A wind to help me. At the locks at La Grange, a steamer, the "Richard," towing two barges came along. They picked me up & threw my canoe in one of the barges. A 100-mile lift. Just fine fortune that we met in the locks. Ate supper with 'em broke up coal for engine. They think, the captain & a girl here, that I'm a hero to be out on this trip &

working along. Oh fiddle—Vanitas vanitatum et omnia vanitas (Vanity of the vanities; everything is vanity.)

After supper it was suggested that we go a-frogging. The captains, two boys and one of the men went in my canoe up a dredge ditch. Went up over 4 miles. I handled the stern. We got 110 frogs. Got back at 12:15. About $20.00 worth of frogs.

AUG 7. Awakened 1 hr after boat had started. I slept inside the steamer. Got up and helped dress frogs. Ate all we could for breakfast & then ate only 27. When we reached Peoria, we went in swimming. I made my first high dive—from the upper deck—and a good one. I was watching James Bradman & his wife—they are a dandy couple. They gave me some addressed cards to make sure I write them.

About 6:00, the "Montauk," a canal boat pulled into Peoria alongside of the "Richard." Captain Hulett knew the captain and said he would get me a tow up the canal & introduced me to Captain LeGault, who said "Sure, I'll take him along glad to." Wasn't that mighty fine of Capt. Hulett.

AUG 8. Packed up my canoe and pulled over to the Montauk. Said good-bye to Capt Hulett and Bob, the pilot, a mighty good fellow. My canoe was hauled on board & I mailed a card for forwarding my mail. Man! How I want my letters from Ardath.

AUG 9. Fine night's sleep. While passing thru one of the locks, 4 young ladies & the mother of two of 'em got on the boat. They kept eying me my coat of tan is attractive. Got acquainted with the mother. She was the limit, scared to death every time one of the girls went near the edge of the boat.

The canal rises until it is 210 ft. above the level of the Ill. River. At one place it is on top of a hill. In the first 27 miles, there are 21 locks. Peat beds along the side of it. One was afire for 6 mos.

AUG 10. Read all day. Was glum, glummer, & glummest all day. I owe so much to everybody. Reached the stopping place at Montauk at 5:30. I mailed letters at the elevator there. Wiped dishes. Wound my watch and slept in pilot house.

AUG. 11. Left the Montauk at 7:30. Paddled very slowly up canal. Was clocked thru into Rock R. at 11:00. Went after my mail. 16 letters and a package from Ardath. How happy I feel. Read her letters first & opened package. It contained candy & jelly—two glasses of her own making. Set up tent. Looks like rain. While I was still a mile down the canal, some men in a barge called, "Hello, there, on your way back? How far did you go?

Have a good time?" That made me feel like I was getting home. Then as I walked down the streets of Rock Falls for my mail, two young fellows whom I didn't remember came out to inquire about my trip. That made it seem still more like home.

Mrs. Williams and Jack brought me a lunch. Mrs. Williams told me I was fleshier, browner, and looked more muscular. She especially admired my arms & shoulders. Told her where I had been. What I'd done on the way and she sighed and said, "My, I wish I had just one half your courage and grit." That's the way everybody along the way speaks. As if I were any better or greater than other boys like me. But anyway I'm going to do my best to live up to the reputation I'm getting. I'm going to be "that boy will make good." Started a letter to Ardath and went to sleep dreaming of her.

AUG 12. Awakened 6:30. Rainy looking. Will camp today. Wrote letters to Ardath, Zelma, Mother, Doc, Sarah, Chick, Natine and mailed card to James Bradman. This morning Mrs. Snyder's little girl brought over some eggs for my breakfast & the boy asked if I would like a cabbage. You bet. Studied Psychology rest of day. Had corned beef & cabbage without the beef for supper. At twilight I looked at the deep blue sky as I lay beside the tent, thought of the Maker of it and of all the world, of the smallness of man. I wound my watch.

AUG 13. In afternoon I lay on the bank & studied German, $2\frac{1}{2}$ lessons. I wonder what will result from this studying. I've studied while drifting along in the canoe, while pulled up on the bank. I've sat beside the campfire and studied, I've studied in old deserted shacks, on river banks, out in the hot sun—even on board a barge in the Ill. River. I've studied while surrounded by a crowd of curious onlookers. I've studied anywhere and everywhere. Now I wonder what I will get out of it. I find it interesting & I know that I am learning. I got almost an education out of Wells "Outline of History." The Psychology book told me many things I already knew & explained them and many I didn't know and gave me clear ideas of how to act & why to act. I like this studying because I feel that I am accomplishing something and am adding to my store of that which is to make me of greater service.

AUG 14. I actually had hard work to crawl out of my blankets at 5:00. Pulled down & packed up, cooked breakfast & pulled out at 10 to 6. The dam at Sterling enabled me to make such good time that around 9:00 I determined to strike out for & reach Oregon (Illinois). Last $\frac{1}{4}$ mile had to wade and pull canoe. At the dam when coming down, I was helpless, I now pulled the canoe up & carried the chest—an utter impossibility a month before. It only took me $\frac{1}{2}$ hr.

One man told me when I was heading for Oregon, "Why that's at least 35 miles from Dixon. Why I'd be afraid to start out for there in my johnboat." Man. Man. How little faith people have in themselves. He wouldn't undertake 35 miles with his motorboat in one day and I was undertaking to paddle 55. At "Grand Detour" there was a fearful current. Got a mile lift with a johnboat. In places, I couldn't make head way paddling. Had to get out & wade for river was shallow. This lasted about 5 miles, that is the wading & paddling alternately.

Paddled until dark before I got into water sufficiently slow to make appreciable progress. About 10:00, out in middle of river, my canoe struck bottom, and before me in starlight I could see a gravel bar. Hopped out & blundered along until I found a two inch depth of water & pulled canoe along for $\frac{1}{4}$ mile. I reached Cable Island where I had camped last July. Pulled canoe up on bank & with blankets in hand went up to the lodge. A camping party there looked me over with a flashlight. Was not tired enough to go to sleep right away & so lay there dreaming a long time. I had reached Oregon, I had paddled over 50 miles, I was not greatly tired. Man! I'm getting well & strong.

AUG 14. [additional entry] When I drew up to the island, I saw lights in the lodge and the shacks & I knew that some party, a large one, had rented the place and that my chances of getting a bed were not very good in as much as I arrived at such a late hr. Clothed only in a bathing suit and appearing after the dark where it would be impossible to get more than flashlight view of me, I was bound to be an object of suspicion. However I determined to ward off suspicion & get a bed by applying my book agent training & the psychology I know.

After pulling the canoe up on the bank, I took my roll of blankets and went up to the lodge and called, despite the fact that I knew he was undoubtedly sleeping 3 miles away, "Hey, Beveridge, come out here, I just got in & want a bed." A half dozen men poured out and after they had looked me over with a flashlight, I asked, "Where the deuce is Beveridge? I've paddled about 55 miles & I'm tired."

One of the men said, "I guess you're in the wrong place." For the purpose of confusing them & bringing about a state of indecision where I could act, I answered in a tone that implied that they were trying to slip something over on me, "Wrong place nothing. This is Cable Lodge & Cable Island, isn't it?" They admitted it and then to complete their confusion and bring about indecision, I said, "Well, I'm pretty thirsty, guess I'll get a drink," and I threw my blankets down on the porch.

One of the men started to tell me where the pump was, but I interrupted immediately and said, "Why it's right around the corner here up on the porch." That remark brought matters to a climax for I could see them turning their heads toward one another. They were wholly at loss, for it seemed I not only knew what I wanted, where I was, but I apparently knew as much about the place as they did. Moreover, the mere throwing of the blankets on the porch gave them the feeling, without their realizing it, that I was at home. This was the very thing I wished, and I stood waiting, expectancy written in my very position. Very naturally and humanly they took the easiest way out of the matter. One of them spoke up, "Why, I've got an extra tent here with a cot in it. If you don't mind, you can sleep in that."

"That's fine, lead me to it." Then to the others, "Good-night," saying it in such a way that they would receive the mental impressions that the incident was entirely closed, thus keeping them from developing fears and suspicions during the night.

Perhaps I could have secured lodging by merely asking for it but all my previous experience tells me that they would have told me to go up town. Moreover, being in a strange part of the country, they would be more than ever likely to send me away. Doing as I did, I secured lodging and by my matter-of-fact take-things-for-granted manner prevented them from worrying or fearing concerning my presence within their camp.

AUG 15. Went to sleep perhaps 11:00 last night. Awakened at 4. Went back to sleep, awake at 5:00 ditto, and after a lot of stretching, got up & looked and laughed and laughed at a comic paper. One of the campers came out, "I'd like to have you take breakfast with us." You bet. Bacon, eggs, milk, prunes. After breakfast, I called up Beveridges. Ralph was tickled to see me & wanted to know about the trip. He says I show improvement physically and then brought me to the house. (His mother) is washing and wanted to know if I had any soiled clothes. What a thoughtful woman.

I read all day. I couldn't help but feel confined and shut in. Every time I tried to look out over the country, the walls obstructed my gaze. After supper Ralph took me down to canoe to fix up things for the night. After introducing me to friends, took me out riding in auto. Drove like the wind. I enjoyed the ride mightily.

AUG 16. Ralph got the day off from work so he could come with me to Bill and Marv's. We paddled slowly, the current was mighty strong. Ralph enjoyed the scenery greatly, and whistled a great deal of the time. Finally at 4:30, we arrived but just then Dr. Beveridge came to get Ralph.

Bill and Marv glad to see me, knew I was coming because a friend had told 'em I was on the way. Pete has grown into a great big beautiful white rooster. Gobbler (the turkey) is molting and a sorry looking sight. Pete is too independent to eat out of one's hand and he bosses the dog, cat, & pigs. During my absence, Marv found a $120 pearl.

Aug 17. Pumped a barrel for water for Marv while he made swill. Wrote 9-page letter to Ardath. Finished memorizing, "I Don't Want to Play in Your Yard." (a children's song by Philip Wingate) Saw article in paper about (William Jennings) Bryan. Made me so disgusted I composed a speech about Bryanism, Darwinism, & Evolution. Memorized "Thanatopsis" (a poem by William Cullen Bryant).

Aug 18. Suddenly Bill asked when I was going home told him I wasn't sure. He said he was going to Rockford in truck in morning and that he could load canoe in and take me above the dam. You bet I accepted.

Aug 19. Got up early, 6:00. Bill had gone to town, so Marv & I ate together for perhaps last time. Packed up, shaved, and sat around until eleven o'clock. Then Bill came, my canoe was loaded in truck & I left the island. They took me down to the steamer landing and put canoe in water. Man! They hated to see me go and I hated to leave. They stood on bank and watched me way up stream and then with a final wave, went back to the truck. Bill made me promise to write.

Current dishearteningly swift. Lots of wading to make progress. At 7:00, making such slow progress, decided to camp. Took blankets and pillows and reconnoitered. Saw camp-fire, wandered over to announce my presence so that nobody would be frightened by finding of me sleeping under a nice thickly leaved tree I had picked out because of the clouds. Got near campfire, yelled, "Hello," & a man off to one side came over. The man was in charge of camp. I told him who I was and that I was intending to sleep under a tree. He said, "I've got a log cabin here & two beds. You can have one." You bet! We fixed up my bed, visited, & listened to (the campers) singing songs.

Aug 20. At 7:30 was already paddling swift current more wading. The twists and turns and bends of that river seemed interminable. Waded in water up to hips and pulled canoe up to foot of dam. There, a member of Salvation Army helped me to portage. Told me not to forget the little helps I had received on the way.

Paddled on. Due to the ever-increasing swiftness of the current, I waded in water up above waist and crept along by degrees in places. Finally reached dam, paused to rest & get stones out of shoes. A boy fishing asked if I needed help you bet! Unloaded canoe, & he grabbed it & walked up the dam & slid it over in a hurry. He carried my chest, loaded canoe & gave me a parting shove. Another thing to be appreciative for!

Wind against me and a growing current. River mighty crooked. It seemed that I never would reach Kilmers. At 6:30, I was pulling up canoe. Fred & Otto came down to welcome me. Complimented my appearance & hustled me in to get supper. 'Tis just 2 mo. since I was last here.

Three years ago today, I was stricken with paralysis. No, only the mistakes I've made would I change if I could relive my life. As for my limp, I believe it has taught me much I would otherwise never have learned.

AUG. 21. Went to factory with Otto. Then out in tobacco field to see if I could help top. Not experienced enough. Went past Ward Bros. Transfer Co. & stopped to see the man who portaged me. He wasn't there but had left word that "that little lame boy with the canoe" was in town. Left my regards for him.

While I was wiping dishes, Mrs. Kilmer told me many things about her dead boy, Charles, showing me unconsciously that while he was living her very life was wrapped up in him. Even now she can not forget him. Now she has just almost her whole soul in her daughter Helen—shields her, protects her from everything that might even be slightly uncomfortable. Even such things as wiping the harder & clumsier dishes. Her greatest pleasure consists of having Helen have a good time. It is the same with Mr. Kilmer. Even as Mrs. Kilmer is the very personification of Mother Love, so is he of Father Love.

AUG 22. Over-walked yesterday laid on couch. In afternoon, a Fuller Brush Co. agent & a companion of his appeared. Listened to his canvas it was punk. He started out fine but died in the middle of it. When money objections came up, he helped it along instead of merely letting it die from lack of attention. Also, he allowed himself to be put on the defensive & stayed there. Even worse he argued. He had his brushes sold, then by the above mistake, lost the sale. Worst of all, he lied. He said upon entering that he had nothing to sell, that he was advertising.

AUG 23. Mr. Kilmer is anxious to have me "stay and rest up. It's doing you good, ain't it?" He and his wife are lovers yet. He is always joking and teasing her and she enjoys it immeasurably. He, Otto and Fred are hauling bricks for the sorghum mill chimney. I have nothing to do but rest, read and enjoy life. Wrote a long letter to Aunt Winifred, telling her of trip and arrangements I'm making for school & my summer studying.

AUG 24. At breakfast table Mr. Kilmer said, "Well, Milt, I've got a job for you!" "Fine. What is it?" "Take the hatchet and a box to sit on and knock the old mortar off those bricks I'm getting from that old building." That's what I've been doing all day. I'm tired.

AUG 25. Decided to stay and work on bricks worked steadily from 7:30 to 5:30. Dreamed of Ardath all the time—of how happy I would be alongside of her when I can be with her, walk and talk with her. Am to start home tomorrow each one of the family asks about it with regret in their voice.

AUG 25. Just before breakfast, Mr. Kilmer came over and dropped a dollar bill in my hand for working on the bricks. I tried to get him to take it back for I wanted to feel that I had done something for him but he absolutely insisted that I accept it.

Fred (the hired man) and I tied the canoe on his car, Mrs. Kilmer fixed up a lunch, I shook hands with everybody and promised to try to come down from Madison. At Janesville, above dams, Fred & I set canoe in, said goodbye and I set out. Reached the Yahara at 12:00. Took me 2 hrs to make first 3 miles to Fulton dam. Waded & shoved canoe a horrible current. Portaged Fulton dam alone in less than half hr.

At Stebbinsville two men portaged me. At Dunkirk I got the engineer to help me. Reached Stoughton at 9:30. It was fun turning & twisting along the river and watching the city lights disappearing and reappearing behind the trees as I came along.

At Stoughton, bumped up against a R.R. bridge too low to go under, crawled out, took blankets & books & went up to (The Rev. R.) Jones' about 10:00. Mrs. Jones was up. Hardly knew me was so dirty. She heated water so I could take bath. Mr. Jones got up out of bed to greet me. Went to bed feeling fine. Kind friends, and I had accomplished what I set out to do.

Wound my watch.

AUG 27. Got up early and had breakfast. Tried to pay or rather, return those $3.00 they gave me on down trip. Couldn't get them to take it. Told me to pass it on. That is what I will do. Will never use it myself. Indeed I do not even need it nor have I, nor would I have used it even if I had needed it.

Called up Ralph Chipman. Ralph and I started out to portage the bridge and dam. I helped at bridge but another fellow helped at the dam. At half past nine left dam at 10:00, Ralph got out and I gave him the $1.65 he gave me on down trip. I never used it and wouldn't anyway. Mightily glad to return it. However, I do appreciate the spirit that prompted the gift.

A couple miles up a motor boat gave me a tow to Lake Kegonsa. Crossed that in ½ hr. Between Kegonsa & (Lake) Waubesa, the river is entirely blocked with bogs. However enough water on top so that with hard shoving, the canoe could be shoved over the grass and rushes.

Took me ½ hr. to cross lake. Stopped at Whitson's. They didn't know me—treated me to plum pie and milk.

Make a home, lad, for the woman who loves you; gather one or two friends about you; work, think, and play, that will bring you Happiness.

J. K. Jerome.

Don't forget.

T. J. Harrington.
Keokuk Lock.
Keokuk, Iowa.
July 19-1922.

Handwritten scraps of paper
stowed in diary:

*Make a home lad, for the woman
who loves you; gather one or two
friends about you. Work, think and
play, That will bring you happiness.*
　　　　—J. K. Jerome

Don't forget T. J. Harrington. Keokuk
Lock. Keokuk, Iowa. July 19, 1922.

Stayed half hour. Set out. Talked to various people on way. On Lake Marona I saw a hydroplane rise from & land on water.

In going thru locks, a launch came in at same time. Asked 'em for tow to middle of Lake Mendota. In middle of lake I undressed and washed my birthday suit then shaved. While still on Marona, I had placed hatchet, roll of blankets on chest & stood firearm upright with camp kettle on it to advertise my return and in case Doc Brooks was canoeing, attract his attention. Paddled up to boathouse.

had good time — improved
at 500 % physically

unburned to hue of an Indian

— 1200 miles — and
did it alone —despite doleful
predictions — I'm proud
of my trip.

"Something attempted, something done, has earned a
night's repose"

May each nights repose be
earned!

The end of a 1200 mile canoe trip
1000 miles paddled
200 ridden on steamers
worked my way
studied hard
had a good time
improved about 500% physically
sunburned to hue of an Indian

1200 miles and did it alone despite
doleful predictions—I'm proud
of my trip.

"Something attempted, something
done, has earned a night's repose."
[from "The Village Blacksmith" by
Henry Wadsworth Longfellow,
1807–1882]

May each night's repose be earned!

Arum, Nevada homestead—
a dirt-floored log cabin where MHE
was born in 1901. The back wall
of the cabin was built into the
mountain. Here, 1903, family and
Mr. Davis. MHE in mother's arm.

MHE'S
PERSONALIZED
BOOK PLATE

MHE designed his own book-
plate with a friend in the 1930s
with symbols to depict events he
considered formative in his life.
Historically, as books became
affordable, decorative bookplates
were popular to paste inside the
front covers of one's books to
indicate ownership.

The seal of the University
of Wisconsin, Madison
where MHE received his
Bachelor's degree in 1924
and both his M.D. and his
M.S. in psychology in 1928.

The Viking Ship symbolizes
MHE's Viking ancestors.

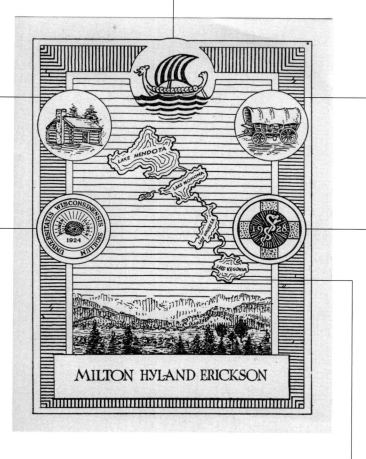

1905 Traveled by covered wagon from
Arum, Nevada, to nearest train station in
Salt Lake City en route to Wisconsin
where the children would attend school.

1928 is the year MHE became a
medical doctor. The staff and snake
together symbolize the staff of
Aesculapius (or Asklepios)—the
ancient mythical god of medicine.

1938 Staff at the county hospital in
Eloise, Michigan, where MHE worked
as a psychiatrist. MHE stands in front
row, third from left.

Chain of lakes near
Madison, Wisconsin, where
MHE attended
University.
He began the
canoe trip that
helped him
recover from his
first episode of
polio on June
15, 1922 on the
northern-most
Lake Mendota.

BETTY ALICE ERICKSON:

Elizabeth Moore, the middle child of an attorney father and a mother who had worked as a teacher of the deaf, had gone to a meeting at Wayne State University while she was still an undergraduate psychology student. Dad had seen her walking up the sidewalk before she entered the building and remarked to a friend, "That's who I'm going to marry."

VINTAGE MHE JOKE

He used to make Mom say this jingle:
"Ask my father," she said when he asked her to wed,
But she knew that he knew that her father was dead,
And she knew that he knew of the life he had led,
So she knew that he knew what she meant when she said,
"Ask my father."

1936–1938

OPPOSITE: Married in Lowell, Wisconsin. Dad and Mom took a driving trip through the American Southwest for their honeymoon.

The Erickson family: Milton, Winifred, Clara, Albert, Florence, Mildred, Clarence. BACK ROW: Effie, Cecelia, Bertha, Edith Carol.

MHE holding his young baby Betty Alice, Eloise, Michigan.

180

Vintage MHE Joke

There was once a mama skunk with two little baby skunks named In and Out. One day In and Out were out playing and Mama was in but went out looking for In and Out. She found Out outside but couldn't find In in or out of the house. She looked and looked and still couldn't find In. So she went back in the house sent Out out to find In and bring him in. Out went out immediately and came back in with In. "How did you find him so fast?" asked Mama Skunk. Out said, "In stinct."

1942–1946

OPPOSITE: MHE and EME with Betty Alice in background, Eloise, Michigan.
PHOTOS: Jerry Cooke

182

Vintage MHE Joke

Once upon a time a lady opened her refrigerator
and found a rabbit sleeping on a shelf.
She inquired, "What are you doing in here?"
The rabbit looked up at her and asked, "Is this a Westinghouse?"
The lady replied that it was.
The rabbit said, "Well, I'm a wabbit and I'm westing."

1951–1954

TOP LEFT: MHE in office at Cypress Street. Photo by Joseph Haywood.

LOWER LEFT: MHE from *The National Cyclopedia of American Biography.*
PHOTO: James T. White & Company

OPPOSITE: The house in Lowell, Wisconsin, where MHE lived as a child
and was stricken with polio as a 19-year-old in 1920.

1951, Family Christmas Card.

1952, MHE sitting on the porch of 32 West Cypress Street, new home
in Phoenix, Arizona.

1954, Family portrait in front of Cypress Street: Allan, Lance, Betty Alice,
Bert, EME, Kristina, Robert, Carol, Roxanna, MHE.

184

KRISTI

ROXIE

BETTY

BOBBY

ALLAN

MILTON

BETTY ALICE MERRY

CAROL

CHRISTMAS

FROM

LANCE

BERT

THE ERICKSONS

VINTAGE MHE JOKE

Once upon a time, all the animals of the North Pole
were sitting around on a iceberg telling stories.
They each spun a yarn and the stories kept going.
Finally, it was the polar bear's turn.
He got up and began to walk off.
The other animals complained, "But you haven't told your story!"
The bear turned and said, "My tail is told."

1954–1957

TOP LEFT PHOTO: *The National Cyclopedia of American Biography.*

OPPOSITE: MHE working in office with daughter-in-law Lillian as subject.
PHOTO: *Parade Magazine*

Chicago ASCH meeting: MHE's sister Bertha Bachman, Seymour Hershman, M.D.,
MHE, William Kroger, M.D.

Family portrait in Phoenix: EME, MHE, Lance, front row Kristina, Roxanna,
Robert, Allan, Betty Alice, Bert.

Photo shoot at Boyce-Thompson Arboretum east of Phoenix for *Parade Magazine,*
MHE and EME.

VINTAGE MHE JOKES

Dad called this the "schizophrenic joke." He claimed small children and schizophrenics liked this one. When my kids were really little, they thought it was funny.

QUESTION: What's the difference between a duck?
ANSWER: One leg is both the same.

In that same vein:
QUESTION: What's the next letter after O T T F F?
ANSWER: S_ _. One, Two, Three, Four, Five, Six.

In fact, small children do tend to get this especially if you move your hand down an imaginary line when you say the letters. Grown-ups don't.

1956–1959

OPPOSITE TOP RIGHT: Herbert Mann, M.D., MHE, William E. Werner, M.D. at New York State Academy of General Practice meeting in New York City. PHOTO: Drucker Hilbert Company

Teaching on board cruise ships.

MHE, Pat McFate, Seymour Hershman, M.D. at Chicago teaching workshop.

VINTAGE MHE JOKE

In order to tell this joke, Dad would hold his hand up with the thumb and little finger making a circle.

QUESTION: What's this?
ANSWER: Thursday.

People wouldn't get it so he would touch his forefinger to his thumb, then the middle finger, the ring finger and then the little finger while reciting, "Monday, Tuesday, Wednesday, Thursday."

1959–1962

BOTTOM LEFT: Portrait used on *Uncommon Therapy: The Psychiatric Techniques of Milton H. Erickson, M.D.* by Jay Haley. PHOTO: Union Tribune Publishing Company.

OPPOSITE: Unique Valentine's Day present: Daddy had the butcher bring over a whole lamb carcass for Mama who loves lamb: chops, shanks, whatever. It was presented on a big heart of tin foil, surrounded with lettuce and colorful vegetables like a big stuffed rabbit holding "reins" of sausage. Mama even loved the picture of it.

EME wearing a silk screen skirt by William Gentry with MHE on board SS Kungsholm.

MHE being observed in his work by doctors with subject in deep trance.

Portrait that was used on *Advanced Techniques of Hypnosis and Therapy,* edited by Jay Haley, published by Grune & Stratton. This was the first effort to compile MHE's major papers.

At a teaching seminar at Lake Louise, Banff, Canada.

190

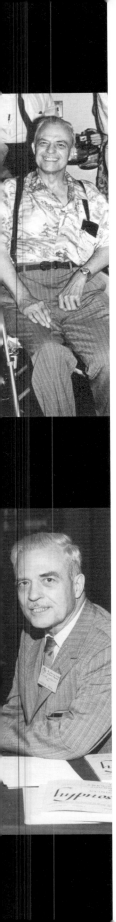

BETTY ALICE ERICKSON:

Dad's long-term friendships all had great intellectual foundations.
Margaret Mead was a family friend for decades. He and Aldous
Huxley were friends for years.

His friendships were deep but the people rarely lived close by. One
of his closest friends who helped the family moved to Arizona, was
John Larson, a psychiatrist who was one of the key inventors of the
polygraph. Dad and Dr. Larson used to have many conversations
about detecting lies. They would talk about observational acuity and
how one could detect different messages from unconscious communications such as eye pupil size, respiration rate, skin color as
influenced by blood flow, and so on. I remember Dad telling me that
people with a conscience always knew when they were lying and had
involuntary responses to lies. People can control one or two of those
responses but cannot focus narrowly enough and broadly enough to
control them all. That's why a lie detector works.

1963–1966

OPPOSITE: Margaret Mead depicted with her trademark shepherd's crook in
the front yard of 32 West Cypress between EME and MHE.

MHE at ASCH professional meeting in Chicago with display of books
and journals.

BETTY ALICE ERICKSON:

Dad had a patient named Ben who had been diagnosed as schizo-phrenic. His goal was to live independently on his rather modest income and to stay out of a mental hospital. After some time with Dad, Ben got an apartment close by and he and my mother rescued a dog from the pound, a very important metaphor for his intervention. Ben named the dog Duke and Duke was his responsibility, even though he lived at out house. Ben had a reason to manage his life—Duke was counting on him. Ben couldn't resent this reason—Duke loved him and was a safe and accepting haven for his love. He would wait at the back gate for Ben to arrive and as soon as he heard Ben approach, he would walk away and act "surprised" when Ben called his name. We finally had to take a series of pictures at Hayward Street to convince Ben that Duke waited for "his master" every morning.

1971–1973

TOP LEFT: Teaching sessions at home.

LOWER LEFT: MHE wearing purple silk shirt to celebrate his 69th birthday. Severely color blind, he was able to truly enjoy only the color purple.

OPPOSITE: Dad with one of his favorite flowers, the night-blooming Cereus. These blooms appeared during the night and faded away as the sun rose.

Duke at Hayward Street. We took photos to show Ben that Duke waits for "his master." (complete story on page 64)

EME, MHE, Roxanna and dog Maura.

MHE and Ernest Rossi, a student, at home in Phoenix.

MHE with daughter Kristina at home on Hayward Street.
PHOTO: John O. Beahrs

194

VINTAGE MHE JOKE

QUESTION: What's green, hangs on the wall and sings like a canary?

ANSWER: A herring.

QUESTION: What do you mean? A herring is not green.

ANSWER: I painted it green.

QUESTION: What do you mean"hangs on the wall?"

ANSWER: I hung it there.

QUESTION: What do you mean"sings like a canary?"

Herrings don't sing.

ANSWER: I just put that in to make it hard.

1974–1977

TOP LEFT: MHE. PHOTO: Pete Nemetsichek

LOWER LEFT: MHE. PHOTO: Rene Bergermaier

OPPOSITE: MHE demonstrating on student during seminar with German group. Marion Moore, M.D. filmed session. PHOTO: Peter Nemetsichek

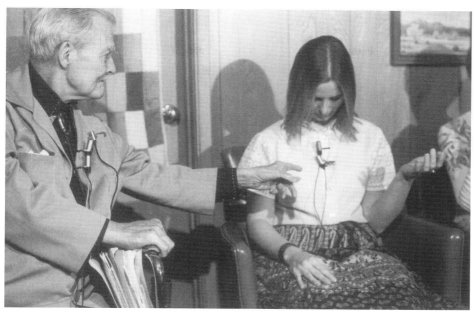

VINTAGE MHE JOKE

QUESTION: What did the chicken say when it saw an orange in the nest?
ANSWER: Oh, look at the orange Marma laid.

1977

TOP LEFT: EME and MHE. PHOTO: Rene Berbermeier

BOTTOM: MHE. PHOTO: Alan Bergman

OPPOSITE: Living room of Hayward Street home with part of MHE's beloved Seri Indian collection of Sonoran Desert ironwood carvings. Jim Hills spent months with the Seri people, and was instrumental in furthering Erickson's extensive collection. (see Hills' recollections of Erickson on page 261). PHOTOS: Alan Bergman

BETTY ALICE ERICKSON:

A real-life exchange that Dad thought was worth repeating:

A scientist had just completed and reported on
a major research project.
A reporter asked him, "But of what use is it?"
The scientist replied, "Of what use is a newborn baby?"

1977–1979

TOP LEFT: MHE. PHOTO: Rene Bergermeier

LOWER LEFT: MHE. PHOTO: John, O. Beahrs, M.D.

OPPOSITE: MHE with Ernest Rossi, after working together.
PHOTO: Rene Bergermeier

MHE with student group. Student and family friend Jan Henley at left.

CHAPTER SIX

A CLINICAL CASE CONSULTATION

IN NOVEMBER 1958, a demonstration interview by Dr. Erickson was filmed by the Gregory Bateson research team at Palo Alto, California. The following is a transcript of the film. A DVD of the interview is included with this book and was contributed by Dr. Wendel Ray, former director of the Mental Research Institute, Palo Alto, and is used with permission of the John Weakland Archive.

Gregory Bateson was present in the room, working the camera, while the rest of his research team observed from behind a one-way mirror. This was the second session Dr. Erickson had with a young man who originally sought help for depression.

DR. ERICKSON: You know I'm curious about one thing: that one-way mirror. I think I would prefer someone light a cigarette… Did you notice that?

CLIENT: Uh-huh.

DR. ERICKSON: Anybody who uses a one-way mirror ought to be careful about that. And I wonder if Andre realizes that you can see that. You know when you hear about the experimental work that they do here, whether they are aware that they can betray themselves through a one-way mirror. Do you remember the first time we met? We were sitting in not-quite this position. I was over on your left side, isn't that right?

CLIENT: On my right side.

DR. ERICKSON: And that's right, on your right side. And let's see. There was Hilgard over slightly to the left of the room.

CLIENT: Yes.

DR. ERICKSON: In the same general relative position where Bateson is right now.

CLIENT: Uh-huh.

DR. ERICKSON: And I don't remember where any of the others were, but they were scattered around. They were rather silent as they listened to what I had to say to you. And one of the things I mentioned to you is this question of feeling yourself, do you recall?

CLIENT: Yes, I remember, yes.

DR. ERICKSON: And as you remember that, do you remember just what happened to you as you recalled it? You felt yourself doing what? [pause] That's right. You felt yourself going into a trance, as you recall, just as you're going into a trance right now. And I'd like to have you feel yourself in a different position, in a different position in this room than you're in right now. And close your eyes and sleep deeply, and feel yourself in a different position in this room, as if you were sitting in a somewhat different way. And Gregory is still there running that [i.e., running the camera], and I'd like to have you feel yourself going deeper and deeper into the trance. And I wonder what you would like to do in the trance state. You were doing some research, I believe, on the primates.

CLIENT: Uh-huh.

DR. ERICKSON: And I'd like to have you think about that, and then I would like to have you wonder what other topic could come up, and I wonder if you would like to look over there, over there. And I wonder what visualization you could achieve as you looked over there. I wonder if you could see a movie, or a screen of some sort.

CLIENT: I can see a screen there.

DR. ERICKSON: You can see a screen. I'd like to have you see a tape of statistics on that screen, and I'd like to have you wonder what they are. They're probably of no particular interest, and then I would like to have you see something besides these statistics. Something of interest; something pleasing. That's right. And begin to see something pleasing and interesting. Very pleasing and very interesting, that involves motion and activity. That's it. Motion and activity—those transformed into something else that's less pleasant, somewhat disagreeable. And it's continuing and I'd like to have you tell me what you sense that motion as. What do you sense that motion as?

CLIENT: I saw someone running. They stopped running and they're on the ground.

DR. ERICKSON: They're on the ground. And now the ground is disappearing. It's another kind of motion, but it's area.

CLIENT: They're falling.

DR. ERICKSON: They're falling. Yes?

CLIENT: Down. They're going down.

DR. ERICKSON: And down. And it isn't going to frighten you now. And now I'd like to have you change that visualization to something else. I'd like to have you discover something entirely different. I'd like to have you discover that your understanding of "yes" and "no" has changed, that the nodding of your head now means

CLIENT: "No."

DR. ERICKSON: and the shaking of your head now means

CLIENT: "Yes."

DR. ERICKSON: Are you sure you understand that?

CLIENT: Yes.

DR. ERICKSON: All right. And how long do you think you'll be able to realize and understand that?

CLIENT: As long as you say.

DR. ERICKSON: As long as I say.

CLIENT: Uh-huh.

DR. ERICKSON: All right. And what are you seeing?

CLIENT: I'm seeing waves along the seashore.

DR. ERICKSON: That's right. And you're seeing waves by the seashore. Do you know how you happen to see those waves by the seashore?

CLIENT: No.

DR. ERICKSON: Would you like to know?

CLIENT: Yes.

DR. ERICKSON: Now I'm going to talk to you and I'd like to have you pay a little bit of attention to me. As I talk to you, do you know how you happened to see the waves by the seashore? You happened to understand that now, and I'm still talking to you, and you're seeing the waves by the seashore. And do you know now? [pause] And you don't know what are the waves doing.

CLIENT: They're tumbling onto the rocks there.

DR. ERICKSON: Yes, and what would a boat be doing if a boat were on the water?

CLIENT: It would be very rough.

DR. ERICKSON: Yes, and what would the boat be doing?

CLIENT: It would be rocking....

DR. ERICKSON: It would be rocking back and forth, wouldn't it?

CLIENT: Uh-huh.

DR. ERICKSON: And I told you to see a scene involving motion. You saw running that came to a halt. And then you saw falling. And then I told you to see an area. And now after you see an area, it's transformed into water with waves. More rapid than my movements, isn't that right?

CLIENT: Uh-huh, yes.

DR. ERICKSON: But do you see how I happened to get you to get that water and waves? [pause] All right? Now the first thing that I did was to build up movement and a not pleasant movement. Was that right? [pause] I suggested a movement and then something not so pleasant. Do you recall?

CLIENT: Yes.

DR. ERICKSON: And you didn't quite like it, did you?

CLIENT: No.

DR. ERICKSON: And I kept on rocking back and forth, in that way, and then I had you see an area, and then you saw rapid movement, rocking of the waves, tumbling of the waves, back and forth. But I had given the overtone of unpleasantness, as you said the water was rough. And so you fitted the unpleasantness into that indirect suggestion, or don't you recognize it as suggestion?

CLIENT: Yes.

DR. ERICKSON: You do now?

CLIENT: I see that as a suggestion now.

DR. ERICKSON: You see that as a suggestion now. How now shall we change it, because we don't need to have the waves rocking anymore?

CLIENT: Something more still.

DR. ERICKSON: Something more still.

CLIENT: Uh-huh.

DR. ERICKSON: For example, um, snow on the mountaintop. It's rather still there, isn't it? It's a quiet day. It's a beautiful sight, isn't it?

CLIENT: Yes.

DR. ERICKSON: Something very, very beautiful. And those mountain prominences, and the valleys. And the lines of the mountains against the horizon, and the lovely hues. And now think of something else that's pleasing. And what do you see? It's something different, totally different. And what do you see?

CLIENT: I see a book.

DR. ERICKSON: You see a book.

CLIENT: Yes.

DR. ERICKSON: And where is that book?

CLIENT: It's on a bookstore.

DR. ERICKSON: And what is in the book?

CLIENT: Words.

DR. ERICKSON: Yes, what else?

CLIENT: It's talking about a war.

DR. ERICKSON: It's talking about a war.

CLIENT: Yes.

DR. ERICKSON: Hmmm, what war?

CLIENT: The last war.

DR. ERICKSON: The last war.

CLIENT: Yes.

DR. ERICKSON: Uh-huh. And what pleasant scene comes to mind now?

CLIENT: Different people in a room.

DR. ERICKSON: And who are the people? What are the people?

CLIENT: They're soldiers and girls.

DR. ERICKSON: Soldiers and girls.

CLIENT: And they're dancing.

DR. ERICKSON: And they're dancing.

CLIENT: Yes.

DR. ERICKSON: Now, how did you get from the mountain to a different scene to the book to the war to the soldiers to the girls to the dancing?

CLIENT: I came down the mountains in Austria.

DR. ERICKSON: Yes.

CLIENT: And there were indications of the war.

DR. ERICKSON: Yes.

CLIENT: And this brought on the bitter scene of the war.

DR. ERICKSON: Yes.

CLIENT: In some club, I think, in London.

DR. ERICKSON: Uh-huh. And now what part of the scene in that room, what part of that scene in the room reminds you rather directly of the mountain scene?

CLIENT: I think the fact that this room is on top of a building. We had to go up many stairs.

DR. ERICKSON: Yes, but what was in that room that suggests the mountain? Now look at every object, animate and inanimate, in the room, and just look at all of that.

CLIENT: I see. There's an advertisement there for ice cream. And on that advertisement there's a mountain drawn in white and pale blue.

DR. ERICKSON: And that's how?

CLIENT: I think so, yes.

DR. ERICKSON: Now, what does the advertisement read?

CLIENT: It says, "Buy Wall's Ice Cream."

DR. ERICKSON: And now where is that advertisement?

CLIENT: This is on the counter at the back of the place where you can get some food.

DR. ERICKSON: And where is this room, really?

CLIENT: This is in London.

DR. ERICKSON: This is in London.

CLIENT: Uh-huh.

DR. ERICKSON: [pause] All right. Now what else in the room, quite different, reminds you of the mountains? Animate or inanimate.

CLIENT: There's one person there who looks very sunburned.

DR. ERICKSON: Yes?

CLIENT: Perhaps he'd been skiing in the mountains, I don't know.

DR. ERICKSON: Uh-huh?

CLIENT: He might have been.

DR. ERICKSON: He might have been. All right.

CLIENT: [pause] He has that suntan which only comes from skiing in the mountains.

DR. ERICKSON: That combination of suntan and windburn?

CLIENT: Yes, definitely that.

DR. ERICKSON: Definitely that. [pause] And what year is this?

CLIENT: I think 1948.

DR. ERICKSON: And who am I?

CLIENT: [pause] You're the person at the table who I'm talking to.

DR. ERICKSON: That's right. And maybe sometime again we will meet.

CLIENT: Maybe.

DR. ERICKSON: You never can tell.

CLIENT: No.

DR. ERICKSON: And what would you have liked to do in 1950?

CLIENT: Perhaps go skiing with you? Perhaps so?

DR. ERICKSON: I think it would be interesting. And where do you think we might go skiing?

CLIENT: [inaudible due to a noise]

DR. ERICKSON: That would be a nice place?

CLIENT: I think so, yes.

DR. ERICKSON: How long have you been skiing?

CLIENT: Oh, about four or five years.

DR. ERICKSON: You really like it?

CLIENT: Very much, yes.

DR. ERICKSON: And in 1952, what do you think you'll be doing?

CLIENT: In 1952, I'll be trying to get into university, I think.

DR. ERICKSON: You will?

CLIENT: I think so.

DR. ERICKSON: And which university do you think you'll try?

CLIENT: London, of course.

DR. ERICKSON: London, of course.

CLIENT: Yes.

DR. ERICKSON: Well, there are other universities, aren't there?

CLIENT: Yes, I agree. [chuckling briefly]

DR. ERICKSON: How many other universities are there, according to your standards?

CLIENT: You mean as far as England is concerned, there's not much there.

DR. ERICKSON: Is that so?

CLIENT: Well, about three in England. That's Oxford and Cambridge and London.

DR. ERICKSON: Yes? But you mentioned the word "elsewhere."

CLIENT: Well, I agreed there were universities outside of England.

DR. ERICKSON: Oh, you agree to that? And where might I think that there were universities?

CLIENT: I don't know about that. I think the good ones are in England.

DR. ERICKSON: Yes, I read that. I actually do think that.

CLIENT: Well, where else would you say there are good universities?

DR. ERICKSON: Well, where else could I say that there are good universities?

CLIENT: You could say America, you could say Germany, you could say France.

DR. ERICKSON: And could I say Germany?

CLIENT: Yes, you could say Germany.

DR. ERICKSON: I could say it, yes, but would I?

CLIENT: Um, well, that depends upon your feelings on this matter, I think.

DR. ERICKSON: And would I say France?

CLIENT: I don't see why not.

DR. ERICKSON: You're being just a bit academic about it, aren't you?

CLIENT: Perhaps so. I mean, it's not exactly the time when universities are at their best in these countries, but

DR. ERICKSON: And where would they be at their best?

CLIENT: Um, England and America at the moment, I assume.

DR. ERICKSON: Uh-huh. Whereabouts in America?

CLIENT: Harvard, especially.

DR. ERICKSON: Harvard, especially. Where else?

CLIENT: Yale. Cornell. These are the only three that one seems to hear about, though I hear there are many more...

DR. ERICKSON: Undoubtedly, there are many more. [pause] The mountain views are very nice, aren't they?

CLIENT: They're wonderful.

DR. ERICKSON: And skiing is very nice.

CLIENT: Yes.

DR. ERICKSON: And if you were to choose a university in America, where would you go?

CLIENT: Um...looking around, I'd always choose one near the mountains.

DR. ERICKSON: Where, for example?

CLIENT: [pause] I don't know. Cornell hasn't too many mountains there, I don't think.

DR. ERICKSON: It's got lakes.

CLIENT: But you can't ski on lakes.

DR. ERICKSON: No, you can't.

CLIENT: I think I'd have to try somewhere west, but I don't know them very well out there.

DR. ERICKSON: Why are mountains there?

CLIENT: They climb mountains, so I think.

DR. ERICKSON: And now let us change the scene. Let's say a mountain's right there, a mountain scene. And I'd like to have you see all of that in the distance. [pause] And it's now approaching October, and the leaves are turning color. And I'd like to have you see that mountain symbolize something. Symbolize something in relationship to something in front of that ice cream advertisement. [pause] And what do you see?

CLIENT: I see something rather cold, austere, something that's very definite.

DR. ERICKSON: And the lines on that mountain scene are changing and the shadows are changing, until you can see more clearly, what it is.

CLIENT: I see a girl.

DR. ERICKSON: You see a girl.

CLIENT: Yes.

DR. ERICKSON: Yes.

CLIENT: [pause] And she's sitting there at the counter, and she's talking to me.

DR. ERICKSON: Yes? And how is she clad?

CLIENT: She's wearing dark green. She has very black hair, wavy hair.

DR. ERICKSON: And what about her cheeks? And her neck?

CLIENT: I think olive color would be the best.

DR. ERICKSON: Uh-huh. How did you first see her face and neck?

CLIENT: Olive color, definitely.

DR. ERICKSON: Is that the way you saw it first?

CLIENT: Yes.

DR. ERICKSON: And what did you mean, cold?

CLIENT: Well, that was more the look on her face, I think.

DR. ERICKSON: The look on her face?

CLIENT: Yes.

DR. ERICKSON: Now how did you get from that mountain and the ice cream advertisement to a girl?

CLIENT: [pause] Mainly through the symbolism because in the symbolism, I saw many of the qualities that she had.

DR. ERICKSON: What were those qualities?

CLIENT: Qualities of independence.

DR. ERICKSON: And do you recall the words that I used in describing that original mountain?

CLIENT: Something standing by itself.

DR. ERICKSON: By itself.

CLIENT: Just the one mountain.

DR. ERICKSON: And snow on the top.

CLIENT: Yes.

DR. ERICKSON: And still. And no movement?

CLIENT: Definitely.

DR. ERICKSON: And then lines?

CLIENT: Uh-huh.

DR. ERICKSON: I didn't say curves, did I?

CLIENT: No.

DR. ERICKSON: No, I didn't.

CLIENT: No, I don't think so.

DR. ERICKSON: No, I didn't. I was very careful to avoid that word, "curves." And I needed to give you time to build up that original suggestion, because I wanted you to see that mountain transformed into curves, and lines, without saying the word "curves." [pause] And the coldness, and the stillness, and the snow. And by itself. And then the lines that could change, and the hues and the colors, and it's autumn.

CLIENT: Yes.

DR. ERICKSON: Now do you see?

CLIENT: Yes, I see.

DR. ERICKSON: Aren't you pleased with your ability to pick up those little cues? I am. I think it's so delightful when you do that. And I think, "André White's mountain." Who is he? [pause] You don't really know, do you? Who am I?

CLIENT: You're the person that I'm talking to at this table.

DR. ERICKSON: That's right. And what year is it?

CLIENT: 1950.

DR. ERICKSON: Uh-huh? And would you like to experience a change of time? This is a curious conversation to get into, isn't it?

CLIENT: Yes.

DR. ERICKSON: You don't mind, do you?

CLIENT: No.

DR. ERICKSON: It would be interesting to experience a change of time?

CLIENT: I think so.

DR. ERICKSON: We read about it in science fiction, and we think about it in our fantasies, and we have it in our dreams. And in our dreams we can dream that we are small children. [pause] And I can dream that and you can dream that. And in the dream you feel yourself a small child, and you sense yourself a small child. That's right. [pause] That's right. And what is your name?

CLIENT: Gordon.

DR. ERICKSON: And how old are you, Gordon?

CLIENT: Nine.

DR. ERICKSON: And who am I?

CLIENT: I don't know. I've not met you before.

DR. ERICKSON: You haven't met me before? That's all right. I'm a friend of some people you know very well. Maybe you can guess who they are.

CLIENT: Mr. Morrissey?

DR. ERICKSON: And someone else?

CLIENT: John.

DR. ERICKSON: You're pretty good at guessing, aren't you?

CLIENT: Yes.

DR. ERICKSON: Aren't you pleased?

CLIENT: Yes, of course. [giggles]

DR. ERICKSON: It's nice to guess right the first two times, isn't it? Well, what did you do yesterday?

CLIENT: I was at school yesterday.

DR. ERICKSON: You did?

CLIENT: Yes.

DR. ERICKSON: Did you enjoy it?

CLIENT: No. I'm sort of not too good.

DR. ERICKSON: Not too good?

CLIENT: No.

DR. ERICKSON: Why?

CLIENT: Well, it's . . . I'm afraid I set a fight with the other lads, you know? [chuckles]

DR. ERICKSON: You don't feel bad about it, do you?

CLIENT: Well, normally I would, but if he'd got lost, I would have felt bad about it.

DR. ERICKSON: Uh-huh. Well, you know, Gordon, some day you're going to grow up. Do you know that?

CLIENT: Not from what my dad keeps saying. [chuckles]

DR. ERICKSON: Well, but you are going to grow up. You know, time is changing. Look at this hand of mine. That's it. Time is changing. And the years are going by, and very soon I want you to rouse up, wide awake, as wide awake as you would be on November the 28th, 1958. Now close your eyes and wake up, as wide awake as you would be on November 28th, just before you eat dinner.

DR. ERICKSON: Hi. Hi. Hi…

CLIENT: It's hot under these mikes, but otherwise quite in good shape.

DR. ERICKSON: Quite in good shape.

CLIENT: Uh-huh.

DR. ERICKSON: Uh-huh? And what are you going to do on Thanksgiving Day?

CLIENT: Go out to dinner. That's the main point.

DR. ERICKSON: You are?

CLIENT: Yes. [laughs]

DR. ERICKSON: That's the main point, isn't it?

CLIENT: You have an excellent Thanksgiving, I gather. We don't celebrate this back in England, but I think it's quite a good idea

DR. ERICKSON: And have you arranged it so that you'll have several invitations to dinner on Thanksgiving Day?

CLIENT: No, just the one. I think the one is enough.

DR. ERICKSON: Well, I can remember a friend of mine who accepted an early Thanksgiving dinner, because they had a plan, his host did, for the afternoon. They just invited him for an 11 o'clock Thanksgiving dinner. His other friends invited him for a 4 o'clock Thanksgiving dinner, so he attended that. And then some others had a late…and he ate nobly at all three.

CLIENT: That's a little more than I could do, I think.

DR. ERICKSON: Well, you've never tried it.

CLIENT: I don't think I'd like to try three. I think one is usually enough. Or, from last year, one was certainly enough.

DR. ERICKSON: Well, I believe one bit of advice is that always take your second, third, and fourth helpings along with the first. [laughter] That way there's no possibility of being frustrated or disappointed.

CLIENT: That's right.

DR. ERICKSON: By the way, do you think you'll go into a trance this afternoon?

CLIENT: Go into a trance this afternoon?

DR. ERICKSON: Uh-huh?

CLIENT: I've been into a trance.

DR. ERICKSON: You have?

CLIENT: I'm certain I have, yes.

DR. ERICKSON: Why are you certain?

CLIENT: Well, I can recall some of the things I've been doing.

DR. ERICKSON: Uh-huh? And have you been watching Gregory?

CLIENT: [laughs] No, not Gregory there. But he's here now.
Gregory Bateson: Cheers.

DR. ERICKSON: Forgetting… [laughter]

CLIENT: He's a quiet sort.

DR. ERICKSON: Uh-huh. It's nice to see him working, isn't it?

CLIENT: Yes, definitely.

DR. ERICKSON: Takes his mind off what you and I were talking about. [laughter]

Gregory Bateson: Well?

DR. ERICKSON: Oh, he's giving me some kind of a signal, but I've been too busy to pay attention to what it is.

CLIENT: He said "well" or something and I don't know quite what he meant by this...

DR. ERICKSON: Do you remember when you went back into a trance?

CLIENT: Yes, I think I recall most of the things.

DR. ERICKSON: We were discussing Andre with smoking, weren't we? Through the one-way mirror.

CLIENT: That's right, yes, regarding how this was a silly thing to do under a one-way mirror.... [laughs]

DR. ERICKSON: Well you even thought not even to breathe behind one of those.

CLIENT: No, certainly not move, I think.

DR. ERICKSON: ...wide awake now?

CLIENT: I feel so, yes.

DR. ERICKSON: You're quite sure of it?

CLIENT: Yes, I'm certain, as far as I know, yes.

DR. ERICKSON: Beginning to have doubts?

CLIENT: [pause] Just a few doubts.

DR. ERICKSON: Uh-huh? All right, well then, lose the doubts.

CLIENT: All right. [laughs] If you say so. [laughter]

DR. ERICKSON: Well, I wish they'd get around to letting us know whether we can leave these hot seats.

CLIENT: Yes, under the hot lights anyway. Something noisy is going on in the background there. [film ends here]

CHAPTER SEVEN

Milton Erickson

A Special Inquiry with Aldous Huxley
into the Nature and Character of
Various States of Consciousness★

Introduction

OVER A PERIOD OF NEARLY A YEAR much time was spent by
Aldous Huxley and by the author, each planning separately for a joint
inquiry into various states of psychological awareness. Special
inquiries, possible methods of experimental approach and investiga-
tions and various questions to be propounded were listed by each of
us in our respective loose-leaf notebooks. The purpose was to prepare
a general background for the proposed joint study with this general
background reflecting the thinking of both of us uninfluenced by the
other. It was hoped in this way to secure the widest possible coverage
of ideas by such separate outlines prepared from the markedly different backgrounds of understanding that the two of us possessed.

Early in 1950 we met in Huxley's home in Los Angeles, there to
spend an intensive day appraising the ideas recorded in our separate
notebooks and to engage in any experimental inquiries that seemed
feasible. I was particularly interested in Huxley's approach to psychological problems, his method of thinking and his own unique use of
his unconscious mind which we had discussed only briefly sometime
previously. Huxley was particularly interested in hypnosis and previous exceedingly brief work with him had demonstrated his excellent
competence as a deep somnambulistic subject.

It was realized that this meeting would be a preliminary or pilot
study, and this was discussed by both of us. Hence we planned to make
it as comprehensive and inclusive as possible without undue emphasis
upon completion of any one particular item. Once the day's work had

★Originally published
in (and reprinted with
permission of) the
*American Journal of
Clinical Hypnosis,*Volume
8, pages 14–33, 1965

been evaluated, plans could then be made for future meetings and specific studies. Additionally, we each had our individual purposes. Aldous having in mind future literary work, while my interest related to future psychological experimentation in the field of hypnosis.

The day's work began at 8:00 a.m. and remained uninterrupted until 6:00 p.m. with some considerable review of our notebooks the next day to establish their general agreement, to remove any lack of clarity of meaning caused by the abbreviated notations we had entered into them during the previous day's work and to correct any oversights. On the whole we found that our notebooks were reasonably in agreement but that naturally certain of our entries were reflective of our special interests and of the fact that each of us had, by the nature of the situation, made separate notations bearing upon each other.

Our plan was to leave these notebooks with Huxley since his phenomenal memory, often appearing to be total recall, and his superior literary ability would permit a more satisfactory writing of a joint article based upon our discussions and experimentations of that day's work. However, I did abstract from my notebook certain pages bearing notations upon Huxley's behavior at times when he, as an experimental subject, was unable to make comprehensive notations on himself, although post-experimentally he could and did do so, though less completely than I had. It was proposed that, from these certain special pages, I was to endeavor to develop an article which could be incorporated later in the longer study that Huxley was to write. Accordingly, I abstracted a certain number of pages intending to secure still more at a later date. These pages that I did remove Huxley rapidly copied into his own notebook to be sure of the completeness of his own data.

Unfortunately, a California brush fire sometime later destroyed Huxley's home, his extensive library containing many rare volumes and manuscripts, besides numerous other treasures to say nothing of the manuscripts upon which Huxley was currently working as well as the respective notebooks of our special joint study. As a result, the entire subject matter of our project was dropped as a topic too painful to discuss, but Huxley's recent death led to my perusal of these relatively few pages I had abstracted from my notebook. Examination of them suggested the possibility of presenting to the reader a small but informative part of that day's work. In this regard, the reader must bear in mind that the quotations attributed to Huxley are not necessarily verbatim, since his more extensive utter-ances were noted in abbreviated form. However, in the essence of their meaning, they are correct and they are expressive of Huxley as I knew him. It is also to be borne in mind that Huxley had read my notations on the occasion of our joint study and had approved them.

Project Initiation

THE PROJECT began with Huxley reviewing concepts and definitions of conscious awareness, primarily his and in part those of others, followed by a discussion with me of his understandings of hypnotic states of awareness. The purpose was to insure that we were both in accord or clear in our divergences of understanding, thus to make possible a more reliable inquiry into the subject matter of our interest.

There followed then a review in extensive detail of various of his psychedelic experiences with mescaline, later to be recorded in his book. (Huxley, A. *The Doors of Perception*. New York: Harper and Brothers, 1954.)

Huxley then proceeded with a detailed description of his very special practice of what he, for want of a better and less awkward term which he had not yet settled upon, called "Deep Reflection." He described this state (the author's description is not complete since there seemed to be no good reason except interest for making full notations of his description) of Deep Reflection as one marked by physical relaxation with bowed head and closed eyes, a profound progressive psychological withdrawal from externalities but without any actual loss of physical realities nor any amnesias or loss of orien-tation, a "setting aside" of everything not pertinent, and then a state of complete mental absorption in matters of interest to him. Yet, in that state of complete withdrawal and mental absorption, Huxley stated that he was free to pick up a fresh pencil to replace a dulled one to make "automatically" notations on his thoughts and to do all this without a recognizable realization on his part of what physical act he was performing. It was as if the physical act were "not an integral part of my thinking." In no way did such physical activity seem to impinge upon, to slow, or to impede "the train of thought so exclusively occupying my interest. It is associated but completely peripheral activity.... I might say activity barely contiguous to the periphery." To illustrate further, Huxley cited an instance of another type of physical activity. He recalled having been in a state of Deep Reflection one day when his wife was shopping. He did not recall what thoughts or ideas he was examining but he did recall that, when his wife returned that day, she had asked him if he had made a note of the special message she had given him over the telephone. He had been bewildered by her inquiry, could not recall anything about answering the telephone as his wife asserted, but together they found the special message recorded on a pad beside the telephone which was placed within comfortable reaching distance from the chair in which he liked to develop Deep Reflection. Both he and his wife reached the conclusion that he had been in a state of Deep Reflection at the time of the telephone call, had lifted the receiver and had said to her as usual, "I say there, hello," had listened to the message, had recorded it, all without any subsequent recollections of the experience. He recalled merely that he had been working on a manuscript that afternoon, one that had been absorbing all of his interest. He explained that it was quite common for him to initiate a day's work by entering a state of Deep Reflection as a preliminary process of marshalling his thoughts and putting into order the thinking that would enter into his writing later that day.

As still another illustrative incident, Huxley cited an occasion when his wife returned home from a brief absence, found the door locked as was customary, had entered the house and discovered in plain view a special delivery letter on a hallway table reserved for mail, special messages, etc. She had found Huxley sitting quietly in his special chair, obviously in a state of deep thought. Later that day she had inquired about the time of arrival of the special delivery letter only to learn that he had obviously no recollection of receiving any letter. Yet both knew that the mailman had undoubtedly rung the doorbell, that Huxley had heard the bell, had interrupted whatever he was doing, had gone to the door, opened it, received the letter, closed the door, placed the letter in its proper place and returned to the chair where she had found him.

Both of these two special events had occurred fairly recently. He recalled them only as incidents related to him by his wife but with no feeling that those accounts constituted a description of actual meaningful physical behavior on his part. So far as he knew, he could only deduce that he must have been in a state of Deep Reflection when they occurred.

His wife subsequently confirmed the assumption that his behavior had been completely "automatic, like a machine moving precisely and accurately. It is a delightful pleasure to see him get a book out of the bookcase, sit down again, open the book slowly, pick up his reading glass, read a little, and then lay the book and glass aside. Then some time later, maybe a few days, he will notice the book and ask about it. The man just never remembers what he does nor what he thinks about when he sits in that chair. All of a sudden, you just find him in his study working very hard."

In other words, while in a state of Deep Reflection and seemingly totally withdrawn from external realities, the integrity of the task being done in that mental state was untouched by external stimuli, but some peripheral part of awareness made it possible for him to receive external stimuli, to respond meaningfully to them but with no apparent recording of any memory of either the stimulus or his meaningful and adequate response. Inquiry of his wife later had disclosed that when she was at home, Aldous in a state of Deep Reflection paid no attention to the telephone which might be beside him or the doorbell. "He simply depends completely on me, but I can call out to him that I'll be away and he never fails to hear the telephone or the doorbell."

Huxley explained that he believed he could develop a state of Deep Reflection in about five minutes but that in doing so he "simply cast aside all anchors" of any type of awareness. Just what he meant and sensed he could not describe. "It is a subjective experience quite" in which he apparently achieved a state of "orderly mental arrangement" permitting an orderly free flowing of his thoughts as he wrote. This was his final explanation. He had never considered any analysis of exactly what his "Deep Reflection" was nor did he feel that he could analyze it, but he offered to attempt it as an experimental investigation for the day. It was promptly learned that, as he began to absorb himself in his thoughts to achieve a state of Deep Reflection, he did indeed "cast off all anchors" and appeared to be completely out of touch with everything. On this attempt to experience subjectively and to remember the processes of entering into Deep Reflection, he developed the state within five minutes and emerged from it within two as closely as I could determine. His comment was, "I say, I'm deucedly sorry. I suddenly found myself all prepared to work with nothing to do and I realized I had better come out of it." That was all the information he could offer. For the next attempt, a signal to be given by me was agreed upon as a signal for him to "come out of it." A secondary attempt was made as easily as the first. Huxley sat quietly for some minutes and the agreed upon signal was given. Huxley's account was, "I found myself just waiting for something. I did not know what. It was just a 'something' that I seemed to feel would come in what seemed to be a timeless spaceless void. I say, that's the first time I noted that feeling. Always I've had some thinking to do. But this time I seemed to have no work in hand. I was just completely disinterested, indifferent, just waiting for something and then I felt a need to come out of it. I say, did you give me the signal?"

Inquiry disclosed that he had no apparent memory of the stimulus being given. He had had only the "feeling" that it was time to "come out of it."

Several more repetitions yielded similar results. A sense of a timeless spaceless void, a placid comfortable awaiting for an undefined "something" and a comfortable need to return to ordinary conscious awareness constituted the understandings achieved. Huxley summarized his findings briefly as "a total absence of everything on the way there and on the way back and an expected meaningless something for which one awaits in a state of Nirvana since there is nothing more to do." He asserted his intention to make a later intensive study of this practice he found so useful in his writing.

Further experiments were done after Huxley had explained that he could enter the state of deep reflection with the simple undefined understanding that he would respond to any "significant stimulus." Without informing him of my intentions, I asked him to "arouse" (this term is my own) when three taps of a pencil on a chair were given in close succession. He entered the state of reflection readily and, after a brief wait, I tapped the table with a pencil in varying fashions at distinct but irregular intervals. Thus, I tapped once, paused, then twice in rapid succession, paused, tapped once, paused, tapped four times in rapid succession, paused, then five times in rapid succession. Numerous variations were tried but with an avoidance of the agreed upon signal. A chair was knocked over with a crash while four taps were given. Not until the specified three taps were given did he make any response. His arousal occurred slowly with almost an immediate response to the signal. Huxley was questioned about his subjective experiences. He explained simply that they had been the same as previously with one exception, namely that several times he had a vague sensation that "something was coming," but he knew not what. He had no awareness of what had been done.

Further experimentation was done in which he was asked to enter Deep Reflection and to sense color, a prearranged signal for arousing being that of a handshake of his right hand. He complied readily and when I judged that he was fully absorbed in his state of reflection, I shook his left hand vigorously, then followed this with a hard pinching of the back of both hands that left deep fingernail markings. Huxley made no response to this physical stimulation, although his eyes were watched for possible eyeball movements under the lids and his respiratory and pulse rates were checked for any changes. However, after about a minute he slowly drew his arms back along the arms of the chair where he had placed them before beginning his reflection state. They moved slowly about an inch and then all movement ceased.

He was aroused easily and comfortably at the designated signal.

His subjective report was simply that he had "lost" himself in a "sea of color," of "sensing," "feeling," "being" color, of being "quite utterly involved in it with no identity of your own, you know." Then suddenly he had experienced a process of losing that color in a "meaningless void," only to open his eyes and to realize that he had "come out of it."

He remembered the agreed upon stimulus but did not recall if it had been given. "I can only deduce it was given from the fact that I'm out of it," and indirect questioning disclosed no memories of the other physical stimuli administered. Neither was there an absent-minded looking at nor rubbing of the backs of his hands.

This same procedure in relation to color was repeated but to it was added, as he seemed to be reaching the state of deep reflection, a repeated insistent urging that, upon arousal, he discuss a certain book which was carefully placed in full view. The results were comparable to the preceding findings. He became "lost,"... "quite utterly involved in it,"..."one can sense it but not describe it,"..."I say, it's an utterly amazing, fascinating state of finding yourself a pleasant part of an endless vista of color that is soft and gentle and yielding and all-absorbing. Utterly extraordinary, most extraordinary." He had no recollection of my verbal insistences nor of the other physical stimuli. He remembered the agreed upon signal but did not know if it had been given. He found himself only in a position of assuming that it had been given since he was again in a state of ordinary awareness. The presence of the book meant nothing to him. One added statement was that entering a state of Deep Reflection by absorbing himself in a sense of color was, in a fashion, comparable to but not identical with his psychedelic experiences.

As a final inquiry, Huxley was asked to enter the reflection state for the purpose of recalling the telephone call and the special-delivery letter incidents. His comment was that such a project should be "quite fruitful." Despite repeated efforts, he would "come out of it" explaining, "There I found myself without anything to do so I came out of it." His memories were limited to the accounts given to him by his wife and all details were associated with her and not with any inner feelings of experience on his part.

A final effort was made to discover whether or not Huxley could include another person in his state of Deep Reflection. This idea interested him at once and it was suggested that he enter the reflection state to review some of his psychedelic experiences. This he did in a most intriguing fashion. As the reflection state developed, Huxley in an utterly detached dissociated fashion began making fragmentary remarks, chiefly in the form of selfaddressed comments. Thus he would say, making fragmentary notes with a pencil and paper quickly supplied to him, "most extraordinary ...I overlooked that ...How? ...Strange I should have forgotten that (making a notation) ...fascinating how different it appears ...I must look....

When he aroused, he had a vague recollection of having reviewed a previous psychedelic experience but what he had experienced then or on the immediate occasion he could not recall. Nor did he recall speaking aloud nor making notations. When shown these, he found that they were so poorly written that they could not be read. I read mine to him without eliciting any memory traces.

A repetition yielded similar results with one exception. This was an amazed expression of complete astonishment by Huxley suddenly declaring, "I say, Milton, this is quite utterly amazing, most extraordinary. I use Deep Reflection to summon my memories, to put into order all of my thinking, to explore the range, the extent of my mental existence, but I do it solely to let those realizations, the thinking, the understandings, the memories seep into the work I'm planning to do without my conscious awareness of them. Fascinating …never stopped to realize that my deep reflection always preceded a period of intensive work wherein I was completely absorbed.... I say, no wonder I have an amnesia."

Later when we were examining each other's notebook, Huxley manifested intense amazement and bewilderment at what I had recorded about the physical stimuli and for which he had no memory of any sort. He knew that he had gone into deep reflection repeatedly at my request, had been both pleased and amazed at his subjective feelings of being lost in an all-absorbing sea of color, had sensed a certain timelessness spacelessness and had experienced a comfortable feeling of something meaningful about to happen. He reread my notations repeatedly in an endeavor to develop some kind of a feeling of at least a vague memory of subjective awareness of the various physical stimuli I had given him. He also looked at the backs of his hands to see the pinch marks but they had vanished. His final comment was, "...extraordinary, most extraordinary, I say, utterly fascinating."

When we agreed that, at least for the while, further inquiry into Deep Reflection might be postponed until later, Huxley declared again that his sudden realization of how much he had used it and how little he knew about it made him resolve to investigate much further into his "Deep Reflection." The manner and means by which he achieved it, how it constituted a form of preparation for absorbing himself in his writing and in what way it caused him to lose unnecessary contact with reality were all problems of much interest to him.

Huxley then suggested that an investigation be made of hypnotic states of awareness by employing him as a subject. He asked permission to be allowed to interrupt his trance states at will for purposes of discussion. This was in full accord with my own wishes.

He asked that first a light trance be induced, perhaps repeatedly, to permit an exploration of his subjective experiences. Since he had briefly been a somnambulistic subject previously, he was carefully assured that this fact could serve to make him feel confident in arresting his trance states at any level he wished. He did not recognize this as a simple direct hypnotic suggestion. In reading my notebook later he was much amused at how easily he had accepted an obvious suggestion without recognizing its character at the time.

He found several repetitions of the light trance interesting but "too easily conceptualized." It is, he explained, "A simple withdrawal of interest from the outside to the inside." That is, one gives less and less attention to externalities and directs more and more attention to inner subjective sensations. Externalities become increasingly fainter and more obscure, inner subjective feelings more satisfying until a state of balance exists. In this state of balance, he had the feeling that, with motivation, he could "reach out and seize upon reality," that there is a definite retention of a grasp upon external reality but with no motivation to deal with it. Neither did he feel a desire to deepen the trance. No particular change in this state of balance seemed necessary and he noted that a feeling of contentment and relaxation accompanied it. He wondered if others experienced the same subjective reactions.

Huxley requested that the light trance be induced by a great variety of techniques, some of them non-verbal. The results in each instance, Huxley felt strongly, were dependent entirely upon his mental set. He found that he could accept "drifting along" (my phrase) in a light trance, receptive of suggestions involving primarily responses at a subjective level only. He found that an effort to behave in direct relationship to the physical environment taxed his efforts and made him desire either to arouse from the trance or to go still deeper. He also, on his own initiative, set up his own problems to test his trance states.

Thus, before entering the light trance he would privately resolve to discuss a certain topic, relevant or irrelevant, with me at the earliest possible time or even at a fairly remote time. In such instances, Huxley found such unexpressed desires deleterious to the maintenance of the trance. Similarly any effort to include an item of reality not pertinent to his sense of subjective satisfaction lessened the trance.

At all times there persisted a "dim but ready" awareness that one could alter the state of awareness at will. Huxley, like others with whom I have done similar studies, felt an intense desire to explore his sense of subjective comfort and satisfaction but immediately realized that this would lead to a deeper trance state.

When Huxley was asked to formulate understandings of the means he could employ by which he could avoid going into more than a light trance, he stated that he did this by setting a given length of time during which he would remain in a light trance. This had the effect of making him more strongly aware that at any moment he could "reach out and seize external reality" and that his sense of subjective comfort and ease decreased. Discussion of this and repeated experimentation disclosed that carefully worded suggestions serving to emphasize the availability of external reality and to enhance subjective comfort could serve to deepen the trance even though Huxley was fully cognizant of what was being said and why. Similar results have been obtained with other highly intelligent subjects.

In experimenting with medium deep trances, Huxley, like other subjects with whom I have worked, experienced much more difficulty in reacting to and maintaining a fairly constant trance level. He found that he had a subjective need to go deeper in the trance and an intellectual need to stay at the medium level. The result was that he found himself repeatedly "reaching out for awareness" of his environment and this would initiate a light trance. He would then direct his attention to subjective comfort and find himself developing a deep trance. Finally, after repeated experiments, he was given both posthypnotic and direct hypnotic suggestion to remain in a medium deep trance. This he found he could do with very little concern then. He described the medium trance as primarily characterized by a most pleasing subjective sense of comfort and a vague dim faulty awareness that there was an external reality for which he felt a need for considerable motivation to be able to examine it. However, if he attempted to examine even a single item of reality for its intrinsic value, the trance would immediately become increasingly lighter. On the other hand, when he examined an item of external reality for subjective values, for example, the soft comfort of the chair cushions as contrasted to the intrinsic quiet of the room, the trance became deeper. But both light and deep trances were characterized by a need to sense external reality in some manner, not necessarily clearly but nevertheless to retain some recognizable awareness of it.

For both types of trance, experiments were carried out to discover what hypnotic phenomena could be elicited in both light and medium deep trances. This same experiment has been done with other good subjects and also with subjects who consistently developed only a light trance and with those who consistently did not seem to be able to go further than the medium trance. In all such studies, the findings were the same, the most important seeming to be the need of light and medium deep hypnotic subjects to retain at least some grasp upon external reality and to orient their trance state as a state apart from external reality but with the orientation to such reality, however tenuous in character, sensed as available for immediate utilization by the subject.

Another item which Huxley discovered by his own efforts unguided by me and of which I was fully aware through work with other subjects, was that the phenomena of deep hypnosis can be developed in both the light and the medium trance. Huxley, having observed deep hypnosis, wondered about the possibility of developing hallucinatory phenomena in the light trance. He attempted this by the measure of enjoying his subjective state of physical comfort and adding to it an additional subjective quality, namely, a pleasant gustatory sensation. He found it quite easy to hallucinate vividly various taste sensations while wondering vaguely what I would think if I knew what he were doing. He was not aware of his increased swallowing when he did this. From gustatory sensations he branched out to olfactory hallucinations both pleasant and unpleasant. He did not realize that he betrayed this by the flaring of his nostrils. His thinking at the time, so he subsequently explained, was that he had the "feeling" that hallucinations of a completely "inner type of process," that is, occurring within the body itself, would be easier than those in which the hallucination appeared to be external to the body. From olfactory hallucinations he progressed to kinesthetic, proprioceptive and finally tactile sensations. In the kinesthetic hallucinatory sensation experience he hallucinated taking a long walk but remaining constantly aware that I was present in some vaguely sensed room. Momentarily he would forget about me and his hallucinated walking would become most vivid. He recognized this as an indication of the momentary development of a deeper trance state which he felt obligated to remember to report to me during the discussion after his arousal. He was not aware of respiratory and pulse changes during the hallucinatory walk.

When he first tried for visual and auditory hallucinations, he found them much more difficult and the effort tended to lighten and to abolish his trance state. He finally reasoned that if he could hallucinate rhythmical movements of his body, he could then "attach" an auditory hallucination to this hallucinated body sensation. The measure proved most successful and again he caught himself wondering if I could hear the music. His breathing rate changed and slight movements of his head were observed. From simple music he proceeded to an hallucination of opera singing and then finally a mumbling of words which eventually seemed to become my voice questioning him about Deep Reflection. I could not recognize what was occurring.

From this he proceeded to visual hallucinations. An [sic (At)] attempt to open his eyes nearly aroused him from his trance state.

Thereafter he kept his eyes closed for both light and medium deep trance activities. His first visual hallucination was a vivid flooding of his mind with an intense sense of pastel colors of changing hues and with a wavelike motion. He related this experience to his Deep Reflection experiences with me and also to his previous psychedelic experiences. He did not consider this experience sufficiently valid for his purposes of the moment because he felt that vivid memories were playing too large a part. Hence he deliberately decided to visualize a flower but the thought occurred to him that, even as a sense of movement played a part in auditory hallucinations, he might employ a similar measure to develop a visual hallucination. At the moment, so he recalled after arousing from the trance and while discussing his experience, he wondered if I had ever built up hallucinations in my subjects by combining various sensory fields of experience. I told him that that was a standard procedure for me.

He proceeded with this visual hallucination by "feeling" his head turn from side to side and up and down to follow a barely visible, questionably visible, rhythmically moving object. Very shortly the object became increasingly more visible until he saw a giant rose, possibly three feet in diameter. This he did not expect and thus he was certain at once that it was not a vivified memory but a satisfactory hallucination. With this realization came the realization that he might very well add to the hallucination by adding olfactory hallucinations of an intense "unroselike" sickeningly sweet odor. This effort was also most successful. After experimenting with various hallucinations, Huxley aroused from his trance and discussed extensively what he had accomplished. He was pleased to learn that his experimental findings without any coaching or suggestions from me were in good accord with planned experimental findings with other subjects.

This discussion raised the question of anesthesia, amnesia, dissociation, depersonalization, regression, time distortion, hypermnesia (an item difficult to test with Huxley because of his phenomenal memory) and an exploration of past repressed events.

Of these, Huxley found that anesthesia, amnesia, time distortion, and hypermnesia were possible in the light trance. The other phenomena were conducive to the development of a deep trance with any earnest effort to achieve them.

The anesthesia he developed in the light trance was most effective for selected parts of the body. When generalized anesthesia from the neck down was attempted, Huxley found himself "slipping" into a deep trance.

The amnesia, like the anesthesia, was effective when selective in character. Any effort to have a total amnesia resulted in a progression toward a deep trance.

Time distortion was easily possible and Huxley offered the statement that he was not certain but that he felt strongly that he had long employed time distortion in Deep Reflection, although his first formal introduction to the concept had been through me.

Hypermnesia, so difficult to test because of his extreme capacity to recall past events, was tested upon my suggestion by asking him in the light trance state to state promptly upon request on what page of various of his books certain paragraphs could be found. At the first request, Huxley aroused from the light trance and explained, "Really now, Milton, I can't do that. I can with effort recite most of that book, but the page number for a paragraph is not exactly cricket." Nevertheless, he went back into a light trance, the name of the volume was given, a few lines of a paragraph were read aloud to him whereupon he was to give the page number on which it appeared. He succeeded in definitely better than 65 percent in an amazingly prompt fashion. Upon awakening from the light trance, he was instructed to remain in the state of conscious awareness and to execute the same task. To his immense astonishment he found that, while the page number "flashed" into his mind in the light trance state, in the waking state he had to follow a methodical procedure of completing the paragraph mentally, beginning the next, then turning back mentally to the preceding paragraph and then "making a guess."

When restricted to the same length of time he had employed in the light trance, he failed in each instance. When allowed to take whatever length of time he wished, he could reach an accuracy of about 40 percent, but the books had to be ones more recently read than those used for the light trance state.

Huxley then proceeded to duplicate in the medium trance all that he had done in the light trance. He accomplished similar tasks much more easily but constantly experienced a feeling of "slipping" into a deeper trance.

Huxley and I discussed this hypnotic behavior of his at very considerable length with Huxley making most of the notations since only he could record his own subjective experience in relation to the topics discussed. For this reason the discussion here is limited.

We then turned to the question of deep hypnosis. Huxley developed easily a profound somnambulistic trance in which he was completely disoriented spontaneously for time and place. He was able to open his eyes but described his field of vision as being a "well of light" which included me, the chair in which I sat, himself and his chair. He remarked at once upon the remarkable spontaneous restriction of his vision, and disclosed an awareness that, for some reason unknown to him, he was obligated to "explain things" to me. Careful questioning disclosed him to have an amnesia about what had been done previously, nor did he have any awareness of our joint venture. His feeling that he must explain things became a casual willingness as soon as he verbalized it. One of his first statements was, "Really, you know, I can't understand my situation or why you are here wherever that may be but I must explain things to you." He was assured that I understood the situation and that I was interested in receiving any explanation he wished to give me and told that I might make requests of him. Most casually, indifferently he acceded, but it was obvious that he was enjoying a state of physical comfort in a contented passive manner.

He answered questions simply and briefly, giving literally and precisely no more and no less than the literal significance of the question implied. In other words, he showed the same precise literalness found in other subjects, perhaps more so because of his knowledge of semantics.

He was asked, "What is to my right?" His answer was simply, "I don't know." "Why?" "I haven't looked." "Will you do so?" "Yes." "Now!" "How far do you want me to look?" This was not an unexpected inquiry since I have encountered it innumerable times. Huxley was simply manifesting a characteristic phenomenon of the deep somnambulistic trance in which visual awareness is restricted in some inexplicable manner to those items pertinent to the trance situation. For each chair, couch, footstool I wished him to see, specific instructions were required. As Huxley explained later, "I had to look around until gradually it (the specified object) slowly came into view, not all at once, but slowly as if it were materializing. I really believe that I felt completely at ease without a trace of wonderment as I watched things materialize. I accepted everything as a matter of course." Similar explanations have been received from hundreds of subjects. Yet experience has taught me the importance of my assumption of the role of a purely passive inquirer, one who asks a question solely to receive an answer regardless of its content. An intonation of interest in the meaning of the answer is likely to induce the subject to respond as if he had been given instructions concerning what answer to give. In therapeutic work I use intonations to influence more adequate personal responses by the patient.

With Huxley I tested this by enthusiastically asking, "What, tell me now, is that which is just about 15 feet in front of you?" The correct answer should have been, "A table." Instead, the answer received was "A table with a book and a vase on it." Both the book and the vase were on the table but on the far side of the table and hence more than 15 feet away. Later the same inquiry was made in a casual indifferent fashion, "Tell me now what is that just about 15 feet in front of you?" He replied, despite his previous answer, "A table." "Anything else?" "Yes." "What else?" "A book." (This was nearer to him than was the vase.) "Anything else?" "Yes." "Tell me now." "A vase." "Anything else?" "Yes." "Tell me now." "A spot." "Anything else?" "No."

This literalness and this peculiar restriction of awareness to those items of reality constituting the precise hypnotic situation is highly definitive of a satisfactory somnambulistic hypnotic trance. Along with the visual restriction, there is also an auditory restriction of such character that sounds, even those originating between the operator and the subject seem to be totally outside the hypnotic situation. Since there was no assistant present, this auditory restriction could not be tested. However, by means of a black thread not visible to the eye, a book was toppled from the table behind him against his back. Slowly, as if he had experienced an itch, Huxley raised his hand and scratched his shoulder. There was no startle reaction. This, too, is characteristic of the response made to many unexpected physical stimuli. They are interpreted in terms of past body experience. Quite frequently as a part of developing a deep somnambulistic trance, subjects will concomitantly develop a selective general anesthesia for physical stimuli not constituting a part of the hypnotic situation, physical stimuli in particular that do not permit interpretation in terms of past experience. This could not be tested in the situation with Huxley since an assistant is necessary to make adequate tests without distorting the hypnotic situation. One illustrative measure I have used is to pass a threaded needle through the coat sleeve while positioning the arms and then having an assistant saw back and forth on the thread from a place of concealment. Often a spontaneous anesthesia would keep the subject unaware of the stimulus. Various simple measures are easily devised.

Huxley was then gently indirectly awakened from the trance by the simple suggestion that he adjust himself in his chair to resume the exact physical and mental state he had had at the decision to discontinue until later any further experimental study of Deep Reflection.

Huxley's response was an immediate arousal and he promptly stated that he was all set to enter deep hypnosis. While this statement in itself indicated profound posthypnotic amnesia, delaying tactics were employed in the guise of discussion of what might possibly be done. In this way it became possible to mention various items of his deep trance behavior. Such mention evoked no memories and Huxley's discussion of the points raised showed no sophistication resulting from his deep trance behavior. He was as uninformed about the details of his deep trance behavior as he had been before the deep trance had been induced.

There followed more deep trances by Huxley in which, avoiding all personal significances, he was asked to develop partial, selective, and total posthypnotic amnesias (by partial is meant a part of the total experience, by selective amnesia is meant an amnesia for selected, perhaps interrelated items of experience), a recovery of the amnestic material and a loss of the recovered material. He developed also catalepsy tested by "arranging" him comfortably in a chair and then creating a situation constituting a direct command to rise from the chair ("take the book on that table there and place it on the desk over there and do it now"). By this means Huxley found himself, inexplicably to him, unable to arise from the chair and unable to understand why this was so. The "comfortable arrangement" of his body had resulted in a positioning that would have to be corrected before he could arise from the chair and no implied suggestions for such correction were to be found in the instructions given. Hence he sat helplessly unable to stand, unable to recognize why. This same measure has been employed to demonstrate a saddle block anesthesia before medical groups. The subject in the deep trance is carefully positioned, a casual conversation is then conducted, the subject is then placed in rapport with another subject who is asked to exchange seats with the first subject. The second subject steps over only to stand helplessly while the first subject discovers that she is (1) unable to move, and (2) that shortly the loss of inability [sic (ability)] to stand results in a loss of orientation to the lower part of her body and a resulting total anesthesia without anesthesia having been mentioned even in the preliminary discussion of hypnosis. This unnoticed use of catalepsy not recognized by the subject is a most effective measure in deepening trance states.

Huxley was amazed at his loss of mobility and became even more so when he discovered a loss of orientation to the lower part of his body and he was most astonished when I demonstrated for him the presence of a profound anesthesia. He was much at loss to understand the entire sequence of events. He did not relate the comfortable positioning of his body to the unobtrusively induced catalepsy with its consequent anesthesia.

He was aroused from the trance state with persistent catalepsy, anesthesia and a total amnesia for all deep trance experiences. He spontaneously enlarged the instruction to include all trance experiences, possibly because he did not hear my instructions sufficiently clearly. Immediately he reoriented himself to the time at which we had been working with Deep Reflection. He was much at loss to explain his immobile state, and he expressed curious wonderment about what he had done in the deep reflection state, from which he assumed he had just emerged, and what had led to such inexplicable manifestations for the first time in all of his experience. He became greatly interested, kept murmuring such comments as "Most extraordinary" while he explored the lower part of his body with his hands and eyes. He noted that he could tell the position of his feet only with his eyes, that there was a profound immobility from the waist down, and he discovered, while attempting futilely because of the catalepsy to move his leg with his hands that a state of anesthesia existed. This he tested variously, asking me to furnish him with various things in order to make his test. For example, he asked that ice be applied to his bare ankle by me since he could not bend sufficiently to do so. Finally, after much study he turned to me, remarking, "I say, you look cool and most comfortable while I am in a most extraordinary predicament. I deduce that in some subtle way you have distracted and disturbed my sense of body awareness. I say, is this state anything like hypnosis?"

Restoration of his memory delighted him, but he remained entirely at [a] loss concerning the genesis of his catalepsy and his anesthesia. He realized, however, that some technique of communication had been employed to effect the results achieved but he did not succeed in the association of the positioning of his body with the final results.

Further experimentation in the deep trance investigated visual, auditory and other types of ideosensory hallucinations. One of the measures employed was to pantomime hearing a door open and then to appear to see someone entering the room, to arise in courtesy and to indicate a chair, then to turn to Huxley to express the hope that he was comfortable. He replied that he was and he expressed surprise at his wife's unexpected return since he had expected her to be absent the entire day. (The chair I had indicated was one I knew his wife liked to occupy.) He conversed with her and apparently hallucinated replies. He was interrupted with the question of how he knew that it was his wife and not an hypnotic hallucination. He examined the question thoughtfully, then explained that I had not given him any suggestion to hallucinate his wife, that I had been as much surprised by her arrival as he had been, and that she was dressed as she had been just before her departure and not as I had seen her earlier. Hence, it was reasonable to assume that she was a reality. After a brief thoughtful pause, he returned to his "conversation" with her apparently continuing to hallucinate replies. Finally I attracted his attention and made a hand gesture suggestive of a disappearance toward the chair in which he "saw" his wife. To his complete astonishment he saw her slowly fade away. Then he turned to me and asked that I awaken him with a full memory of the experience. This I did and he discussed the experience at some length making many special notations in his notebook elaborating them with the answers to questions he put to me. He was amazed to discover that when I asked [him] to awaken with a rentention of the immobility and anesthesia, he thought he had awakened but that the trance state had, to him, unrecognizably persisted.

238

He then urged further work on hypnotic hallucinatory experiences and a great variety (positive and negative visual, auditory, olfactory, gustatory, tactile, kinesthetic, temperature, hunger, satiety, fatigue, weakness, profound excited expectation, etc.) were explored. He proved to be most competent in all regards and it was noted that his pulse rate would change as much as twenty points when he was asked to hallucinate the experience of mountain climbing in a profound state of weariness. He volunteered in his discussion of these varied experiences the information that while a negative hallucination could be achieved readily in a deep trance, it would be most difficult in a light or medium trance because negative hallucinations were most destructive of reality values, even those of the hypnotic situation. That is, with induced negative hallucinations, he found that I was blurred in outline even though he could develop a deep trance with a negative hallucination inherent in that deep trance for all external reality except the realities of the hypnotic situation which would remain clear and well defined unless suggestions to the contrary were offered. Subsequent work with other subjects confirmed this finding by Huxley. I had not previously explored this matter of negative hallucinations in light and medium trances.

At this point, Huxley recalled his page number identification in the lighter trance states during the inquiry into hypermnesia and he asked that he be subjected to similar tests in deep hypnosis. Together we searched the library shelves, finally selecting several books that Huxley was certain he must have read many years previously but which he had not touched for twenty or more years. (One, apparently, he had never read, the other five he had.)

In a deep trance with his eyes closed, Huxley listened intently, as I opened the book at random and read a half dozen lines from a selected paragraph. For some, he identified the page number almost at once and then he would hallucinate the page, and "read" it from the point where I had stopped. Additionally, he identified the occasion on which he read the book. Two of the books he recalled consulting fifteen years previously. Another two he found it difficult to give the correct page number and then only approximating the page number. He could not hallucinate the printing and could only give little more than a summary of the thought content; but this, in essence, was correct. He could not identify when he had read them but he was certain it was more than twenty-five years previously.

Huxley, in the post-trance discussion was most amazed by his performance as a memory feat but commented upon the experience as primarily intellectual with the recovered memories lacking in any emotional significances of belonging to him as a person. This led to a general discussion of hypnosis and Deep Reflection with a general feeling of inadequacy on Huxley's part concerning proper conceptualization of his experiences for comparison of values. While Huxley was most delighted with his hypnotic experiences for their interest and the new understandings they offered him, he was also somewhat at a loss. He felt that, as a purely personal experience, he derived certain unidentifiable subjective values from Deep Reflection not actually obtainable from hypnosis which offered only a wealth of new points of view. Deep Reflection, he declared, gave him certain inner enduring feelings that seemed to play some significant part in his pattern of living. During this discussion he suddenly asked if hypnosis could be employed to permit him to explore his psychedelic experiences. His request was met but upon arousal from the trance he expressed the feeling that the hypnotic experience was quite different than was a comparable "feeling through" by means of Deep Reflection. He explained that the hypnotic exploration did not give him an inner feeling, that is, a continuing subjective feeling, of just being in the midst of his psychedelic experience, that there was an ordered intellectual content paralleling the "feeling content" while Deep Reflection established a profound emotional background of a stable character upon which he could "consciously lay effortlessly an intellectual display of ideas" to which the reader would make full response. This discussion Huxley brought to a close by the thoughtful comment that his brief intensive experience with hypnosis had not yet begun to digest and that he could not expect to offer an intelligent comment without much more thought.

He asked urgently that further deep hypnosis be done with him in which more complex phenomena be induced to permit him to explore himself more adequately as a person. After a rapid mental review of what had been done and what might yet be done, I decided upon the desirability of a deep trance state with the possibility of a two-state dissociative regression, that is, of the procedure of regressing him by dissociating him from a selected recent area of his life experience so that he could view it as an onlooker from the orientation of another relatively recent area of life experience. The best way to do this I felt would be by a confusion technique (Erickson, M. H., The confusion technique in hypnosis, This JOURNAL* 1964, 6, 269–271.[)] This decision to employ a confusion technique was influenced in large part by the author's awareness of Huxley's unlimited intellectual capacity and curiosity which would aid greatly by leading Huxley to add to the confusion technique verbalizations other possible elaborate meanings and significances and associations, thereby actually supplementing in effect my own efforts. Unfortunately, there was no tape recorder present to preserve the details of the actual suggestions which were to the effect that Huxley go ever deeper and deeper into a trance until "the depth was a part and apart" from him, that before him would appear in "utter clarity, in living reality, in impossible actuality, that which once was, but which now in the depths of the trance, will, in bewildering confrontation challenge all of your memories and understandings." This was a purposely vague yet permissively comprehensive suggestion and I simply relied upon Huxley's intelligence to elaborate it with an extensive meaningfulness for himself which I could not even attempt to guess. There were, of course, other suggestions but they centered in effect upon the suggestion enclosed in the quotation above. What I had in mind was not a defined situation but a setting of the stage so that Huxley himself would be led to define the task. I did not even attempt to speculate upon what my suggestions might mean to Huxley.

It became obvious that Huxley was making an intensive hypnotic response during the prolonged repetitious suggestions I was offering when suddenly he raised his hand and said rather loudly and most urgently, "I say, Milton, do you mind hushing up there. This is most extraordinarily interesting down here and your constant talking is frightfully distracting and annoying."

For more than two hours, Huxley sat with his eyes open, gazing intently before him. The play of expression on his face was most rapid and bewildering. His heart rate and respiratory rate were observed to change suddenly and inexplicably and repeatedly at irregular intervals. Each time that the author attempted to speak to him, Huxley would raise his hand, perhaps lift his head, and speak as if the author were at some height above him, and frequently he would annoyedly request silence.

After well over two hours, he suddenly looked up toward the ceiling and remarked with puzzled emphasis, "I say, Milton, this is an extraordinary contretemps. We don't know you. You do not belong here. You are sitting on the edge of a ravine watching both of us and neither of us knows which one is talking to you; and we are in the vestibule looking at each other with most extraordinary interest. We know that you are someone who can determine our identity and most extraordinarily we are both sure we know it and that the other is not really so, but merely a mental image of the past or of the future. But you must resolve it despite time and distances and even though we do not know you. I say, this is an extraordinarily fascinating predicament, and am I he or is he me? Come, Milton, whoever you are."

There were other similar remarks of comparable meaning which could not be recorded, and Huxley's tone of voice suddenly became most urgent. The whole situation was most confusing to me, but temporal and other types of dissociation seemed to be definitely involved in the situation.

Wonderingly, but with outward calm, I undertook to arouse Huxley from the trance state by accepting the partial clues given and by saying in essence, "Wherever you are, whatever you are doing, listen closely to what is being said and slowly, gradually, comfortably begin to act upon it. Feel rested and comfortable, feel a need to establish an increasing contact with my voice, with me, with the situation I represent, a need of returning to matters in hand with me not so long ago, in the not so long ago belonging to me, *and leave behind but* AVAILABLE UPON REQUEST *practically everything of importance,* KNOWING BUT NOT KNOWING *that it is* AVAILABLE UPON REQUEST. And now, let us see, that's right, you are sitting there, wide awake, rested, comfortable, and *ready for discussion of what little there is.*"★★

★★Amer. J. *Clin. Hyph.*

Huxley aroused, rubbed his eyes, and remarked, "I have a most extraordinary feeling that I have been in a profound trance, but it has been a most sterile experience. I recall you suggesting that I go deeper in a trance, and I felt myself to be most compliant, and though I feel much time has elapsed, I truly believe a state of Deep Reflection would have been more fruitful."

Since he did not specifically ask the time, a desultory conversation was conducted in which Huxley compared the definite but vague appreciation of external realities of the light trance with the more definitely decreased awareness of externalities in the medium trance which is accompanied by a peculiar sense of minor comfort that those external realities can become secure actualities at any given moment.

He was then asked about realities in the deep trance from which he had just recently aroused. He replied thoughtfully that he could recall vaguely feeling that he was developing a deep trance but that no memories came to mind associated with it. After some discussion of hypnotic amnesia and the possibility that he might be manifesting such a phenomenon, he laughed with amusement and stated that such a topic would be most intriguing to discuss. After still further desultory conversation, he was asked *a propos* of nothing, "In what vestibule would you place that chair?" (indicating a nearby armchair.) His reply was remarkable. "Really, Milton, that is a most extraordinary question. Frightfully so! It is quite without meaning, but that word 'vestibule' has a strange feeling of immense anxious warmth about it. Most extraordinarily fascinating!" He lapsed into a puzzled thought for some minutes and finally stated that if there were any significance, it was undoubtedly some fleeting esoteric association. After further casual conversation, I remarked, "As for the edge where I was sitting, I wonder how deep the ravine was." To this Huxley replied, "Really Milton, you can be most frightfully cryptic. Those words 'vestibule,' 'edge[,]' 'ravine' have an extraordinary effect upon me. It is most indescribable. Let me see if I can associate some meaning with them." For nearly 15 minutes Huxley struggled vainly to secure some mean- ingful associations with those words, now and then stating that my apparently purposive but unrevealing use of them constituted a full assurance that there was a meaningful significance which should be apparent to him. Finally he disclosed with elation, "I have it now. Most extraordinary how it escaped me. I'm fully aware that you had me in a trance and unquestionably those words had something to do with the deep trance which seemed to be so sterile to me. I wonder if I can recover my associations."

After about 20 minutes of silent, obviously intense thought on his part, Huxley remarked, "If those words do have a significance, I can truly say that I have a most profound hypnotic amnesia. I have attempted Deep Reflection, but I have found my thoughts centering around my mescaline experiences. It was indeed difficult to tear myself away from those thoughts. I had a feeling that I was employing them to preserve my amnesia. Shall we go on for another half hour on other matters to see if there is any spontaneous recall in associa- tion with 'vestibule,' 'edge' and 'ravine?'"

Various topics were discussed until finally Huxley said, "It is a most extraordinary feeling of meaningful warmth those words have for me, but I am utterly, I might say frightfully, helpless. I suppose I will have to depend upon you for something, whatever that may be. It's extraordinary, most extraordinary."

This comment I deliberately bypassed but during the ensuing conversation Huxley was observed to have a most thoughtful puzzled expression on his face, though he made no effort to press me for assistance. After some time, I commented with quiet emphasis, "Well, perhaps now matters will become available." From his lounging comfortable position in his chair, Huxley straightened up in a startled amazed fashion and then poured forth a torrent of words too rapid to record except for occasional notes.

In essence, his account was that the word "available" had the effect of drawing back an amnestic curtain, laying bare a most astonishing subjective experience that had miraculously been "wiped out" by the words "leave behind" and had been recovered in toto by virtue of the cue words of "become available."

He explained that he now realized that he had developed a "deep trance," a psychological state far different from his state of Deep Reflection, that in Deep Reflection there was an attenuated but unconcerned and unimportant awareness of external reality, a feeling of being in a known sensed state of subjective awareness, of a feeling of control and a desire to utilize capabilities and in which past memories, learnings, and experiences flowed freely and easily. Along with this flow there would be a continuing sense in the self that these memories, learnings, experiences, and understandings, however vivid, were no more than just such an orderly meaningful alignment of psychological experiences out of which to form a foundation for a profound pleasing subjective emotional state, from which would flow comprehensive understandings to be utilized immediately and with little conscious effort.

The deep trance state, he asserted, he now knew to be another and entirely different category of experience. External reality could enter but it acquired a new kind of subjective reality, a special reality of a new and different significance entirely. For example, while I had been included in part in his deep trance state, it was not as a specific person with a specific identity. Instead, I was known only as someone whom he (Huxley) knew in some vague and unimportant and completely unidentified relationship.

Aside from my "reality," there existed the type of reality that one encounters in vivid dreams, a reality that one does not question. Instead, one accepts such reality completely without intellectual questioning and there are no conflicting contrasts nor judgmental comparisons nor contradictions so that whatever is subjectively experienced is unquestioningly accepted as both subjectively and objectively genuine and in keeping with all else.

In his deep trance, Huxley found himself in a deep wide ravine, high up on the steep side of which, on the very edge, I sat, identifiable only by name and as annoyingly verbose.

Before him, in a wide expanse of soft dry sand was a nude infant lying on its stomach. Acceptingly, unquestioning of its actuality, Huxley gazed at the infant, vastly curious about its behavior, vastly intent on trying to understand its flailing movements with its hands and the creeping movements of its legs. To his amazement, he felt himself experiencing a vague curious sense of wonderment as if he himself were the infant and looking at the soft sand and trying to understand what it was.

As he watched, he became annoyed with me since I was apparently trying to talk to him, and he experienced a wave of impatience and requested that I be silent. He turned back and noted that the infant was growing before his eyes, was creeping, sitting, standing, toddling, walking, playing, talking. In utter fascination he watched this growing child, sensed its subjective experiences of learning, of wanting, of feeling. He followed it in distorted time through a multitude of experiences as it passed from infancy to childhood to school days to early youth to teenage. He watched the child's physical development, sensed its physical and subjective mental experiences, sympathized with it, empathized with it, rejoiced with it, thought and wondered and learned with it. He felt as one with it, as if it were he himself, and he continued to watch it until finally he realized that he had watched that infant grow to the maturity of 23 years. He stepped closer to see what the young man was looking at, and suddenly realized that the young man was Aldous Huxley himself, and that this Aldous Huxley was looking at another Aldous Huxley, obviously in his early fifties, just across the vestibule in which they both were standing; and that he, aged 52 was looking at himself, Aldous, aged 23. Then Aldous, aged 23 and Aldous, aged 52, apparently realized simultaneously that they were looking at each other and the curious questions at once arose in the mind of each of them. For one the question was, "Is that my idea of what I'll be like when I am 52?" and, "Is that really the way I appeared when I was 23?" Each was aware of the question in the other's mind. Each found the question of "Extraordinarily fascinating interest" and each tried to determine which was the "actual reality" and which was the "mere subjective experience outwardly projected in hallucinatory form."

To each the past 23 years was an open book, all memories and events were clear, and they recognized that they shared those memories in common, and to each only wondering speculation offered a possible explanation of any of the years between 23 and 52.

They looked across the vestibule (this "vestibule" was not defined) and up at the edge of the ravine where I was sitting. Both knew that that person sitting there had some undefined significance, was named Milton, and could be spoken to by both. The thought came to both, could he hear both of them, but the test failed because they found that they spoke simultaneously, nor could they speak separately.

Slowly, thoughtfully, they studied each other. One had to be real. One had to be a memory image or a projection of a self-image. Should not Aldous, aged 52, have all the memories of the years from 23 to 52? But if he did, how could he then see Aldous, aged 23, without the shadings and colorations of the years that had passed since that youthful age? If he were to view Aldous, aged 23, clearly, he would have to blot out all subsequent memories in order to see that youthful Aldous clearly and as he then was. But if he were actually Aldous, aged 23, why could he not speculatively fabricate memories for the years between 23 and 52 instead of merely seeing Aldous as 52 and nothing more? What manner of psychological blocking could exist to effect this peculiar state of affairs? Each found himself fully cognizant of the thinking and the reasoning of the "other." Each doubted "the reality of the other" and each found reasonable explanations for such contrasting subjective experiences. The questions arose repeatedly, by what measure could the truth be established and of how did that unidentifiable person possessing only a name sitting on the edge of a ravine on the other side of the vestibule fit into the total situation? Could that vague person have an answer? Why not call to him and see?

With much pleasure and interest, Huxley detailed his total subjective experience, speculating upon the years of time distortion experienced and the memory blockages creating the insoluble problem of actual identity.

Finally, experimentally, the author remarked casually, "Of course, all that could be left behind to become AVAILABLE at some later time."

Immediately there occurred a re-establishment of the original posthypnotic amnesia. Efforts were made to disrupt this reinduced hypnotic amnesia by veiled remarks, frank open statements, by a narration of what had occurred. Huxley found my narrative statements about an infant on the sand, a deep ravine, a vestibule "curiously interesting," simply cryptic remarks for which Huxley judged I had a purpose. But they were not evocative of anything more. Each statement I made was, in itself, actually uninformative and intended only to arouse associations. Yet no results were forthcoming until again the word "AVAILABLE" resulted in the same effect as previously. The whole account was related by Huxley a second time but without his realization that he was repeating his account.

Appropriate suggestions when he had finished his second narration resulted in a full recollection of his first account. His reaction, after his immediate astonishment, was to compare the two accounts item by item. Their identity amazed him, and he noted only minor changes in the order of narration and the choice of words.

Again, as before, a posthypnotic amnesia was induced, and a third recollection was then elicited, followed by an induced realization by Huxley that this was his third recollection.

Extensive detailed notations were made of the whole sequence of events, and comparisons were made of the individual notations, with interspersed comments regarding significances. The many items were systematically discussed for their meanings and brief trances were induced to vivify various items. However, only a relatively few notations were made by me of the content of Huxley's experience since he would properly be the one to develop them fully. My notations concerned primarily the sequence of events and a fairly good summary of the total development.

This discussion was continued until preparations for scheduled activities for that evening intervened, but not before an agreement on a subsequent preparation of the material for publication. Huxley planned to use both Deep Reflection and additional self-induced trances to aid in writing the article but the unfortunate holocaust precluded this.

Concluding Remarks

IT IS UNFORTUNATE that the above account is only a fragment of an extensive inquiry into a nature of various states of consciousness. Huxley's state of Deep Reflection did not appear to be hypnotic in character. Instead, it seemed to be a state of utterly intense concentration with much dissociation from external realities but with a full capacity to respond with varying degrees of readiness to externalities. It was entirely a personal experience serving as apparently as an unrecognized foundation for conscious work activity enabling him to utilize freely all that had passed through his mind in Deep Reflection.

His hypnotic behavior was in full accord with hypnotic behavior elicited from other subjects. He was capable of all the phenomena of the deep trance and he could respond readily to posthypnotic suggestions and to exceedingly minimal cues. He was emphatic in declaring that the hypnotic state was quite different from the Deep Reflection state.

While some comparison may be made with dream activity, and certainly the ready inclusion of the "vestibule" and the "ravine" in the same subjective situation is suggestive of dream-like activity, such peculiar inclusions are somewhat frequently found as a spontaneous development of profound hypnotic ideosensory activity in highly intellectual subjects. His somnambulistic behavior, his open eyes, his responsiveness to me, his extensive posthypnotic behavior all indicate that hypnosis was unquestionably definitive of the total situation in that specific situation.

Huxley's remarkable development of a dissociated state, even bearing in mind his original request for a permissive technique, to view hypnotically his own growth and development in distorted time relationships, while indicative of Huxley's all-encompassing intellectual curiosity, is suggestive of most interesting and informative research possibilities. Questioning post-experimentally disclosed that Huxley had no conscious thoughts or plans for review of his life experiences nor did he at the time of the trance induction make any such interpretation of the suggestions given him. This was verified by a trance induction and making this special inquiry. His explanation was that when he felt himself "deep in the trance" he then began to search for something to do and "suddenly there I found myself—most extraordinary."

While this experience with Huxley was most notable, it was not my first encounter with such developments in the regression of highly intelligent subjects. One such experimental subject asked that he be hypnotized and informed when in the trance that he was to develop a profoundly interesting type of regression. This was primarily to be done for his own interest while he was waiting for me to complete some work. His request was met and he was left to his own devices while sitting in a comfortable chair on the other side of the laboratory. About two hours later he requested that I awaken him. He gave an account of suddenly finding himself on an unfamiliar hillside and, in looking around he saw a small boy whom he immediately "knew" was six years old. Curious about this conviction about a strange little boy, he walked over to the child only to discover that that child was himself. He immediately recognized the hillside and set about trying to discover how he could be himself at 26 years of age watching himself at the age of 6 years. He soon learned that he could not only see, hear, and feel his child-self, but that he knew the innermost thoughts and feelings. At the moment of realizing this, he felt the child's feeling of hunger and his wish for "brown cookies." This brought a flood of memories to his 26-year-old self, but he noticed that the boy's thoughts were still centering on cookies and that the boy remained totally unaware of him. He was an invisible man, in some way regressed in time so that he could see and sense completely his childhood self. My subject reported that he "lived" with that boy for years, watched his successes and his failures, knew all of his innermost life, wondered about the next day's events with the child and, like the child, he found to his amazement that even though he was 26 years old, a total amnesia existed for all events subsequent to the child's immediate age at the moment, that he could not foresee the future any more than could the child. He went to school with the child, vacationed with him, always watching the continuing physical growth and development. As each new day arrived, he found that he had a wealth of associations about the actual happenings of the past up to the immediate moment of life for the child-self.

He went through grade school, high school, and then through a long process of deciding whether or not to go to college and what course of studies he should follow. He suffered the same agonies of indecision that his then-self did. He felt his other self's elation and relief when the decision was finally reached and his own feeling of elation and relief was identical with that of his other self.

My subject explained that the experience was literally a moment by moment reliving of his life with only the same awareness he had then and that the highly limited restricted awareness of himself at 26 was that of being an invisible man watching his own growth and development from childhood on, with no more knowledge of the child's future than the child possessed.

He had enjoyed each completed event with a vast and vivid panorama of the past memories as each event reached completion. At the point of entrance to college the experienced [sic (experience)] terminated. He then [sic (than)] realized that he was in a deep trance and that he wanted to awaken and to take with him into conscious awareness the memory of what he had been subjectively experiencing.

This same type of experience has been encountered with other experimental subjects, both male and female, but each account varies in the manner in which the experience is achieved. For example, a girl who had identical twin sisters three years younger than herself, found herself to be "a pair of identical twins growing up together but always knowing everything about the other." In her account there was nothing about her actual twin sisters, all such memories and associations were excluded.

Another subject, highly inclined mechanically, constructed a robot which he endowed with life only to discover that it was his own life with which he endowed it. He then watched that robot throughout many years of experiential events and learnings, always himself achieving them also because he had an amnesia for his past.

Repeated efforts to set up as an orderly experiment have to date failed. Usually the subject objects or refuses for some not too comprehensible a reason. In all my experiences with this kind of development in hypnotic trances, this type of "reliving" of one's life has always been a spontaneous occurrence and with highly intelligent well-adjusted experimental subjects.

Huxley's experience was the one most adequately recorded and it is most unfortunate that the greater number of details, having been left with him, were destroyed before he had the opportunity to write them up in full. Huxley's remarkable memory, his capacity to use Deep Reflection and his ability to develop a deep hypnotic state to achieve specific purposes and to arouse himself at will with full conscious awareness of what he had accomplished (Huxley required very little instruction the next day to become skilled in autohypnosis) augured exceedingly well for a most informative study. Unfortunately the destruction of both notebooks precluded him from any effort to reconstruct them from memory because my notebook contained so many notations of items of procedure and observation for which he had no memories and which were vital to any satisfactory elaboration. However, it is hoped that the report given here may serve, despite its deficiencies, as an initial pilot study for the development of a more adequate and comprehensive study of various states of consciousness.

CHAPTER EIGHT

ERICKSON, THE HEALER: REFLECTIONS
BY FRIENDS AND COLLEAGUES

SANDRA SYLVESTER

A licensed psychologist, Sylvester has conducted training in clinical hypnosis since 1979 and used medical applications of hypnosis throughout her career. Specializing in working with people with neurological impairments, she has authored a set of cassette *The Relaxation Series*. Author of *Living with Stress*, she has contributed to various texts, including *Fear and the Management of Pain, Self-Healing, Milton H. Erickson: The Wounded Physician as Healer* and *Erickson Approaches in Medicine*. Sylvester enjoys gardening and playing the violin.

MILTON ERICKSON WAS the most integrated person I have ever met. He was totally comfortable in his own skin, and he had a way of being with you so that you, too, were completely comfortable with who you were. Being with him was like wearing a glove that had become so molded to your hand that you no longer felt it to be separate from yourself.

I first met Erickson when I was a doctoral student at the University of Arizona and he would invite me to Phoenix to visit with him and his family. Our first afternoon visit was in his living room. Every flat surface was filled with beautiful and distinctive Seri ironwood carvings and other interesting art objects. Erickson was sitting in his stuffed chair and he motioned to me to sit next to him in his wheelchair that was at a 90 degree angle to him. (The only other place to sit was a love seat on the other side of the room.)

As we sat and talked, Erickson asked me, "And who is that little girl over there?" gesturing to the area where the television was. I looked over and could see myself as a very young child, about three or four years old. We talked about this for a while and I described what I was seeing and then I became confused. He noticed the confusion and asked, "What is happening now?" I told him that if I looked down at my legs, I could see them in the wheelchair, hanging down and touching the floor, but if I sensed my legs without looking at them, they were cross-legged and I was sitting in a bucket of water in our backyard as a three-year-old child. Then, if I looked around the room, I could see the television and the ironwood carvings or I could experience my inner experience and also be sitting in the bucket and feel the water on my feet and butt, as if I were sitting in six inches of water. I could switch between these two states instantly, so my conclusion was that this was not a true regression experience! He laughed good-naturedly at my naive comments and then explained that this was the difference between an integrated experience and a psychotic experience. In psychosis, you get stuck. In integration you can move between these experiences. This began my journey into understanding hypnotic experience, and so began my friendship with Milton Erickson.

Erickson completely changed my understanding of mental illness. I stopped seeing it as a state of being, a label cast in concrete, a lifelong sentence, and began to see it as a state of stuck-ness in a dynamic process which could change dramatically and quickly if the key to unlock the stuck-ness could be found. I also learned that the key was held in the hand of the person who was stuck. It was fear, primarily, that prevented one from opening his or her hand and using the key. Erickson taught me to disarm the fear with humor, comfort in life experiences, cajoling, and especially modeling alternate behaviors.

As a therapist-in-training, being with Erickson taught me to look at the human experiences I share with psychotherapy clients and build from these rather than look at what divided us.

He taught me profound truths about life in the most simple ways. He started me on my first cactus garden. One day, he said, "Sandy, go into the kitchen and get the largest, sharpest knife you can find and come with me." We went into his cactus garden, which was informally positioned along the perimeter of the lawn and at the sides of the house, garage, and guest house. He studied each cactus and showed me how to slice a pad or a branch off this cactus and that one. We then took these assorted cactus parts to the side of the house where we dusted sulfur powder on the seeping surfaces of the slices. He said that the sulfur would cause the open slice to dry and become scarred and that it was from this scarred-over wound that new roots would grow. He said if you don't have sulfur, the wound will heal by itself, but the sulfur will help it heal quicker. He told me to watch this wound and once the wound was healed, I could plant this cactus in my own garden. The metaphors for life are obvious in this lesson and they have helped me immeasurably.

I started my first garden in Tucson with the cuttings from that day. From time to time, Erickson would ask me how my garden was growing. That was all he said. He left it to me to discover that this simple lesson applied to any wound: First you see the wound, then, if you can, you do or say something to help heal. Then you wait, as long as necessary for the wound to scar over, then allow new roots to grow. Erickson tended to start a person going in a direction and then let them go. He knew that their own inner process and inner motivation would take over from there.

Since that time, I always tend a garden, and now that we live in Sacramento, I keep a wonderful Japanese style garden and koi pond. A Japanese garden gives special consideration to the unique beauty of each individual plant and also the relationship between each plant and the rocks, other plants, and the spaces between them. Taken altogether, they create a place of balance, ease, and serenity.

Each season in the garden has unique needs, rhythms, and feelings. When I spend time in this garden each day, I listen for the rhythm. When the garden was young, I learned that the easiest time to pull weeds is after a rain and when they are small. If I neglect the garden and let the weeds grow, they take root and it is very difficult to get them out. It takes much longer and the job is a struggle and not very pleasant. But, if I am willing to spend a few minutes several times a week pulling young weeds in the early morning, the task is easy and pleasant. Once the plants in the garden mature, weeds become much less of a problem because they can't get to the soil they need because other plants are growing in that place.

I learned that you can only train a tree in the spring when there is soft new growth. If you try to train the tree later in the season, you will break it. Most of gardening is waiting for the appropriate time to do something. By listening to the plants and being in balance with them, you learn when the time is appropriate.

One time, when I was teaching in San Francisco, I was given a freshly caught Pacific Salmon. I called Erickson and asked him if he liked salmon. He said he loved salmon, and I told him I had a surprise for him when I returned home. I had to figure out how to get this fish to Phoenix on the plane, so I had one of the students freeze it as hard as a brick. When it was time to leave San Francisco, I wrapped the fish in two days of newspapers for insulation and sealed it in a brown paper grocery bag and hand-carried it on the plane. Luckily, the salmon stayed frozen until I was ready to drive to Erickson's.

When I got to there, I took over the kitchen and cooked a big dinner. I baked the whole five-pound salmon, made a cold sauce of curried dill, olive oil, mayonnaise, steamed a bunch of spinach and made a fresh salad. We cleared the dining room table and set the table for this feast. Erickson mentioned that Ernie Rossi was in town. I asked him if he wanted to invite Ernie over for dinner. He looked at me and said, "What! And share MY salmon?" So Milton Erickson, Betty, and I enjoyed the salmon for dinner. After we finished dinner, I began to prepare the leftover fish for the refrigerator. I removed the skeleton in one piece. Erickson stayed in the kitchen and took the skeleton and carefully extracted every single morsel of salmon from the backbone with a fork. These he ate with relish. This relish and delight and savoring pleasure is a memory of Erickson that I cherish.

Sunday afternoons I would often join Erickson as he watched *Wild Kingdom*. He loved this program and I enjoyed sitting with him. However, in my mind and in my thoughts, there was conflict.

I wondered, "What am I doing here? This is a waste of time, I have to study, and here I am watching *Wild Kingdom*. I should be doing something 'productive.'" But then, out of respect I would finally turn off my judgments and guilt, settle down, and just be and allow myself to get into the rhythm of the moment. Erickson was totally involved in the drama.

One time, I commented about how hard it was for me to see so much death on this program. Erickson said, "You know, I am going to die someday." In an instant, I could feel tears welling up and flooding my eyes. I felt as if my head would explode. I could barely breathe. I was stunned.

When I was finally able to speak, I told Erickson that I could not talk about this. I just could not do it. He just smiled and nodded his head. We never discussed this again.

Several weeks later, I went tide pooling for several days at Rocky Point, Mexico with friends. It was the first time that I had seen bioluminescence in the sea. I could hardly contain my excitement. It was so beautiful! In the middle of the night, when the waves would break before they reached the shore, there was this incredible blue-green light all along the breaking wave. We began to play in the water. We splashed the water and it would explode in this blue-green light. It would glow for a moment on our bodies. Each burst of bioluminescence lasted only for an instant, and then there was another and then another and another. It lasted every night, all night, as long as it was dark.

I was scheduled to teach in Cleveland when I returned from Mexico, so it was several days before I was able to call Erickson. I called him from Cleveland on a Friday, and told him about my experiences. He told me about the two times in his life that he had seen bioluminescence. It was a wonderful conversation. We chatted for 20 minutes or more, which was extremely unusual—our phone conversations rarely lasted more than a few minutes. In the course of our conversation, he asked when I was coming home. I told him I would be home on Sunday and that I would come to see him soon and bring the pictures that I had taken in Mexico. He was silent for what seemed like a long time. Then he said, "OK."

The following Monday morning, just after I arrived at my office, I received a call asking me to come to Phoenix, that Milton was in a coma. He was dying.

How do you make such a journey? …I'm not sure how I made it to Phoenix that day.

Each of us grieves in a very private place. I went through the motions of daily life, but I found myself far away in my thoughts. I decided that I would do the cooking and remain in the background while the family began to arrive. Someone from the family was in the ICU waiting room all of the time. You could only go into Erickson's room for a few minutes each hour. So we took turns. I do not have much memory of those days. My mind was somewhere else.

I was convinced that Erickson knew that he was going to die when I spoke to him on the phone that Friday. This was the best phone conversation we had ever had. He was animated and engaged and happy. And then, there was that long unusual silence when he learned that I would not be home until Sunday. I felt that he knew that we would never talk again in words.

Some people dream about Erickson. I do not. I have conversations with him in my head. My life has been forever changed by having known him. I am constantly surprised by fundamental changes in how I deal with things. For example, I learned almost one year ago that I have major artery disease in my brain and that I will probably die of a massive cerebral hemorrhage. What I do not know is when. What totally surprised me is that I am not afraid. I don't know why I am not afraid to die, but I am not. This amazes me. I've always been a "scaredy cat." In fact, Erickson used to call me that. Now I am not.

When I learned about my artery disease, after the initial shock, I heard Erickson in my head saying, "Well, are you going to do anything different with your life now that you know this?" I said, "No, I'm satisfied with my life. I'll just continue." Sometime later, he asked, "Will there be anything that you would regret not having done?" I said, "Yes, I would have wanted to play the violin again." He said, "Well..." So now I am playing the violin.

When he was alive, Erickson gave me so much of himself so generously. I wanted to do something for him to repay him for his kindnesses. One day I figured out something I could do. I had developed a multimedia presentation on the seasons of life for a holistic health conference that we were running in Tucson. I wanted to bring this to Phoenix for Erickson to see.

The presentation was short, only about 15 minutes, but those were the days before computers were used, and so to put on this presentation I needed to haul a large screen, two slide projectors, a cassette tape deck, and two speakers to Phoenix. I asked another doctoral student to come with me to help with all this equipment. We needed about 40 minutes to set up and test and prepare the family room for the presentation. When we were done, we called Erickson and Betty and Roxanna (who was visiting at the time) to take their seats. We darkened the room and began the show. When it was over, Betty and Roxanna said how much they'd liked it. Erickson, however, was silent. Then he said very softly, "May I see it again?" I felt my heart leap! Finally, at last, I was able to do something for Erickson.

After the second showing, he asked if we could stay for a while before driving back to Tucson. We said, yes. Then he turned to Betty and said, "Betty, a new resort, The Pointe, just opened near here. I am told they have a very good restaurant. I want you to take the girls there for dinner tonight."

I was crestfallen. Erickson noticed my expression and asked what was wrong. I told him that I wanted to give him something to repay him for all that he had given me. And just when I thought that I had done that, he turned around and gave me something more. He looked at me very seriously and held me with his gaze and said very slowly, "Sandy, there is no such thing as repayment or keeping score in friendship. Now go, and have a wonderful time on me."

JIM HILLS

Jim Hills operates the Arizona-Sonora Desert Museum Gift Shop and Book Store in Tucson, Arizona, and has continued to be active with the Seri Indians by conducting research with them, and by working closely with organizations in both Mexico and the United States to provide protection for the Ironwood tree. His company, Native & Nature, Inc., was awarded the 1998 National Wildlife Federation Conservation Achievement Award for its corporate leadership in educating customers about the environment and native traditions by using a unique bio-regional approach to merchandising. Jim credits Erickson for his successes in business, as well as his improved interpersonal relationships with neighbors, family, and friends.

THE FIRST TIME I heard of Milton Erickson was sometime between 1971 and 1972. I was selling Seri Indian woodcarvings to the Matthew Center Art Shop at Arizona State University and the manager, Astrid Thomas, told me, "We have a collector who's buying these wonderful carvings of yours (see photo, page 198) and if you come across anything special be sure and let me know. We'll try to get it to him. I really want to give you his name, but then we wouldn't have our sales."

For several years I sold carvings to the shop and Milton went there and bought them.

In the summer of 1973, I spent three-and-a-half months with the Seri Indians in Mexico along the northeastern shores of the Sea of Cortez, introducing new concepts and ideas to them on how to push their art into a different direction. It was a psychological quandary for me: because of my training in anthropology, I wondered whether I should be tinkering with their lives in this manner. However, my colleagues, including noted directors of museums, said they'd already been pushed into the modern world and they needed all the financial help they could get. This is how I justified my actions in those early years of working with the Seri.

I spent the summer of 1973 working with 10 different Seri artists, introducing different ideas like flying birds floating over a chunk of knurled ironwood supported via a thin steel wire, or an osprey seated on top of a cardon cactus eating a fish, seals on a rock, birds with turned heads, or curved-tailed shark and dolphin. By the end of the summer I had acquired hundreds of fabulous new carvings that, for the first time, had "movement" integrated into them. Since these carvings were so innovative, I thought it best not to wholesale them separately to different sites. Instead, my wife and I set up an exhibition at the Hassayampa Inn in Prescott, Arizona, and sent out 500 invitations, one of which went to Astrid Thomas. She responded, "I have a collector who is quite frail, but you really ought to send him an invitation." I did.

The show opened on a Friday evening and the first person in line was a gentleman with intense dark brown eyes and white hair, dressed in a purple jumpsuit with a large purple bolo tie He was seated in a wheelchair pushed by his wife, Betty. I introduced myself, and that is when I first met Milton Erickson. Milton and Betty had driven all the way up to attend the show and Milton had bought a couple of thousand dollars of art. We were stunned. I never had sold that much to any one person. As he left, he said, "If you get anything unique, let me know."

I immediately called Astrid and asked if it would be a problem selling directly to Milton, and she said it was fine. This was in the fall of 1973. When I look back at my notes and remembrances of Milton it seemed that we really didn't start building a relationship until about 1975, but between 1975 and 1979 our meetings were constant, frequent, and very intense. We gave each other things on each trip. He gave me his books and money, and I left him with woodcarvings and stories about the Seri Indians.

I visited him several times a year, showing him carvings, and we'd talk. His collection grew and he made jokes about how he'd have to build another room onto the house to hold the carvings, but that Betty would not tolerate it. Nevertheless, he did end up putting shelves all over his living room to hold his ever-expanding collection.

Knowing someone's significance isn't always immediate. The fact that Milton wore purple clothes, could stare through concrete with his intense dark brown eyes, and was at times very bizarre, was fine with me. I didn't mind his eccentricity. I knew he was some sort of "hypno-psycho-therapist." Milton never talked much about who he was in the field, but every time I came down, there was someone there and he would introduce us. The first person I met was Ernest Rossi, and on each trip it seemed I met another student or client. This went on for a number of years.

I slowly learned that Milton was well-known throughout the world and that people were coming from all over to see him. I remember an airline flight where I sat next to an Asian man who was reading a book on psychotherapy. I asked if he had heard of Milton Erickson and he quickly acknowledged that he knew his work. I then began telling my story to him. After we got off the plane, I literally had to run and hide in the airport bathroom to get away from the man. That's when I began to fully realize how important Milton was.

"What in the hell am I doing here?" I asked myself. Then I realized I was with Milton because of the carvings and that we enjoyed being with one another. Milton and I mostly talked about anthropology, particularly the Seri culture. One afternoon he mentioned that he had a friend coming for a conference in a couple of months. He asked if I would like to meet her and join them for dinner. I said I'd love to. Some months later I received a call and made plans to show up for dinner. I didn't know who the person was, but Milton said she was an anthropologist. He met me at the door and I immediately noticed that Betty and the woman were in the kitchen peeling potatoes. I looked more closely and said to myself, "Oh my God, it's Margaret Mead." I had always loved the work of Gregory Bateson. He was one of my early interests and I knew that they had been together at one time and I thought, "Whew, Margaret Mead, this is wonderful."

You have to understand where I was in my life at this time. I was considered an Indian trader, a position not that well respected in professional circles. I was a marginalized person in the eyes of most of the people I dealt with. Not only that, I was working primarily with Indians in northwestern Mexico who were marginalized. I had degrees from Arizona State University in anthropology and a master's degree in geography, but wasn't teaching or doing "valuable research," just hanging out with a bunch of Indians, laughing a lot, and buying their stuff. I always felt slighted and uncomfortable about how I was seen by others during that time. I remember a director of a California Museum telling me my life was heading down a blind path: no life insurance, no career, and no retirement. I felt they were saying that there was no value to my work. I felt that what I was doing had validity, but very few people in my culture really appreciated it or saw it. However, Milton obviously saw it.

I worked a lot as a commissioned buyer for the Heard Museum collections and provided items for their gift shop. That evening after dinner with Margaret Mead, Milton said, "You know, Jim, I'm not feeling very well. Would you accompany Betty and Margaret to the Heard Museum for the event?" That was the first time I had heard that there was going to be an event at the Heard. I agreed and I walked with those two ladies, arm-in-arm, and when we entered, everyone was waiting, wringing their hands for Margaret Mead. All the notables looked up, including the director of the museum, who saw Margaret first and announced, "Margaret is here." Then he saw me, and I will never forget the stunned look on his face. It was something like, "What is Jim Hills doing with Margaret Mead?" I believe Milton deliberately set this up and with that one simple act, I was instantly granted credibility. From that moment on everyone at the Heard Museum saw me in a different light, but more importantly, I began to "see" myself differently.

That's just one of the ways Milton worked. He was a genius. When he'd give me one of his books, he would always write some words on the inside. He once wrote, "To Jim Hills, Ph.D." He knew I didn't have a Ph.D., but he knew what he was doing. He wrote in another book,

"Jim, when we get together, everything comes out right." He was doing this subtle work to build me up, and at the same time we were opening up to one another. I considered Milton a very good friend.

I always felt that when I came into the room, he'd light up and so would I. When I look back at my times with him, I must admit that at first it took money to get me to go there, but it wasn't money that kept me coming back. He was truly a wonderful fellow.

Toward the end of his life—I believe in 1979—I said, "Milton I have some personal issues. Could I pay to have a session with you?" And he respectfully replied, "I don't normally take clients now, but I'll do it for you." We set up an appointment and I came back a couple of weeks later. I remember him asking, "What are you after? What are you trying to do here?" I told him, "The problem is that I have a hard time getting over the hump. I'm great at starting things and I have plenty of good ideas. I'm a smart guy, but I just have a hard time pushing through and finishing things." He spoke to me for an hour. By now I knew some of the techniques he used, particularly his references to the growing of tomato plants from seeds. And in that session he talked a lot about the growing of tomatoes from seeds. Frankly, at the end of the session I thought he was nuts, or worse, senile. I had no idea what he'd done, or whether I had been hypnotized, or even if he'd done anything. OK, fine. I accepted it and left his office a bit disillusioned. But it didn't take long to realize that something had gone on and that he had done something. Within a week I found myself obsessed with doing things right and finishing them quickly. Today I don't necessarily finish things quickly, but I always finish them. I only needed that one session. There have been times when I have actually cursed Milton because sometimes I don't want to be obsessed with finishing a task. But I have to finish everything I start. I attribute this to Milton, because I did not have that characteristic prior to that session with him.

He loved to hear me talk about the Seri Indians: their traditions, their connection to the land, their use of songs and dance, and what

traditional Seri shamans had told me. He was interested in everything. When I gave him a carving, we would talk about it. For
example, when I gave him a carving of an osprey, we'd talk about
how it flies, how it can see forever, how it turns its head when it is
looking at something, that sort of thing. I think that Milton would
use the carvings I brought to him as a way of expanding his world. It
was a way he could move out of his little house on Hayward Avenue
and become an osprey, a seal, an owl, a roadrunner, or a coyote.

One time I told him the story of how I ran up behind a trotting
coyote that was looking for something to eat along the beach.
I touched his tail and then observed the look on his wily face as he
turned and saw me running like a mad man, bent over, reaching for
his tail. After that story, Milton sometimes called me "coyote."
We talked like that.

He was particularly interested in how the Seri related to their land
and their sense of place. We talked about the Seri cultural tradition
that takes place with a new birth in the community. In the old days,
the maternal grandmother would rub the placenta with ash and bury
it in a location near where the infant was born. It would be buried
about elbow deep in the sand and then rocks would be piled on top
with a cactus planted on top. When he heard this, Milton
immediately said, "Ah, so they have a placental connection to the
earth." We would talk about how their placental burial connected
them to place and how, as an adult, a person could return to the
exact spot of their placental burial and look at how much the cactus
had grown over the past 20 years—kind of like the way we make
pencil marks on a door frame marking the growth of our kids.

The Seri's homeland is vast, comprising hundreds of square miles,
but desolate, with little water. It's also dangerous, particularly years
ago before radios, roads, trucks, dependable boats, and motors.
However, none of the Seri I knew was ever afraid of this land, seen as
"hostile" by "outsiders." Milton once observed, "A Seri is connected
to the earth in a spiritual fashion that gives them the same sense of

confidence and safety when they walk from the top of a mountain down to the ocean that we have when we walk with safety and confidence from our bedroom to the kitchen." The Seri say that when they are "home," their "spirit touches down."

One of the carvings Milton obtained from me was what I called an environmental contextual piece. It was carved out a huge chunk of ironwood 10 inches wide, 18 inches long, and up to 8 inches thick. In it the carver had placed a dolphin pod and a pack of sharks chasing seals swimming through ironwood waves—as we might see them in the water from a boat. "You know," said Milton, "that seal is in fear of the shark, and that dolphin is the mother calling to her pup." He also liked the owl carvings I brought him, particularly the ones made by Aurora Astorga. They had gigantic eyes and Milton would talk about their "owlness," and their ability to see well at night. He loved winged bird carvings and bought many "flying" birds. When we got together, it was as if we both learned to see the world with expanded eyes and fly to realms of experience that were outside the walls of his house.

Another thing Milton loved about the woodcarvings was their tactile feel. He told me that he would invite his clients and students to touch them. I have always believed the Seri have a way of putting "sealness" into a carving of a seal, or "birdness," or "sharkness," that non-native carvers cannot do. "You can feel its sealness or owlness," he'd say. That was one of the main reasons he loved them so much. He was always talking about how they felt.

Ironwood is a slow growing tree. It's a desert legume and grows in areas where there is very little water. It is highly adaptive to the desert and is considered a "nurse plant" for many other plants. For example, the saguaro cactus grows under the branches of the ironwood. In desert conditions, ironwood trees can live for centuries and a long living plant like a saguaro can begin its life under an ironwood's leaves with increased ability to survive. The ironwood provides it shade, moisture and added nitrogen in the soil, and protection from freezing. By growing under the branches of a long living ironwood tree, many plants increase their longevity. Milton always enjoyed reflecting on this.

I knew a shaman among the Seri Indians, and both he and Milton had a deep way of seeing. For example, Milton would take the story about the placenta and expand that little bit of information into a complete knowledge about how people felt about their world. Similarly, Fernando would talk about a gentle breeze blowing out of the south and discuss how that subtle movement of air was associated with a whole complex of winds and how the winds were connected to the Seri's understanding of the cosmos.

Milton would speak about tomatoes, mist, fog, and things like that with seemingly little association to the subject at hand. He was definitely an American shaman. At times, I thought Milton and the shamans were nuttier than fruitcakes and absolutely in the ozone. Imagine spending an hour with a world-famous someone while he talks in a monotone voice, with little to no inflection, about tomato seeds. I often found myself waiting for something to happen. I'd think, "I'm waiting to be hypnotized. What's the deal with this story about a plant? Get moving."

Fernando, the Seri shaman, talked a lot like Milton. He was seldom direct, always beat around the bush, and referred to the darndest things. He would talk about his four days in a cave where a flower would float in from the outside and engulf him, pick him up, and rock him back and forth. I'd wonder what he was talking about. The so-called objective part of my mind would declare that this was nonsense, while another part of me was listening because I wanted to know more and I realized that I hadn't allowed myself to break through. This kind of experience took place with both Milton and Fernando. I now know that they both had *acucama* or "spirit power."

Milton wanted to know what Fernando said to me. I told him how Fernando went up to a cave and fasted. Fernando said he had to be very strong and focused. "If you are not, you'll die," he said.

Then I told Milton what Fernando had told me:

"After four days of fasting, a flower will come. You can't accept the first flower because it is a black one. It's a big flower. It floats through the mouth of the cave and opens up asking you to submit. You have to fight that flower off. Then a little bit later comes a white, yellow, or red flower. Those are the flowers that you can let into your life. They come in and cradle you, and rock you gently. They help you have visions. Then the visions give you songs. After you have finished all of this, you are very weak, but you fly home."

Milton listened to such stories, and the only comment he would make would involve tying pieces together, bringing forth a fuller sense of context. He never told me whether he had experiences like that. He may have. He didn't talk about "shamanism," but we talked a lot about the experiences of people who called themselves shamans. He was interested in what they went through. One of the shamans claimed to have flown to the moon. He carved a piece that depicted his lunar journey. Milton ended up owning that carving.

After Milton expanded my view of the world, I was surprised to find that I had lost most of my childhood fears associated with the wilderness and large groups of people. Milton and the Seri taught me that being myself was my greatest strength. I found I could travel through unknown parts of the world—the desert or New York City—without any fear, doing so in the same way that I move from my kitchen to the living room.

Milton gave me the gift of seeing beyond the obvious. I learned that 20% of truth is found in the words people say. The other 80% is in their body expression. I now can learn more about a person by watching them walk into a room than from talking with them for two hours. When I dream of Milton, I see him in a wheelchair, staring at me with his intense dark brown eyes. He taught me that everything is OK in life. There is no need for any of us to feel like we are not fine.

Milton and I always talked in his living room that overflowed with wood carvings. I remember telling him how I thought the Seri Indians viewed my relationship with them. I said I was like a court jester. I'd show up in the village; we'd laugh together, talk about life; and then I'd leave them some money. My relationship with Milton was also sort of like that. We'd come together, have a few laughs, expand each other's view of world, and I'd leave with some earned cash and learned wisdom. I was there, in part, to help bring him outside of his house. I was an extension of his eyes, providing a link to a larger world. In turn, he helped plant the mysteries of the outside world more deeply into my inner being, making me more able to grow with the recognition that I have kinship with not only tomato plants and ironwood trees, but eagles, seals, owls, and coyotes, the very fabric of life. ❋

CARL HAMMERSCHLAG

A Yale-trained psychiatrist, author, teacher, and healer, Hammerschlag has spent more than 20 years working with Native Americans. His work has been critically acclaimed books: *The Dancing Healers, The Theft of the Spirit,* and *Healing Ceremonies.* A leading proponent of the practical applications of the science of psychoneuroimmunology or mind-body-spirit medicine, he is a faculty member at the medical school of the University of Arizona.

ERICKSON WAS a well-known psychiatrist by the 1960s. But I never heard a word about him when I was in medical school at the Upstate Medical Center in Syracuse, or in my residency at Yale in New Haven, Connecticut. Psychiatry was beginning to move toward neuro-chemical explanations for the gamut of the human experience. Hypnosis and trance states were relegated to romantic myths of an archaic age.

I discovered Erickson only after joining the Indian Health Service in the mid-1960's. I spent 20 years in Indian country, most of them as Chief of Psychiatry at the Phoenix Indian Medical Center. Working with Native American medicine men, I saw things for which my training had not prepared me. Traditional healers could cure patients in varying states of psychological disintegration, in ways I'd never been taught in medical school.

Using ceremonies, myths, and sacred objects, shamans cured the disabled and the psychotic. The hypnotic fires of all-night meetings, with drumbeat and prayer songs, the weaving of ritual, myth, and symbols into ceremonies of awesome healing power—I didn't understand a word of the spoken language, but I could feel its impact. The symbolic world clearly opened up channels to the unconscious mind. The shamans' dramatic power changed people faster than I could with drugs and psychotherapy.

This process was difficult to explain in the traditional language of psychiatry (projection, incorporation, identification). It was only when I met Erickson that I began to understand and ultimately learn to speak this nontraditional language. I discovered Erickson through the writings of Jay Haley. When I learned he lived in Phoenix, I sought him out. Here was a psychiatrist who understood my experiences with clarity and translated what I was seeing into a profound awakening that had enormous practical application in my work.

Erickson revealed to me these guiding principles of healing. A healer will:

1. See beyond a patient's pathology, illuminate and mobilize his strengths, and help him move beyond his limitations;

2. Find ways to open up a channel into the unconscious mind and get patients to see their reality differently. Using stories, symbols, shared myths, and prescribing rituals, ceremonies, even ordeals, healers get people to look at the familiar in new ways;

3. Uniquely craft a healing experience for each individual in which both the patient and the healer are totally involved in the experience. There is no dispassionate, distant, unavailable transferential object to work through one's neurosis.

Erickson was proud that he had Indian blood. He sponsored a scholarship at Phoenix College for Native American students who retain the practices and language of their tribal traditions. He was the keeper of a Navajo medicine bundle (*ji' ish*) which contained the medicine man's most sacred healing totems. In all my years in Indian country, I had never seen the contents of an entire one. I asked Erickson if he had ever looked inside it, and he said with a twinkle, "You get to see everything, when it's time."

A healer is more than a good doctor. A good doctor can make the diagnosis and prescribe the appropriate treatment; a great doctor can make the diagnosis, treat the patient, and also add a preventative component that teaches the patient how to avoid exposure to trauma and pathogens. A healer can do all of that and, in addition, make a personal connection with the patient in a way that touches them at a soul level.

How did Erickson get initiated into the shamanic journey? He got polio at age 17 and suddenly found himself paralyzed. Unable to move, he had time to observe people and learn to understand and speak the language of nonverbal communication. This was the beginning of his appreciation of the principle of utilization. It didn't matter what happened to you, only that you learned something from it, which was its own reward. Playing the hand you'd been dealt meant that what was once a curse could become a blessing. Erickson never stopped learning. At 57 he was stricken with post-polio syndrome and learned to face the world with slurred speech and weakened muscles.

All healers have the capacity to see things from beyond an ordinary perspective. When healers look at patients, they see not only their pathology (Western medicine's forte), but also their strengths. Healers use whatever symbols and language the patient speaks, in order to mobilize those strengths and move them beyond their limitations. Everything in the natural universe has potential for symbolic value, because symbols acquire meaning only when you supply them with their power.

A friend of mine watched a Navajo Roadman (a spiritual leader in the Native American Church) take out a fluid-filled vial and sprinkle some drops onto a patient. Later, my friend asked the healer what the stuff was. The Roadman said it was very powerful medicine and then dropped the subject. The next morning, while my friend was drinking from a water bottle, the Roadman took it from him and poured a few drops from the bottle into a teaspoon. Holding the bottle in one hand and the teaspoon in the other, the Road Man looked at the bottle and said, "If you drink this when you are thirsty it's water." Then, turning to the teaspoon he said, "When you need it for healing it's medicine." Symbols only have meaning when what you bring to them supplies them with power.

Erickson knew that if you re-examine everything you know, you might see it from another perspective. If you can move beyond your ordinary consciousness, and suspend your preconceptions, you can create new endings to old stories.

All healers find ways to penetrate the unconscious without direct interpretation. They know that conscious mechanisms of defense can keep patients from understanding the most insightful interpretation. Healers create a symbolic language that speaks uniquely to each patient and illuminates the undefended areas of the mind. Using stories, rituals, ceremonies, even ordeals, healers make a connection with a patient's soul that opens up channels of healing.

Early in his career, Erickson worked at Worcester State Hospital in Rhode Island. One of the patients was a harmless catatonic schizophrenic who was called "Jesus Christ #1." Having ground privileges, JC #1 wandered the campus draped in a white bed-sheet prayer shawl blessing everything and everyone. One day, when Erickson was out walking, he came upon JC #1 who said to him, "Blessings on you my son." Erickson thanked him, and then told him he was also seeking a blessing for the other doctors at the hospital. They needed to take a break from their strenuous work and exercise. They needed to replenish themselves so they could take care of patients.

Unfortunately, the tennis courts were not in good shape. He told JC #1 that he understood he had the power to bless things and make them beautiful. These tennis courts were God's creation and he could save them and the doctors. JC #1 said he was here to serve mankind and if Erickson could get him the right tools, he could do the job.

JC #1 became the court-keeper, gardener, and carpenter; he kept the grounds beautifully and was greeted by the entire hospital community with respect and appreciation. If you can speak the patient's language, you can tell the story in a way that helps them mobilize their strengths.

All healers create sacred space for their work. This does not mean a religious tabernacle, but a place that is different from ordinary space. A setting that invites people to come in and open themselves up in a way that encourages a soulful connection. Erickson's waiting room and office were filled with magical symbols—a dried stingray was twisted into a crucifix and hung from the ceiling. On a bookshelf was a pelvic bone that looked like a skull with flashing lights for eyes, and everything came with a story. This was a sacred space that encouraged the journey into the unexplored mind.

All healers create a partnership with their patients. They under-stand that it is both of them together who make the healing work happen, and that there are lots of other helpers (people, flowers, animals, fire, and drumbeat). Everything in the natural world provides the symbols that can intensify one's healing power. Erickson didn't mind if some saw him as odd; he thought it was a blessing that helped him see the world from a unique perspective.

Healers do not separate themselves from the therapeutic experience, they are right there with the patient. They are not detached, unrespon-sive, trasferential objects; they are totally involved in the event.

A friend of Erickson asked him to visit his aunt if he ever spoke in her city. The aunt had become increasingly depressed and now was reclusive. She no longer went to church or spoke to anyone. When Erickson was in her city, he visited her in her home and asked if she would guide him around. Slowly, she led him from room to room. In one of them, he noticed three well-cared-for African violets. Each was a different color and next to them was an empty pot in which she was clearly going to propagate another plant. This lady was a talented horticulturist, and Erickson told her he knew these were delicate plants and easily destroyed by the slightest neglect. He said he wanted to prescribe something for her, but before he did so, he wanted her word that she would fulfill it. She agreed to do it.

He told her that there were 13 different hues of African violets and that she was to go to a specific florist who needed a talented African violet lady to help save them. Then he told her to purchase pots and transplant leaves to grow more. When she had an adequate supply, he wanted her to put them in gift pots and send one to every baby born to a member of her church. Then, to every member of her church who was hospitalized. She kept her promise and moved beyond her despair.

To totally participate in the healing event does not always involve preparing for the event; it just requires spontaneity and a willingness to take creative leaps of faith.

Erickson was a healer. He provided me with a structure that helped me move beyond my boundaries and own my own power. He encouraged me, as he did all his students, to tell the story our own way, and not mimic his; to be authentic and use whatever works into our healing repertoire.

On one of our last times together, I gave him a Hopi Sun Kachina and told him it reminded me of his influence on me. He provided the light that helped me shift my need for certainty and enjoy the free-flight into the unconscious, where the magic of our work is realized.❅

EDWIN DRUDING

After four years in the U.S. Army during World War II, Druding earned his B.A. and M.A. in education and psychology in 1950 from Arizona State University, where he taught during the last year of his master's program. He joined the staff of Phoenix College in 1952 where he continued to teach through 2002. In 1975, he earned his Ph.D. from A.S.U. He met Milton Erickson in 1949, and established his own practice in 1950. He is still actively practicing as a psychologist.

"COME TO MY HOUSE, Tuesday evening, eight o'clock. Don't be late!" Those were the first words I received from Dr. Erickson.

"Do you have a card?" I asked.

"I don't have cards," he replied.

"What is your address?" I asked.

"If you're interested, you'll find it," he replied.

How much easier it would have been for him to state, "32 West Cypress." But "If you're interested, you'll find it." was the beginning of the most transformational journey of my life. I considered myself a reasonably serious, mature student. I had four years of military service and was accustomed to following orders. My academic training in psychology had familiarized me with all of the schools of psychology. I leaned heavily toward Carl Rogers' non-directive approach.

I did not know whether Erickson's reply was merely rude or a test for me. As it turned out, it was one of countless tests.

I found his address in the phone book and located it so I would be on time for the appointment. When I arrived, I was admitted by Erickson's wife, Betty. She asked me to have a seat on the couch in the living room. Several of Erickson's children joined me and engaged me in conversation. Soon the children disappeared and were sent to bed, and at about 10 o'clock, Erickson came out of his office, looked at me, and asked, "What are you doing here?"

I replied that I had an appointment with him and began to remind him of our conversation. He interrupted me: "Tuesday evening, my house, eight o'clock. Don't be late!" As I tried to defend myself for having been there on time, he turned and walked out of the room.

This scenario repeated itself for the next two weeks. After my third fruitless visit for two hours in his living room, talking only with his children, Erickson said "Why do you keep coming back?"

"I believe that you have a purpose for this," I replied.

"You're ready!" he answered. "Next Tuesday, eight o'clock. Don't be late."

I'd passed one of the tests that Erickson gave to prospective students at that time in his life. The next Tuesday, and for many Tuesdays thereafter, I arrived at his house at precisely eight o'clock. He would hand me with a case file without the patient's name and tell me to read it. I felt that if he had wanted me to take notes, he would have said so.

My very first encounter with Erickson was at an Arizona State College psychology club meeting in the fall of 1949 where he demonstrated hypnosis by placing his young daughter, Betty Alice, in a trance. He had her hold her arm out to her side for an indeterminably long time.

When he questioned her, she indicated that her arm was at her side. He continued his discussion about the medical uses of hypnosis and stated that he personally used it to control pain. That word "pain" caught my attention. I had sustained serious injuries in World War II and I had refused to take pain medications even though they were supplied by the VA. After the meeting, I approached Erickson and told him I was a disabled vet and interested in learning about pain control.

Erickson subsequently taught me that I could reflect on something exciting or frightening—my war experiences, for example—and adrenaline would be released just as though it were a real situation. Hormones were released if my thoughts turned to something erotic. "Now," he reasoned, "if the brain can be tricked into releasing fluids from the appropriate glands, what about the endorphins that block pain? What if by your own mental control you can reduce the amount of pain by 10 percent? Then you only have 90 percent to handle. If you increase that control to 25 percent then there is only 75 percent of the pain to bear. But if you can push that envelope to 50 percent, then you can HALF the pain or you can HAVE the pain!"

I have repeated those words to hundreds of patients with great success. He said to validate the pain; it is there and it is real, not imagined. But you are in control of it if you want to be.

My education with Erickson was eclectic:

He taught me how placebos work, citing numerous examples of

how medications would not work when patients did not want them to work and how a placebo would work if the patient was convinced that it would.

Where medical interventions failed, Erickson healed. In my own practice, I saw a couple who asked me to see their daughter. Immediately following the birth of that girl's son, she developed a paralysis in her hand. Her fingers were rigidly fixed over her palm. This had persisted for six years. Medical doctors had failed to help. I referred her to Dr. Erickson who talked to her in her very calming hypnotic manner. He asked her what she was holding so tightly in that hand. She said it was her deep, dark secret. He confidently asked her if she trusted him with that secret. He told her that he would keep it in his hand so that she could have that hand free. She transferred that "secret" to Dr. Erickson's hand and he held it for her. She was able to open and move that hand more freely as time went on. It was stiff at first but it gradually loosened up. The secret was that her father was the father of her child.

In 1950, a young Washington, D.C., psychiatrist, Linn Fennimore Cooper (a direct descendent of the famous James Fennimore Cooper), came to speak to Erickson. He was interested in conducting an experiment that was partially funded by what eventually became the U.S. Space Agency. The scope of the experiment was time distortion with hypnosis. One of the questions the military was investigating was how traveling around in space with many sunrises and sunsets in a 24-hour period might affect the mind and body.

At that time, I was in the graduate program at Arizona State College. Erickson asked me to recruit some reputable students who would be trained as subjects for the experiment. These subjects were paid during their training as well as the experimental period, and I was paid to train several of the subjects. The findings of the experiment were published in several professional journals and a book co-authored by Cooper and Erickson, *Time Distortion in Hypnosis* (Baltimore: Williams and Wilkins, 1954; Crown House Wales, 2002).

Strangely, none of the cases Dr. Erickson had me review had the slightest reference to hypnosis or hypnotherapy. At one visit, long into my association with him, he asked, "What was your REAL reason to visit me?" I replied that I had hoped to learn about hypnosis and the treatment values of hypnotherapy. He asked, "Why haven't you said something to me about this?" I said, "I imagine that you had a purpose in not sharing that with me." My answer must have pleased him because his answer was "You're ready!"

Erickson admitted his fallibility: Because he had severe allergies to horsehair, he had instructed his sons to remove their riding clothes on the outer porch after going horseback riding. On one occasion, the boys returned several hours after going and walked through their dad's office. The sight of their riding clothes and the association with their plans to have been riding caused Erickson to have a severe allergy attack.

Erickson asked the boys why they intentionally disobeyed the procedure of removing their clothes on the porch. They informed him that when they called the stables, no horses were available, so they had just visited their friend down the street. Physician, heal thyself.

Erickson sometimes would ask me to respond to a specific case, and other times would present me with hypothetical cases. Sometimes he praised my intuitive abilities. Other times he would shoot me dead in the water because I had overlooked some important factor in the case. How I learned from him!

Erickson influenced me in more than just treatment but in the true healing processes of mind, body, and soul. He was not a church-oriented man but I believe that his spirituality transcends any of the religious leaders alive today. I thank God for that invitation I humbly accepted: "Come to my house Tuesday evening eight o'clock. Don't be late." ❋

ERNEST LAWRENCE ROSSI

Recipient of the Lifetime Achievement Award for Outstanding Contributions to the Field of Psychotherapy, given by the Milton H. Erickson Foundation in 1980 and the American Association of Psychotherapy in 2003, Rossi has published 24 books and 150 scientific papers on therapeutic hypnosis, psychotherapy, dreams, and the creative process. His publications have been translated into numerous languages. His work in the area of the connection of mind and body in the healing process has been groundbreaking. His latest book, *A Discourse with our Genes*, integrates fundamental concepts of biology, medicine, neuroscience and psychology.

WHEN I KNEW and studied with Erickson, he was in his seventies. It was during the last eight years of his life when he was permanently confined to a wheelchair. I was a young man in the full flush of his strength and health, and I had gone to Erickson to learn about what I imagined were the "strange and dark mysteries" of hypnosis. Little did I realize that he had a lot more to teach. It wasn't until a few years ago, when I experienced a stroke at the age of 69, that the full meaning of Milton H. Erickson's stature as person and inner teacher finally became clear to me. Let me tell you the story of this realization.

I awakened very early one morning with a strange sluggishness, stiffness, and awkwardness of movement. I was incredibly uncoordinated: I could not stand steady on my feet; it was a struggle to dress and my right leg felt so weak and limp that I could not put on my trousers. It wasn't till my wife, Kathryn, awakened later that I realized I had badly slurred speech. A quick check in the mirror revealed that the right side of my face was pulled down out of its normal symmetry. I now knew I was experiencing a stroke. Kathryn called the doctor and rushed me to the hospital. From that time to the present I have had a series of dreams that are clearly related to my stroke, recovery, and Erickson's unique approach to creative rehabilitation.

During the second week of my recovery I had this dream and memories of Erickson that began to guide my rehabilitation.

A small, lonely, emergency radar on an infinite, desolate, and dusty plain seemingly coughs, sputters a bit, and then begins sweeping the sky rapidly in a circular pattern—frantically but futilely seeking a response. Gradually, in the far distance, I see a response beginning to develop as an output image on a computer screen. The image is a 3-D wire mesh outline of a human head circulating so one can get a complete 360-degree view of the interior of the head. With growing excitement I realize that it is a MRI image of my own head that may enable me to see the exact area of my brain that was damaged by the stroke. I start to go lucid in the dream: I realize that I am dreaming and if I can slow down the rotating image enough I will be able to see exactly where the damage is to better guide my rehabilitation program. The rotating image does indeed slow down and I am just about to see the damaged area in my left cerebral hemisphere when I realize, "Oh, no, I am waking up!"

My many occupational and rehabilitation therapists congratulated me on my positive attitude toward rehabilitation. But they really didn't know half the story. My body was still very weak and uncoordinated. I had to hold onto the banister with two hands trying to get up and down stairs haltingly. If I tried to walk backwards I fell down. I couldn't skip or whistle. My driver's license was taken away and I was no longer allowed to cross the street by myself. My wife winced with worry as she watched me use both my arms to lift and haul my somewhat limp right leg into and out of our van. Paradoxically her worried wince evoked a grim satisfaction in me as I suddenly recalled the analogous situation about 30 years earlier when I lifted the Erickson out of his wheelchair into his family's old station wagon to take him for a drive through the deserts around Phoenix to visit rock shops, which we both loved. On those occasions the situation was reversed since I was the one who winced with worry lest I hurt Erickson as I hauled him about.

Erickson, ever the healing mentor, tried to reassure me with his jaw firmly set in grim satisfaction as he told me yet another story about his efforts at self-rehabilitation from his lifetime of coping with polio. Life, he would explain, actually is a continuous process of rehabilitation. Every day and every moment when you consciously choose to work cheerfully and creatively with your handicap rather than complain—literally gives you a leg up. Getting in and out of an auto is utilized as another opportunity to gain yet another increment of muscle coordination and strength. He called this the essence of his naturalistic or utilization approach whereby the process of actively coping with one's symptoms and problems guides and facilitates real physical healing as well as further psychological development. Erickson was a living example of creative rehabilitation. This is the source of Erickson's greatest legacy of healing to us all, although I could not appreciate its significance 30 years ago.

During my third week of recovery a neurologist filling out a routine medical form asked if my stroke resulted in a loss of physical strength so that I can no longer do my job. I grimly grinned at him with my best Ericksonian attitude and humorously responded, "Well, I'm not exactly an iron foundry worker you know." That night I had the following dream.

A huge Paul Bunyan-type man is using gigantic iron pliers and tongs to manipulate small metal objects. He is going to teach me how to do it skillfully. I am experiencing great awe that he notices me and I feel very grateful about the prospect of his help.

I interpreted this dream figure to be analogous to my occupational therapist who was facilitating my damaged hand-eye coordination recovery by giving me many tasks involving puzzles, picking up small metal objects with tweezers, etc. I told him this dream and explained my interpretation: Paul Bunyan is a metaphor of an inner implicit healing process operating via activity-dependent gene expression and brain plasticity (the growth and reorganization of synapses and neurons in the brain) that hopefully are now being activated by all this occupational therapy to repair my brain.

He had never heard of this new neuroscience concept of activity-dependent gene expression and Erickson's lifetime of creative rehabilitation. During this period I read and re-read Erickson's early paper (1970/1980) about facilitating recovery from trauma by encouraging patients to replay their dreams in a more therapeutic fashion:

"Dream the same dream with the same meaning, the same emotional significance, but with a different cast of characters. This time maybe it won't be so dark. Maybe you can see a bit more clearly. It won't be pleasant, but maybe it won't hurt so much. So go ahead as soon as you can and have your dream." Within four minutes the dream developed; 20 minutes later, streaming with perspiration, Edward said, "It was bad. It was awful bad. But it didn't hurt so much." ...Again he was asked to dream the same dream, but to dream it with less pain, less discomfort, and to dream more clearly—to see the characters more plainly. His fingers tightened on my hand, and the dream developed immediately. The observed behavior was essentially the same. The duration was again about 20 minutes. (pp. 62–63)

Such intense states of psychobiological arousal that we now know could evoke gene expression, brain plasticity, and recovery from trauma were characteristic of many of Erickson's (1948/1980) case histories, which he described as follows:

"Therapy results from an inner resynthesis of the patient's behavior achieved by the patient himself. ...this experience of re-associating and reorganizing his own experiential life that eventuates in a cure, not the manifestation of responsive behavior, which can, at best, satisfy only the observer. ...Not until sometime later did the therapist [Erickson] learn by what train of thought he had initiated the neuro-psycho-physiological process." (pp. 38–39, italics added).

During this period I awakened one morning with grateful tears when I imagined a powerful figure pounding a huge, glowing, gold ingot on a mighty anvil with flashing lightning leaping about. I feel empowered as I witness his methodical pounding whenever I call him forth in my imagination. On one level it is an awesome experience—a drama that I feel to be deeply healing. On another level, I recognize that this positive emotion is good for me so I try to replay it as long as I can. This inner drama wherein I am both healer and healed reminds me of Erickson's emphasis on the value of such multi-level states in psychological development and healing.

My dream series of creative rehabilitation and Erickson continues even today in ever surprising and delightful ways. In the early days of our relationship when I would drive him about through the deserts to the rock shops, I always dreamt that Erickson was driving and I was the passenger. It gave me great pleasure at the time when I told Erickson of this peculiar reversal in my dreams, which probably reflected the deeper truth that Erickson was in fact the driver in our relationship. With a twinkle in his eyes Erickson quietly murmured, "That may change in time." Indeed, it has. In my most recent dream I am the driver for the first time, as Erickson smiles at me from the passenger seat. ❋

Betty Alice Erickson:
Erickson was always interested in working with the police and did so from the beginning of his professional career until close to the end of his life. He had great regard for law enforcement officers and respected their abilities to deal effectively with a vast variety of people. He especially admired the ability that so many law enforcement officers have of observing people quickly yet carefully in order to make decisions about their responses. Leonard Zingg and Erickson developed a friendship based on Zingg's interest in hypnosis.

LEONARD D. ZINGG

Retired Phoenix police detective, Zingg spent 28 years in various law enforcement positions from uniformed patrol to supervisor of the polygraph section. Trained to use hypnosis for memory enhancement in criminal cases, he also taught courses on the psychology of interrogation, interview techniques, and communication at Arizona State University, Phoenix College, the Phoenix Police Academy, and numerous other police agencies. FBI trained and certified, Zingg has personal experience using hypnotic techniques to calm excited and violent people in life-threatening situations.

I FIRST MET Dr. Erickson in 1979 when I was one of a large group of police officers to be invited to his home for a lecture on hypnosis.

At that time, I was a lieutenant with the Phoenix Police Department in the Squaw Peak Precinct. I had been assigned to the polygraph section and, for six years, conducted polygraphs, interrogated criminal suspects, and interviewed victims and witnesses to determine their truthfulness regarding crimes. It was during one of these interrogations that I developed an interest in hypnosis: I was questioning a female suspect accused of calling in bomb scares to banks. As the interrogation progressed, she suddenly said to me, "I don't know what is happening to me, but right now, I would tell you anything that I knew."

This reinforced my theory that there was a certain amount of hypnosis involved in any effective interrogation. The interrogator establishes a mindset in the suspect that, for a period of time, intensely focuses him or her. The suspect is unable to think of anything except what is happening and the interactions with the interrogator. For all practical purposes, the two are alone in the world and the suspect can speak freely. I believe that everyone will talk if you find the right key.

The Department sent me to school so I could learn to hypnotize victims and witnesses who were unable to recall specific information concerning a crime. I also took a psychology class at Phoenix College, and the professor who was a hypnotist invited me to his house to learn more. During one of my visits, he conducted a hypnosis session with me. I was somewhat disappointed as I expected a more dramatic experience. I felt like I could have gotten up and walked out at any time. After the session, I considered the idea that either I was not a good subject or I had a misconception about hypnosis. I was curious to find out which was true and began reading.

The more I learned, the more I realized how little I knew. So when I heard that a group of officers was meeting with Dr. Milton Erickson, a noted authority on hypnosis, I joined them.

Upon arriving at Dr. Erickson's home, we were directed to a small house at the rear of the main house. Dr. Erickson was wheeled into the room by his wife. He was dressed in purple. I immediately connected this with royalty, as I recalled that historically, only royalty were allowed to wear purple. I thought this was a subtle yet brilliant strategy to let everyone know who was in charge. (I didn't know Erickson was color-blind and that purple was a color he could see well. And maybe he liked that color.) I had found during my police career and especially during interrogations, it was imperative to present the perception that the officer and/or the interrogator is always in control.

Dr. Erickson appeared to be a small man with a soft voice but there was something about him that transcended his physical stature and his quiet demeanor. He appeared confident, without being arrogant, perceptive without the attitude of seeming to know it all, and in control, without any overt action or words that established his control.

I had to smile when I looked at him. I had taken numerous psychology classes and read numerous books and articles on psychology, and this man had it all. I had graduated from a law enforcement interrogation college in Chicago in the mid '70s and taught *The Psychology of Interrogation* at the Phoenix Police Academy and other law enforcement agencies around the valley. I was very familiar with body language and voice inflection and I was seeing a master of both.

As I watched Dr. Erickson, I thought, "This man is totally suited to his calling." It was as if he had invented everything about himself— just the way a person would do, if that were possible.

I have always found it advantageous for others to underestimate, rather than overestimate me. During any training or seminar, I usually sit towards the rear of an audience and try to blend in unnoticed. On this day, I made my way to the middle rear of the group, thinking I would become obscure and be able to take in all of the information being processed, without providing any output. Everyone was in civilian clothes and there were no outward signs that anyone was of higher rank— or even a police officer. Right from the start, however, Dr. Erickson spotted me and asked me to come up front and sit near him. I was reluctant to do so, but did as I was asked. After speaking for some time, Dr. Erickson used me as an example and had me focus my attention on the figure of a horse on a shelf at the rear of the room until it appeared to me that the horse was running.

This was a great induction technique for me as I was born and raised on a farm in the Midwest and worked with horses. I also rode horses and saw horses running on many occasions. During the induction, Dr. Erickson gave me the option of leaving my eyes open or closing them when it was more comfortable for me to do so. Of course, it was more comfortable to close my eyes as the object that I was staring at was above eye level and after a while my eyes became tired. During the session, Dr. Erickson levitated my arm. He then regressed me back to my early days in grade school, while he explained his actions to the group. He asked me to verbalize what was happening, and I gave a detailed description of where I was and what was occurring at the moment. It was as though I had been transported back in time.

Several people were concerned about me holding my arm up in the air while Dr. Erickson continued his lecture. They commented that it must be uncomfortable and questioned him about it. I was not in any discomfort, however, and I was mildly amused as Dr. Erickson continued speaking as though he had not heard or understood their concern or their questions. This was one of many times that Dr. Erickson did not answer a question directly. Instead, he let you answer your own question through a story or a parable. It reminded me of politicians who never answer the question that was asked, but rather, the question that they wished you had asked.

I have often regretted not paying more attention to what was being said while I was the subject of hypnosis by Dr. Erickson, but I was in my own little world. It would have required more energy to listen than I was prepared to give at the time.

Following his lecture, the group departed but Dr. Erickson asked me to stay and wheel him into the main house. Once there, he proceeded to show me his ironwood collection that he was very proud of. He told me that people had heard that he collected ironwood figures and sent them from all over the world.

I have no idea what Dr. Erickson saw in me or why he singled me out and took time to privately explain things, but it didn't seem odd. At the time, it seemed normal. I felt very comfortable in his presence, even knowing that he was a noted psychiatrist, hypnotist, and author and that I was no one of importance.

Dr. Erickson explained the origin of each figurine, and after some time, Mrs. Erickson came in and reminded him that he should not tire himself and that it was time for him to rest. Reluctantly, I said that I should be going but I asked if I could return for another visit. Dr. Erickson said I should.

Erickson's residence was in the patrol area that I supervised, and over the next few months, I would occasionally stop by to see him. I was concerned about his health and tried not to take up too much of his time. I refrained from asking numerous questions about hypnosis. Mrs. Erickson suggested that I read his books rather than get too deeply involved in specific cases, and I readily agreed.

On one occasion during my brief visit, Dr. Erickson asked me if I wanted to meet his "girlfriend." Of course I said I did and he showed me a cylindrical object that looked like a stove pipe with a light hanging inside. The cylinder had a flexible plastic window in the middle. He told me to look in the window and I would see his girlfriend. When he turned on the light inside the cylinder, I could see the image of the head of a woman. As I moved my head, she appeared to blow kisses. It was a hologram and he seemed to enjoy showing it to me.

I learned early on that it was not wise for me to ask too many questions concerning hypnosis as I never got a straight answer. It was sometimes frustrating to ask what I thought was a simple question and get a story that would sometimes go on until I forgot what the question was. But often, several days later, I would recall some parts of Erickson's story, and get the answer to my question. Dr. Erickson was answering my questions by a story or parable so I had to figure out the answers myself.

One of Dr. Erickson's stock prescriptions for personal problems was to climb Squaw Peak. People's problems would be resolved by merely climbing up and down. Or maybe Erickson knew they would solve their problems just by the focus and effort involved in doing something different. I often wondered what obstacle he would have used had Squaw Peak not been so close and noticeable, but I am sure he would have just developed another method.

I learned so much more from this incredibly intelligent and talented man than I can specifically recall at this writing. But his teachings have been demonstrated in the positive results experienced by the many people who have come to me for hypnosis over the years. I and many others will forever be grateful to Dr. Erickson for his unselfish contribution to society. ✵

STEPHEN LANKTON

A licensed clinical social worker practicing in Phoenix, Arizona, Lankton is adjunct faculty at Arizona State University. A recipient of the Lifetime Achievement Award for Outstanding Contributions to the Field of Psychotherapy from the Erickson Foundation, he is past president of the American Hypnosis Board for Clinical Social Work. Lankton studied with Milton Erickson for five years. He has authored and edited 16 books including *Tales of Enchantment*, *The Answer Within*, *Enchantment and Intervention*, *Practical Magic*, and *The Ericksonian Monographs*.

The Meeting

I SHOULD BEGIN by mentioning that I did not journey to Phoenix to meet Dr. Erickson with any need for a hero or a guru or an expectation of changing my life. I first learned of Erickson in 1976 when I read a small book by Jay Haley called *Strategies of Psychotherapy*. However by the time I finished graduate school, I had long forgotten that I'd ever read the book. It was through Gregory Bateson and the team at Palo Alto that I became reacquainted with

Erickson; he had been the object of their studies for eight years preceding the development of the double-blind theory.

I was under the impression that Erickson had died long before I finished graduate school, but Dr. Bateson assured me that Erickson was quite alive and living in Phoenix, Arizona, and he urged me to contact him for the answer to the questions I was asking. I knew next to nothing about hypnosis when I had arranged my first meeting, so I spent the next few months reading every professional book about hypnosis that I could get my hands on. I also read everything that had been published about Erickson up to that time. Sadly, while I could understand the use of direct suggestion aimed at symptom removal (which characterized the majority of hypnosis being done at that time), I could not understand the approach or interventions that Erickson was using. My attitude as I flew to Phoenix for that first meeting was one of curiosity and nothing else.

Conveying That No Limitations Exist

By 1976, I had trained with many famous therapists: I was personal friends with Dr. Bill Kell as MSU, his family, and others in the department and at the psych clinic; and I had attended many conferences with still other therapy teachers who had achieved national and international renown. However, Erickson's presence and the ambience surrounding my first visit evoked an entirely new and unexpected part of me.

Erickson seemed to be physically limited to such a degree that I wondered whether he had the energy to conduct the training we were undertaking. His limbs looked weak, his eyes were often moist, and the skin below his eyes often showed a redness which seemed more indicative of a sick individual than a healthy one. I struggled to resolve an apparent incongruity: On one hand, Erickson was a person who had earned, and was due, a great deal of respect as a professional. On the other hand, he appeared incapable of holding his own due to physical frailty. However, as he began to speak, it was clear that he possessed an uncommon tenacity, and I instantly understood that he had overcome greater adversity than I would ever have in my life, and I recognized that his academic and professional achievements were well beyond anything I would ever achieve. This was a very powerful individual in whose presence I could make no excuses about my limitations. That is, if Erickson asked about my goals or ideals, there would be no adequate excuse for why I had fallen short in any area.

It's not that the excuses would be inadequate for Erickson, but rather they would be inadequate for me! Something about his countenance evoked in me an intense feeling that any shortcoming that I might complain about was my choice in life. Nothing could possibly have been the result of anyone else's behavior toward me—not my parents' 'failures,' not poverty or education or illness of any kind, not geography or politics. After meeting Erickson, I could no longer honestly complain about anything. I would have to engage in an incredible deceit to claim that there was something I couldn't achieve if I only wanted to. And I concluded that any failure to have achieved something in the past was simply my choice. This was an extremely sobering experience.

This heightened sense of personal responsibility carried with it an additional new burden—an implicit question that defined the context of our subsequent meetings: What did I want to achieve?

It was not that Erickson asked me this question; it was that the context begged the question. Erickson had not just achieved incredible career goals; he had achieved incredible family accomplishments. If a person so limited from polio had been able to achieve everything he intended and perhaps even more, then in my case, the sky could be the only limit. Suddenly, perhaps for the first time in my life, I awakened to the understanding that I could choose any goals or any life path that I would like and there were absolutely no limitations that would prevent me from accomplishing them except those which were imposed upon me by myself.

Erickson did not accomplish this impact on me by means of any trick or technique. He accomplished it simply by being himself and bringing with him a history of having been himself more than most other people have ever been themselves!

Conveying an Atmosphere of Creativity
Erickson's interpersonal impact was different from anything I had experienced. Much has been said about his techniques (I invite the reader to investigate any of the books by Lankton, Zeig, Gilligan, Yapko, and many others about Erickson's approach to therapy), but I intend to bypass those types of analysis and present a more subjective experience. I experienced Erickson as a very nonjudgmental person who, paradoxically, held very high values. I experienced him as a person who listened carefully to and watched closely—not in a threatening manner—everything I said and did. When he spoke, it seemed as if he brought his experience of living, modulated by his experience in psychiatry, to focus directly on what he had perceived about me. I felt an admiration or perhaps a reverence for how much he seemed to respect me, and that in turn magnified my expectations of myself.

Erickson's glee and joyfulness regarding almost anything that I said (or anyone else present said) created a very accepting atmosphere. This is not to say that he conveyed a permissive attitude about anything one might do. His value system was quite strong and he did not in any way condone criminal or hurtful activities. But his curiosity and readiness to explore the creative edge in those around him enriched the atmosphere.

In my visits with Erickson I pretended that my curiosity pertained to his professional skill. It was true, I was enormously curious about things that I didn't understand. And it was more than just a little bit true that I did not understand Erickson's approach to therapy. However, more importantly, I also did not understand his approach to me.

Erickson seemed extremely caring and concerned with my improvement, yet it was quite clear to me that if I were to change in any way it was entirely up to me. Usually, when people care for you they encourage you to change, but Erickson was definitely not exerting any energy in that direction. That is, if I wanted to go back to University of Michigan to earn a Ph.D., if I wanted to write a book, if I wanted to buy a cabin in the mountains and become a recluse, or if I wanted to buy a Subway franchise, it seemed as if Erickson would caringly find value in any decision I chose. He would not, however, exert any energy to influence any particular decision. He waited.

I was most curious about how I was responding to this man. I was quite close to my own father. I was staying with him while I visited Erickson. My father was an incredible man and quite a role model. For me, Erickson was not a father figure but more of a catalyst for change. In fact, from my anthropological studies, I took him to be sort of a shaman in his role in the culture.

The Role of Shaman

Years before I met Erickson, I studied the characteristics of a shaman from an anthropological perspective. The role of the definitive healer has not changed over centuries. A shaman is a person in the community who has the ability to motivate an ill person in a manner that brings him back into the flow of nature so that the change will restore health. Nowadays, we consider a qualified change agent to be a person with a professional degree, a state license, and special skills to be a physician or psychotherapist. But many licensed professionals fail more than they succeed. Many are only performing a "job" and they help only as much, or perhaps a bit more, than a kindly neighbor. Still others prescribe a life of drug-dependence that has questionable short-term results and dubious long-term consequences. A licensed professional can be molded over time, but a true shaman is not cut from a common mold.

Over the period 1970 to 1976, I collected knowledge about the role of a shaman, and I discovered that shamans stand apart from common tribal people due in part to several characteristics. I had these characteristics in the back of my mind when meeting Erickson, and I couldn't shake the idea that he was one of the true shamans in America.

A Shaman is a person who:
- excels at influencing others
- tends to others in pain
- is believed to have mysterious powers
- originates from a select cast (who have survived when others have not) perhaps by the will of God
- has perhaps survived injury
- goes into some sort of trance state
- undergoes rigorous training
- falls ill or goes crazy
- is treated by other medicine men
- is taught secret rituals
- observes the tribal taboos
- makes sacrifices
- reveals his dreams or trance learnings
- is told when he/she is ready to practice
- knows "secret words" not known to the general people
- knows "magic formulas" not known to the general people
- is known to take credit for cures
- reserves the right to act as if a given situation is not real
- reserves the right to not conform to social conventions

Much has been written about Erickson's illness, pain, healing, sacrifices, psychiatric learnings, and practice. Those experiences are consistent with the above list of shamanic characteristics.

My first observations of Erickson revealed aspects of his persona that are so well known that they probably go without saying. Shamans need not conform to social convention, and at this Erickson excelled. When I first contacted him by telephone, he answered directly, "Yes?"

I was speechless. I had expected a secretary and a delay of the usual bureaucratic barriers.

"I was calling for Milton Erickson," I said haltingly.

"This is he," he answered in a low, gravelly, poorly enunciated voice.

"I understand there are two Milton Ericksons in Phoenix," I said.

"I am calling for Dr. Milton H. Erickson, M.D., the psychiatrist?"

"This is he," answered Erickson.

"I am familiar with your work from the writings of Jay Haley and Gregory Bateson," I said. "Dr. Bateson recommended I call you. I want to invite you to teach as part of my training group for professionals in Michigan."

"I can't travel. I'm in a wheelchair," said Erickson.

"I'm sorry I can't hear you very well, I think we have a bad connection."

"I'm paralyzed. I'm in a wheelchair," repeated Erickson.

"You're paralyzed, in a wheelchair," I said. "I'm sorry, I can't hear you well, I think we have a bad connection."

"We don't have a bad connection, my damn lips are paralyzed!"

"You're lips are paralyzed."

"That's right. If you want to meet me, you will have to come here to Phoenix. Write a letter suggesting some dates."

"Write a letter suggesting some dates?"

"That's right."

And he hung up the phone. There was no "hello," "goodbye," "nice to meet you," or any other conventional formality of phone calling. It was a total break with convention and a total disruption of my expectations.

Does the tribal shaman exempt him/herself from convention because they live in a different world or as an attempt to begin the process of change by disrupting expectations? My experience in this unconventional beginning was mixed and uncomfortable. I was surprised and curious, but at the same time I was filled with trepidation. Erickson was unpredictable; I was uncomfortable, and this was likely to continue and become even more uncomfortable when I visited.

I like to get feedback that I am not offending, and, in fact, pleasing. Lacking that feedback, I feel unsure. I recall a quote from Carlos

Castenada, presumably directed to him from Don Juan: "The average man seeks certainty in the eyes of onlookers and calls that self-confidence. The warrior looks for certainty in his own eyes and calls that humbleness." (Castaneda, page 15, 1974). In my case, I did not find certainty from my initial phone contact with Erickson. Whether or not this was his plan, the experience threw me back onto myself. If I were to have any confidence at all, it would come from me.

When I finally arrived in Phoenix, I found a man dressed in purple from head to toe—a wardrobe more like pajamas than the clothes of a training psychiatrist—and then he began speaking. Now, all psychotherapists and psychiatrists use secret words as is done by shamans—we have a vocabulary not known by or understood by the common person. But in addition to these secret words, Erickson added countless others. His words held people spellbound. He spoke in a tone, rhythm, and language that I had not heard before. I had to listen carefully to make sense of his words, and the harder I listened, the less my mind could be distracted. There was even a melody to his voice. The range of tone, while uncommon, did not seem overly dramatic or inappropriate. Just engaging.

I often found myself unable to draw conclusions from what Erickson said, and it was in his speech that I often found him true to the shamanic characteristic of acting as if the situation was not real. I was unable to distinguish whether he was speaking about others or me. I recall Jay Haley's account of communication (Haley, 1963). In any communication there will be sender, a receiver, a message, and a context in which it is taking place. This can be described as having four parts:

    a) I
    b) am communicating this
    c) to you
    d) in this situation.

Haley's thesis is that in a hypnotic language the speaker must communicate in such a way as to deny, or at least fail to affirm, one or more of these elements. Erickson would mention what he said to others, even when it seemed to apply to me. He spoke of what others said, even though it could have been him speaking. He told stories that were about other people in other situations, and yet, these often applied to me. I was unsure if he realized the parallels or not. With Erickson's shift in pronouns, discussions of others in the form of case stories, and use of ambiguity, it seemed as if he often invited me into a state of self-examination. At times, it was so intense or profound that I tuned him out and sort of relived earlier times to extract feelings, ideas, or other impressions. When I returned to hearing him again, I often had no idea what he was saying or how much time had passed. In earlier times, I'm certain this would have been considered speaking magic formulas, as they resulted in profound changes in my manner of thinking and behaving in the late 1970s and thereafter.

Finally, Erickson spoke to his trainees from the trance he maintained. In fact, one time I actually asked if that was what he did. He replied, "Of course I do. If I wasn't in trance with all of you, I'd be bored to death!" While this is a humorous reply, one can only wonder to what extent it explains his heightened intuition. Many of us who visited Erickson reported his almost psychic ability to know our background. While Erickson vehemently denied the existence of psychic powers, he repeatedly dazzled me and others with comments that could not be explained by conventional "knowing." Thus, the shamanic characteristic of gaining special knowledge in trance or having mystical powers is fulfilled.

After 25 years, I still find myself in circumstances hearing something he said. I chalk this up to the fact that ambiguous comments can take on more then one meaning. He once said to me, "And my voice goes everywhere with you and changes into the voice of your parents, your teachers, your playmates and the voice of wind and the rain…" It seems as if his prediction was correct.✳

Betty Alice Erickson:

Neither Dan Short nor Teresa Robles ever met Erickson in person. But each feels he is present in their lives. It is remarkable how Erickson's healing influence and loving spirit still envelopes so many. People around the world are deeply dedicated to giving to others some of what they feel Erickson gave so freely to everyone.

It is significant that virtually everyone who knew him directly or through his recorded words and image, or through the words of others, or even by the impersonality of the printed page, feels his presence and his healing spirit.

It is understandable that people have difficulty using the limited abilities of words to delineate exactly what Erickson did—how his being affected them. Perhaps Jeffrey Zeig came close to expressing it when he said in his Convocation Address at the 9th International Ericksonian Congress, "He taught us how to be just by being."

DAN SHORT

A licensed psychologist in private practice in Scottsdale, Arizona, Short is graduate faculty at Ottawa University and a supervisor for graduate internships. A leading scholar on Erickson's work, he was associate director of the Milton H. Erickson Foundation as well as editor of the Milton H. Erickson Foundation *Newsletter* for five years. A presenter at international conferences, he has published on brief therapy and created the Short Assessment System. His current book, *Hope and Resiliency*, co-authored, with Betty Alice Erickson and Roxanna Erickson Klein, is a comprehensive description of Erickson's work.

"I had many patients write a letter to me, explain that they want help…and not mail it…they went through that formal conscious process of asking for help and then their unconscious would answer them. So when I am just a memory, you still write to me and your unconscious can answer your letter."
—Milton H. Erickson, M.D., 1974

FOR ME ERICKSON'S PRESENCE has always been indirect. In the same way that a distant light illuminates objects in a fog, Erickson's heroic life story not only expanded my worldview but also helped me see some of the hidden good in my own life. Though it is challenging to become intimately acquainted with someone who is no longer living, I have always felt that I gained much through meeting Erickson.

In the same way that I learned to love Socrates through the eyes of Plato, my admiration for Erickson initially grew from the chronicling of Jay Haley and then others such as Ernest Rossi and Jeff Zeig who apprenticed under Erickson. Many years later, I had the opportunity of working with the Milton H. Erickson Foundation Archives. While digitizing this material, I was immersed in hundreds of hours of audio recording. Every day for two years, I listened to Erickson speak. I transcribed his words, made connections between the overarching ideas, visualized his hypnotic demonstrations, and spent much of my day and night in and out of trance. When I left the archives, Erickson's voice would go with me.

My encounters with Erickson have occurred on various levels of consciousness. The most intriguing occurred at night. During the darkness, the restless part of my mind was searching for home. It has been this way since the disintegration of my childhood family. I am honored to know the widow Erickson and have visited Erickson's house in Phoenix on many an occasion. But in my dreams Erickson's house is different; it is more like the place I lived as a four-year-old boy. In the dream I remember most clearly, I am taking a long journey up a hill and, once inside the house, I walk up a long flight of stairs. Somewhere at the top I am hoping to find Erickson. The feeling associated with these images is one of intense anxiety as if waiting to be judged. When I find Erickson, he does not say a word. He simply looks at me, kindly and expectantly. This visual memory yields profound encouragement and the understanding that the rest is up to me.

I have also encountered Erickson through hundreds of written case studies describing his clinical work and the touching stories of his fatherly interactions with his children. After reading these, it is natural to imagine the feeling of the connection that existed between Erickson and those he helped. I seriously doubt that I am the only person to vicariously enjoy, through Erickson, the special type of security that can only be known in relation to a strong father figure.

In modernity, this experience with a father as one's hero is rare. Perhaps as a result of over-correction from outdated authoritarian practices, today's fathers are portrayed in the popular media as bumbling, childlike figures that require a great deal of caretaking by their wives and children. Even worse, with the demands of an industrial society, the father has been absent from the home, banished to a cubical where he spends his time performing subordinate tasks that lack meaning. At the end of the day, nothing heroic has been accomplished. There are, of course, exceptions, but in general this culture lacks pride in the family and has little interest in its deposed patriarchy.

When I first started reading about Erickson, I had an insatiable appetite for his heroic healing stories. Similar to the way that a malnourished child eats plaster off the walls to get more calcium, I devoured Erickson's case studies to strengthen my psychological constitution. Characterized primarily by acts of altruism, these stories illustrate how Erickson approached life's challenges with cunning and determination. He had an iron will and a velvety softness in the way he approached the needy and the weak. I was someone who grew up without a father in the home, and Erickson's indirect presence provided a secure foundation that I would eventually use to grab hold of aspirations that formally seemed out of reach.

This father strength is the same that I hope to convey to my children. I enjoy placing my son or my daughter on my shoulders while walking around. This way they can see the world from a higher vantage point than my own. While writing this paper, I asked my five-year-old son about his experience with me as his father. He responded, "I am glad that I am so smart...I asked you to carry me just before the sting-ray bit your foot." I interpreted his reply as meaning that he felt upheld by his father. At this young age, his trust in his own goodness is still inseparable from his father's abilities and the fact that he will unquestionably benefit from them. I credit my relationship with Erickson for helping me to feel that I have much to offer those who have come into my life.

Reading about Erickson's unique accomplishments has richly contributed to my ability to recognize opportunities for creative problem solving. But not all of the literature has been equally satisfying. What I found more difficult to swallow were the books that concerned themselves mainly with the dissection of Erickson's technique and the invention of new jargon. In the same way that ethologists eventually recognized that more information is gained from an animal that is studied in its natural habitat, rather than one reduced to small pieces on a lab table, I find that Erickson is better viewed as a forest than a twig. The former offers a false sense of superiority while the latter inspires awe.

The other way that I indirectly experienced the life of Erickson was through his progeny. Shortly after reading Jay Haley's book, I discovered that Erickson's daughter, Betty Alice, was conducting therapy and training in the city where I lived. So I immediately sought her out. Even though I was young and new to clinical practice, she expressed a strong interest in my ideas and confidence in my developing abilities. The experience was nourishing, like fruit from a really good tree. Shortly thereafter, I had the additional pleasure of becoming acquainted with another of Erickson's daughters, Roxanna. I quickly came to respect her discernment and candor. My time with these two unique individuals has been very rewarding as they have reflected aspects of their father that I would have otherwise missed.

Another connection I have with Erickson is through my writing. Serving as editor for the Milton H. Erickson Foundation *Newsletter* for five years, I gained a better appreciation for simplicity in written communication. There was a lot of work involved in making contributors' articles easy to read and absorb. When I wrote my introductory comments, they were designed to be concise and to the point. It is not possible to write this way without thinking about the essence of what is being discussed. This skill was recently taken to new levels when I coauthored a full-length book about Erickson with Betty Alice and Roxanna. Much is learned through the exercise of putting thought to written word. While writing about this wounded healer who had so much hope and resiliency, I found myself becoming less concerned with my personal issues and more aware of the meaning that is derived from empowering others.

Lastly, I would say that I have encountered Erickson by seeking to emulate his pioneering spirit and appreciation for discovery. Erickson's stubborn refusal to tell others how to live their lives, or exactly how to practice psychotherapy, has forced me to find my own individual path. Erickson's mysterious style of communication and idiosyncratic behaviors remind us that human uniqueness defies scientific reductionism. His flexibility and readiness to act in seemingly contradictory ways makes it impossible to confine his work to a procedural cage. Although freedom means more responsibility, it also provides more room to grow. Now with less learned helplessness and greater strength of will, I find myself riding the same wind on which Erickson soared. ✺

TERESA ROBLES

Born in Mexico City, Robles has an M.A. in social anthropology, and a Ph.D. in clinical psychology as well as training in Systemic Family Therapy. She founded the first Erickson Institute in her country as well as the Centro Ericksoniano de Mexico. Robles has introduced the Ericksonian approach throughout Mexico as well as in Latin America and Europe where she frequently teaches. She has written many books which have been translated into several languages, including *Concert for Four Brain Hemispheres in Psychotherapy.*

I AM AN ANTHROPOLOGIST as well as a psychologist and it is partly from the anthropological approach that I write. What is a healer? What characteristics does a he have? How does a person become a healer? Perhaps most important, how does a healer work?

In traditional cultures, a healer is an extraordinary man—a man greater than the ordinary. He influences others, helping them to heal by themselves. He may use different methods and techniques, but he really is like a musical tone that upon vibrating, makes all the tones around vibrate in that frequency.

In 1987 I spent a week at the Milton H. Erickson Foundation looking at Dr. Erickson's videos. Every time he began to speak, I went into trance and stayed there until the end of the video. After that week, I returned to Mexico very different, with much more inner peace.

And still now when I am teaching, showing one of his videos, although I must stay "awake" in my role as a teacher, Erickson's voice and especially his image, sitting in his wheelchair looking down, make me feel better, and I am certain that something inside me changes.

I have a picture of Dr. Erickson in my office. In my first sessions with clients, I explain that the techniques we'll use were created by him. And very often in other sessions they comment, "Dr. Erickson's picture transmits a lot of peace." The tuning fork makes others vibrate at its pitch....

A healer creates these pitches because he vibrates with the rhythms of nature. He is aware of all nature's cycles. Always after night, day comes; the tempest passes and calm arrives. We need to sow and wait for plants to grow and then to harvest. A healer is aware of the rhythms of nature; he is part of it, he feels one with nature.

Sometimes, healers have suffered grave illnesses, are physically handicapped or have lived through near-death experiences. Their strong desire to overcome their illnesses and handicaps lead them to develop capacities beyond the ordinary.

Among the Huicholes Indians, future healers meet their guides as a white eagle or a blue deer in their dreams. Pablo de Tarso (later San Pablo) fell off his horse, was blinded by a light, and listened to a voice; after that he changed his life. In Western cultures, the extraordinary man is a healer because with only his presence, he makes others "vibrate" as he does. What he does or what he says is a mere support. Teresa de Ávila would say, "With only a few words he transmits so much; he transmits peace."

In Mexican traditional cultures, there is a moment during sunset known as "the slot between worlds," through which we can cross from one world to the other. Our tradition is that healers go out from their bodies, becoming animals or natural elements. Then they meet others in dreams and protect those people during their journeys. We believe healers always ask permission from the spirit of the person before beginning to work. Without that, they know they cannot achieve anything.

I didn't have the opportunity to know that extraordinary man who was Milton H. Erickson while he lived. But I know him through the films and the words of those who knew him. And I recognize him as a man who produced (and produces) changes in others with just his presence. I say this without diminishing Dr. Erickson's techniques, his strategies, and the psychotherapeutic approaches he gave us that have so radically changed psychotherapy.

Erickson grew up on a farm and always had some sort of garden. He was able to feel and live the rhythms of nature. He never lost this ability despite being part of the modern, academic world.

He had many handicaps; he was color blind, deaf to some tones, and dyslexic. His little classmates looked at him as different. Erickson told us that his teacher got mad because she was not able to make him understand the differences between the letter "m" and the number "3." Suddenly one day, in a ray of light, he saw that "m" was like a horse standing on all four legs with its head bent down to the ground, and the "3" was like a horse standing on its hind legs. He said the flash of light was so strong and brilliant that he could only distinguish the "m" and the "3" amid that explosion of light.

Years later, while he was reading the dictionary, column by column trying to find the words he needed, the flash of light appeared again and "showed him" that the dictionary was listed in alphabetical order. I don't know if this light that Erickson saw was similar to the light our culture says Pablo de Tarso saw. I find it interesting, however.

The story of Erickson, paralyzed with polio, lying in bed, asking his mother to place a mirror in a position that allowed him to look at the sunrise is well known. He lived through the night and, saw the sunrise and then remained in a coma for some time. We don't know what happened when he was disconnected from this reality, but it is interesting that Erickson looked in a mirror. In many old cultures, mirrors are considered as an entrance to the world of the dead, a "slot between the worlds." Don Juan, the Yaqui Shaman would tell us that the young Milton went to the world of the dead and returned with a mission. Or maybe he would say that he flew to the sun and took energy from it for healing.

When he was paralyzed after he came out of the coma, he was "a mind without body." How many other times did he leave his body, when it was filled with pain, when he was confined to his wheelchair and he let his mind travel to other realities? Did part of him always remain connected with the external world? How many times have we listened to him inviting his clients to become a mind without body, training them to enter in trance? In my culture, healers transcend their physical bodies and work in other dimensions, like a mind without a physical body.

The theoretical framework of quantum physics states that other realities co-exist with the physical world we know so well. We can switch from one to another through dreams and through amplified states of conscious. Perhaps the Ericksonian hypnotic trance can be defined as an amplified state of conscious, another slot between different worlds. It is in those realities where the Spirit of the healers meet the Spirit of their clients and their guides.

Dr. Erickson used to ask his patients in trance "and there, who am I?" In his well-known case, The February Man, Dr. Erickson modified Miss S.'s story of solitude and emotional lack, entering into her trance and creating from there a new life story for her. With her, in this "new life;" he was the February Man.

I invite you to imagine that when he suggested to his clients, "And my voice will go with you and can change into the voice of your parents, your playmates, your schoolmates, your neighbors, into the voice of anything you wish, into the sounds of the birds, the lake, the river, the wind…" he was connecting with the conscious energy-matter that projects rivers, the rain, the wind, and the different characters of the stories of his clients. In this way, the influence continued and was made known to them.

I believe Dr. Erickson was a healer. As shamans ask permission from the Spirit of their clients for healing them, Dr. Erickson looked to the unconscious mind of his clients before beginning to work. Like traditional healers, he met his clients in the waking dream he developed with them, the hypnotic trance. Then, as a mind without a body, in a different dimension, he helped them to change. They changed from their Spirit, their unconscious mind, and even from the source of the projections that all our reality is.

I didn't personally know this extraordinary man. I did not live the experience of vibrating in his presence. But I have felt his vibration and his strength through his writings, his tapes, and films. In my dreams, in very special moments while dreaming asleep or dreaming awake, I know him. Dr. Erickson continues alive in the dream world. ❖

JOHN O. BEAHRS

Professor of psychiatry at Oregon Health and Science University and staff psychiatrist at the Portland VA Medical Center, Beahrs studied hypnosis with Ernest Hilgard as well as with Milton Erickson. A three-time recipient of the Milton H. Erickson Award of Scientific Excellence for Writing in Hypnosis given by the ASCH, Beahrs has authored three books and numerous articles. His principal academic focus is in studying consciousness and volition. He is also interested in music composition and the great outdoors.

"THERE IS NOTHING particularly fancy about what I do. It's just simple common sense psychology." With these words, Milton Erickson summarized the essence of his work to a first-year psychiatry resident honored to be studying with the master, awed by the elegant complexity of what are now known as "Ericksonian techniques." Since that early 1971 encounter, I have come to see Erickson's statement as literally true, and perhaps the best summary one could make. If so, the missing theory of Ericksonian psychotherapy is none other than the basic psychology of everyday living.

Consider the implications of this premise. It is not true to say that Erickson eschewed basic theory. I have long been troubled by this widely accepted myth. Although eschewing theory is claimed to justify being open to each patient as a unique individual, it carries a corresponding risk—that technique could reduce to ungrounded manipulation, vulnerable to its practitioners' prejudices and hidden agendas. Erickson truly was a master of interpersonal manipulation, but none who knew him would ever have considered him to be ungrounded. Where was his grounding? In strong unswerving family values which ensured that his manipulative skills would be put to constructive use. The psychology and the values are equally essential.

Erickson summarized his therapeutic methodology to me as a threefold maxim. First, "join the patient's system, and gain rapport." Second, given this rapport, "modify the patient's productions, thereby gaining control." Finally, utilize this control to foster desirable change. He illustrated this maxim with 16 elegant case anecdotes in a marvelous 1959 paper on "utilization techniques," which remains my choice assignment when introducing Ericksonian psychotherapy to trainees (Erickson M.H.: "Further techniques of hypnosis—utilization techniques," *American Journal of Clinical Hypnosis*, 2:3-21, 1959). Many will recognize the maxim as the essence of good leadership—again, common sense psychology. Exactly how it operates is less than obvious, however.

Common sense psychology is elusive. Otherwise, its mysteries would be known to all scientists; every psychotherapist would utilize them; and Milton Erickson's special contributions would evaporate as routine. Anticipating subsequent lines of research that are slowly catching up, Erickson sensed that much of what we call consciousness and volition are deceptive, and he learned through practice how to utilize these features to enact therapeutic change. Here are several high points, each of which illustrates one facet of his utilization of common sense psychology grounded in strong personal values.

Different peoples' psychologies are intermeshed. One can influence another, to the degree that the two become aligned, or in "rapport." This is mutual suggestion, the essence of hypnosis. Erickson appreciated the extent to which this process pervades everyday living, and utilized it in contexts seemingly remote from the hypnosis lab.

Consciousness is complex. We humans often want something and its opposite, equally honestly and intensely. Opposing levels may paralyze one another with internal conflict, or sabotage one another with outcomes that benefit neither. Erickson emphasized a need to treat all "parts" even-handedly, with respect—an internal democracy, so to speak. This value-based premise enabled him to establish rapport at many hidden levels, prerequisite to interventions that followed. He often cautioned potentially resistant patients to "go slow," for example. Rapid change often ensued.

Different people speak unique "languages." These serve to communicate with insiders, and obfuscate communication with outsiders. Part of respectful treatment was to decipher these secret codes, and speak patients' languages to the extent possible. He was thereby more likely to be experienced as an insider, and granted rapport.

The form of psychological realities varies with how they're defined within their interpersonal milieu. Rigidity can be redefined as integrity, for example; wishy-washy as open-minded, or resistance as an assertion of autonomy. Having already won for himself a role in a patient's system, reframability imparted new options for changing the system's balance, e.g., by redirecting attention from one level to another, or reframing a problematic aspect of selfhood as an advantage. Patterns of approach and avoidance, one's so-called psychodynamic forces, could thereby change at a single stroke.

The experience of conscious will has remarkably little to do with our voluntary muscles actually moving. More of life is lived at unconscious levels, with consciousness as an add-on that probably serves social regulatory functions. Milton Erickson also anticipated and utilized this counterintuitive fact. In many cases, for example, "resistance" to desired change arose less from unconscious counter-motivations than from a need for the illusory conscious to save face. Where this occurred, Erickson employed his legendary techniques for "depotentiating consciousness," always with respectful provision for face-saving. When freed from interference, unconscious processes were drawn toward more salutary balance on their own.

Now consider a psychotherapy case in progress. By skilled selective attention, reframing, and face-saving, the stage has been set. Profound intrapsychic and behavioral change is now likely to occur, as if by itself. Just how, to what extent and in what direction is indeterminate, however—or probabilistic. We can only manipulate the odds. Equally important, is to bias the parameters in such a way that the now-imminent change is likely to occur in a more desirable direction. This biasing is essentially value-driven. What differentiated Milton Erickson from problematic manipulators such as despots or cult leaders, was the desirability of his personal values. What were these values, and why was their implementation so therapeutically efficacious as well as desirable?

Milton Erickson was a family man. Beyond respect, multilevel communication and trusting unconscious wisdom, a more explicit modulating role was granted to family values. They work because they are fundamental to human nature. Evolutionary biologists are identifying them in the twin principles of "kin altruism" and "in-group reciprocity." Erickson fostered both. He was openly devoted to his own family, and many of his celebrated case anecdotes can be interpreted as facilitating family relationships in his clientele.

Reciprocity is explicit in his exhortation to therapists to thank their subjects for successful hypnotic performances. It is clear that family values contributed an essential grounding element to Erickson's common sense psychology.

To consider "Erickson as healer" points even further beyond the specifics just described. "Therapeutic personalities" are defined partly through the extent that their own unconscious states of mind "resonate" with those of others, facilitating therapeutic effects in ways far more difficult to explicate. Such resonance cannot be coached, or consciously planned. It "just happens," seeming to well up from the deeper springs of a person's basic being. After working with a particularly difficult case dilemma, Erickson would sometimes "awaken" to find detailed process notes, with near-complete amnesia for a session that had just transpired. When necessary, Erickson would call on his own trusted unconscious to take over, and the requisite resonances would then flow.

How has Milton Erickson impacted me and my own work? That he did so quite profoundly is beyond dispute. Exactly how and in what directions, I'm less sure. As a budding theorist, I had sought his tutelage, already committed to studying the paradoxes of consciousness and volition, already convinced that hypnosis offered a key to the lock. As a mature academician, I am now studying the implications of viewing consciousness and volition as shared self-deception, evolved in order to promote social cooperation where interests conflict. As a therapist to be, I had hoped to become more skilled at hypnosis. I ended up developing a therapeutic style of challenging patients at their most conscious levels to define who they are, what they stand for, and where they're headed—then utilizing this self-defining process as a vehicle for therapeutic change. As a person, I became ever more committed to basic family values—always my intrinsic bias.

Erickson's influence was intangible. Just as important as his explicating his techniques, were the extent to which I felt valued and respected at all levels, the extent to which he shared his own family with me, and his challenging me to develop who I was in my own unique way. After reviewing a draft of an award-winning paper, he had openly criticized me for giving him more credit than he wanted. "It's your work!" he insisted. As I reflect on his influence, I think that its very intangibility expresses this influence and his values as well as anything else I could say. I clearly recall his unabashed delight while he was wielding his influence skills on me, just as he delighted when demonstrating his work with third-party subjects. But the product was always mine, and solely my own. This was his respect, his skill, and his values—all exemplified.✤

ALIDA IOST-PETER AND
BURKHARD PETER

Alida Iost-Peter became a psychologist and psychotherapist after having been a school teacher. She is cofounder of M.E.G. and a close coworker of her husband Burkhard Peter. She translated several of Erickson's books and articles into German, and is copy editor of the journal *Hypnose und Kognition*.

Burkhard Peter, Ph.D., has had a private psychotherapy practice in Munich, Germany, since 1976. He is cofounder and codirector of the Institute for Integrative Psychotherapy (IIT) in Munich. From 1978–1984 he was founding president of the Milton Erickson Society for Clinical Hypnosis, Germany (M.E.G.); 1992–2000 he was a board member of the International Society of Hypnosis (ISH). He is editor and co-editor, author and co-author of two journals (*Hypnose und Kognition*; *Hypnosis International Monographs*), six books, and more than 100 articles and book chapters on hypnosis and hypnotherapy and its applications in psychotherapy. He is a fellow of the American Society for Clinical Hypnosis (ASCH) and has been awarded the Lifetime Achievement Award for Outstanding Contributions to the Field of Psychotherapy by the Milton H. Erickson Foundation, and the Pierre Janet Award for Clinical Excellence by the International Society of Hypnosis (ISH). He conducts seminars and workshops on hypnosis and hypnotherapy for M.E.G. and other societies and institutions and maintains a lectureship on hypnosis at the University of Munich, Department. of Clinical Psychology.

Alida:

IN SEPTEMBER 1978, a group from Germany—Wilhelm Gerl, Burkhard Peter, and I—visited Milton Erickson at his place in Phoenix. We had heard about him, when Stephen Gilligan and Paul Carter had been here in Munich at our Institute for Integrated Therapy to give a workshop on Ericksonian hypnosis.

It was my first trip to America. I was curious to see the country, to visit Milton Erickson, and to get to know his work, which I had heard was spectacular. I was also a bit worried: My first husband had left me; I had been working with him in management training and now I had to find a new professional orientation; I was considering going back to the university to get an academic degree as a psychologist; I was in love with Burkhard but I was not sure that we could get along so well for the rest of our lives; and, I was pregnant! So I secretly hoped to find some solutions for my future life.

Stephen and Paul had instructed us what to tell Erickson about ourselves and what to remain silent about—for instance, that we were not married

When we arrived at Dr. Erickson's home, Mrs Erickson welcomed us. I immediately liked her warm and lovely nature. Then we sat down in Erickson's lecture room. He had already started his work and there were several students from all over the world. A young lady from Australia was sitting at his right side with an arm-levitation, and while she remained frozen with her mind obviously far away, Erickson asked us to tell something about ourselves. I felt very embarrassed and when he looked at me in his special inquiring and disturbing way, I was sure that he knew more about me than I myself did.

Erickson suggested I regress to a child's age, but somehow I felt the need to resist, not to behave like an obedient believing child. I made up my mind not to sit there like this Australian lady with her arm levitated.

I felt a bit uncomfortable. We had walked in the hot Phoenician sun for more than half an hour from our motel, and when we entered Erickson's office, it felt like a refrigerator—at that time we Europeans were not used to air conditioning.

For two or three days we sat, listening to Erickson. It was unbelievable that this older man in his purple suit, in his wheelchair with his undeniable health problems was able to teach and to demonstrate for more than four hours—at the end of which we felt completely exhausted.

I was not able to understand too much because of my rather poor school English and Erickson's American pronunciation, restricted by the consequences of his former polio attacks. The more I could not understand, the angrier I got. When he asked me whether I had experienced hypnosis and asked if I wanted to do it now, I complained about my difficulties understanding him—I had come the long way from Germany to learn from him.

He invited me to sit by his side and I did so with a pounding heart. He asked if I wanted to go in a trance now or later. He grasped my wrist and lifted my arm, and when he let it go, it fell like a stone. Remembering my plan not to do an arm-levitation, I crossed my arms and my legs. He looked at me, smiling, and said to the audience: "What a nice kind of resistance!" From this moment on I must have been in a trance. Burkhard and Wilhelm later told me that Erickson used an induction for age-regression to take me to when I first went to school and learned to read and write:

I found myself sitting in an old Egyptian school watching the teacher writing signs with a kind of stone on a blackboard and pointing at them with a stick and letting us, the pupils, repeat the names of the signs. We all sat there like the figures on the reliefs of the pharaoh's tombs in the pyramids. I was trying hard to learn to read the hieroglyphs. I followed them with my finger from right to left, and all at once I got it; I could comprehend easily and I was very happy.

I came back to the present with a laughter and when I looked around, I was aware that all the other participants in Erickson's group were laughing too.

What is most amazing is that from then on I was able to understand and follow Erickson quite easily—even when we spoke on the
telephone between the States and Germany.

Several times Erickson took us to his private room after the
seminars. There, he showed us objects from his playful, amusing,
curious, and remarkable collection, and he was delighted with our
surprise and amazement. I had grown up without my father who
had died when I was two, and I felt a bit like a little girl whose father
shows her important things and teaches her about meaning.

When we got back to Germany, Burkhard and I married and
had our daughter Shoshannah, I studied psychology, became a
psychotherapist, and I am especially proud to have translated books
by Erickson into German.

Burkhard:
MY STORY IS much shorter, as I still have a profound amnesia for
some of the time we spent with Erickson—especially for that period
in time he worked with me. What I do remember from this special
amnesiac period is that he suddenly, and, in my opinion without any
contextual reason, out of the blue so to speak, asked me, where was
I the first time I was in a trance. I was totally confused and tried hard
to give an answer but was only able to utter some obviously confused
sentences describing some real places in great detail. I stopped with
some anger when others in the room began laughing loudly instead
of being interested in all my "special" details. It was then that I realized something must be wrong—that I was not really awake and that
my trying hard in giving details about places was not right. Only
then did I recognize that I obviously had been in a trance.

The morning after, during one of our breakfasts in our motel,
I asked Alida and Wilhelm whether we should ask Erickson for
permission to use his name for a hypnosis society in Germany. We did
ask, and he replied, "You may use my name in any way you find
appropriate." Indeed, this was a very high compliment, and we have

worked hard to deserve it—eventually founding the Milton Erickson Society of Hypnosis, Germany (M.E.G.). Since that time in Phoenix, my entire life has been devoted to and infiltrated by hypnosis, both professionally and personally.

I don't want to claim that this is only due to an amnesiac period of about 30 minutes. I still have very vivid memories of this week we spent with Erickson. I know that modern Ericksonian hypnotherapy developed as a consequence of his professional and personal influence. On a personal level, I cannot say that he healed a special disease I suffered from at that time. I also do not want to say that he suggested an idea to found M.E.G. during that amnesiac period. I just want to say that I remember very precisely his face and his voice when he said to me with his special meaningful way of looking at someone: "Do the best you can." Whenever it gets hard in my personal life I remember this. Whenever I have physical pain, I remember him and can use self-hypnosis to alleviate it. He is a personal icon to me.❋

PHIL AND NORMA BARETTA

Frequent faculty for both the ASCH and the Erickson Foundation, the Barrettas also teach regularly in Europe. Their private practice specializes in Brief Ericksonian hypnotherapy, neurolinguistics, and uncommon therapeutic intervention strategies.

Norma is a clinical psychologist, a consultant and fellow of the ASCH. She is a diplomate of the International Academy of Behavioral Medicine and a member of the Southern California Society of Clinical Hypnosis.

Philip is a licensed marriage and family therapist. In 1989, he was honored by the ASCH and received the status of "Special Member" before marriage and family therapists were eligible for membership. He is a consultant for the ASCH, a diplomate of the International Academy of Health Care Professionals, a member of CAMFT and the SCSCH.

The Barrettas are celebrating over 57 years of productive togetherness.

OUR ASSOCIATION WITH Milton Erickson began long before we met. When we began to study hypnosis, his name kept reappearing.

We got to know him through the words of Jay Haley and John Grinder and Richard Bandler and through some of his own writings.

In 1973, we wrote a letter addressing it merely to: Dr. Milton Erickson; Phoenix, Arizona. Certainly we believed he was so famous that the Phoenix post office would deliver the letter, and we were horrified when it came back boldly stamped "Undeliverable As Addressed."

We kept on reading, studying, and, to some degree, learning. We met John Grinder who told us, "You have to meet the 'old man' and you have to do it now."

We had heard Erickson had a waiting list over a year long, but John said, "I'll call him. When can you go?"

"Immediately."

"Good," said John. "I'll arrange it." The next morning he gave us a phone number. "Telephone on Monday, precisely at noon, Arizona time. He's expecting your call."

A voice picked up on the second ring, and when I heard it, I went into a trance. Milton Erickson had answered the phone! He said, "This is Norma Barretta, is it not?"

It took me about 30 seconds to remember my name. "This is Norma Barretta," I said. "John Grinder told me to call you."

"I've been waiting for your call," Dr. Erickson responded. "When can you come?"

"Whenever you say."

"Good. Here's Betty. She'll tell you when." Mrs. Erickson came on the phone and asked, "Can you come next Monday?"

"Next Monday?" My God! We thought we'd have to wait a year and she says next Monday.

Next Monday was an impossible date, but we rearranged our lives and flew to Phoenix. Thus began our "Moments with Milton."

Our group was small that first time—only five people—a rare treat, we learned later. It was never to be so intimate again; later visits were shared with no less than 10 to 12 people from all over the world.

On our first day, there was a woman from Southern California who had to re-take her licensing exam. She wanted Dr. Erickson to hypnotize her so she could pass the test. John Grinder had told me (Norma) I should sit in a green chair and I was in it. Dr. Erickson looked at me and said, "You'll have to move for now."

"You'll have to move for now." An embedded command? The beginning of a healing? Erickson had written, "...give the patient the opportunity to make use of his capacities to function...."

Another woman came in and Dr. Erickson continued to talk, just continued talking. We watched him intently, waiting for him to do the hypnotic work. Then we glanced over and saw that the new woman was in a profound trance, although neither of us had heard any of the linguistic patterns designed for induction. And the rest of us were in somewhat of a trance as well.

Several years later we met the woman who had sat in the green chair, and she informed us that she had passed her exam. Had Erickson's words had a "healing" effect on her? Did he "cure" her inability to pass her examination?

On the second day of our meetings with Erickson, there were only four of us. We sat in the little office where the desk was located, and someone asked, "Can I record this?"

"Do you doubt your ability?" replied Dr. Erickson.

We thought about that and immediately went into a trance. "What in the world did he mean?" Perhaps two hours later, while Erickson was talking, we realized the person should have said, "MAY I record this?" Nine words had induced a profound trance. There was no doubt that Erickson was clever with words, and from that moment on, both of us caught the linguistic fervor.

The rest of that morning he wove a tale that described both our lives. He just started to talk: He described a young couple in a setting that matched the setting in our early lives. With minimal information about us, he wove a tale about a Slavic girl (Norma is Polish) and a boy of Mediterranean heritage (Phil is of Italian descent). He described Norma's interactions with her parents and some of the early events in our lives that nobody else knows. It was uncanny and a revelation of Erickson's remarkable sensory acuity. We must have been very responsive to what he was saying and he must have noticed and built on that. In his words, he "…relied on the capacity of the individual to furnish the cues, the information…the patient can find a way if given the opportunity."

In retrospect, we believe we know how he did it—he had a great deal of sensitivity, and he "read" us, weaving a tale that had elements out of our cores. Erickson was an excellent observer and an exquisite teacher—one of those masterful guides who could keep people on the "main road" of their lives. If asked how he did it, we know he would say, "There's nothing magical about what I did."

Was he a "healer?" We don't think so—not in the sense that he "healed" or "cured" others. He was a great teacher of healing and he elicited that ability to heal in everyone he encountered. He made it a totally "inside" job. ✴

C. ALEXANDER SIMPKINS AND
ANNELLEN SIMPKINS

The Simpkins are clinical psychologists in private practice specializing in hypnosis and meditation. They studied hypnosis with G. Wilson Shaffer, Milton Erickson, and Ernest Rossi. They have done research in hypnosis and are the authors of 20 books including *Effective Self-Hypnosis, Self-Hypnosis for Women, The Simple Series, Ten Easy Lessons Series on Eastern philosophies, Meditation from Thought to Action* with an audio CD, and *Timeless Teachings from the Therapy Masters.* Their books have won numerous awards and have been translated into numerous languages. They are active in the Milton H. Erickson Foundation *Newsletter* as reviews editors.

IT HAS BEEN A NUMBER OF YEARS since we sat in Milton H. Erickson's presence, listening and watching the master at work. But the unconscious mind isn't limited by chronological time. So we turn to our unconscious minds to reclaim our experience of Erickson as healer. And now the time spent with Erickson can be present to draw on. We see him sitting in his chair at the desk, turned toward us, dressed comfortably in his purple suit, with crocheted booties on his feet. He has a dignified, yet relaxed way of sitting in his chair, gently holding his hands together. We have just arrived for our first visit with Erickson, a one-hour appointment scheduled for 11 a.m., not expecting that this first hour will stretch into an entire week and then many more years!

Erickson makes us feel at ease from the first moment by welcoming our young daughter. Now with a charming smile on his face, he watches our daughter play quietly near him on the floor. Little did we know that first day that he would teach our whole family how to use our unconscious minds productively. We all would look forward to visits with Dr. Erickson.

We tell him that we both have our M.A. degrees and are working on our Ph.D.s. We explain that we are seeing clients at the counseling center of our university doing hypnotherapy, under supervision. Our discussion is not just limited specifically to hypnosis and therapy, permitting Erickson's uncanny utilization methods to facilitate our work in many ways. For example, we tell him that we both enjoy practicing magic and misdirection. He tells us that he loves magic and asks to see some. So Alex performs a heads and tails guessing game with a coin under a cup. But on the third try, when Alex lifts the cup, a large red rubber ball is there, instead of the expected coin. Erickson laughs heartily, enjoying the surprising illusion. He says, "Direction of attention is one of the fundamentals in hypnosis. I like to re-direct attention inwards to an object of imagination rather than to the outer surroundings." With a swift sleight of mind he turns our magic trick into a learning opportunity.

We ask Erickson a question that we asked of our most significant teachers, "Do you believe human nature is good or bad?" Erickson's answer reveals his unique perspective, reflected in his creative way of working with patients. He answers, "I believe there is something of value within people that needs to be expressed." He will show us how his therapy makes this happen.

He calls in Mary who has come for therapy. "Annellen," he says, "Hypnotize Mary." He observes carefully as she induces a trance using suggestions for relaxation, comfort and inward focus. After a few minutes, Erickson awakens Mary and asks her, "How do you feel after being hypnotized by Annellen?" He looks at her significantly as she recounts her experience, blinking and nodding. Erickson masterfully and subtly guides her back into trance. He says, "You can see that with her recollection of trance she begins to slip back in. I merely direct her ever so gently, and her unconscious does not rest." We watch him carefully to try to observe exactly what he is doing. Erickson senses our gaze and says, "Watch Mary, not me! All the answers are right there in her."

When we eventually leave the room so that he can work privately with Mary, we have already been transformed. Erickson has subtly given us greater confidence in our capacities to hypnotize and work with attention, and yet this is only the beginning.

In a little while he ushers us and the other students sitting in the waiting room back into his office. Erickson introduces us to the group, "This is M.A. and M.A." (Pronounced as Ma and Ma). He finds humor at many levels of meaning. The group of students all chuckle. They gracefully include our daughter in the learning. We begin to relax even more deeply as his stories unfold and our learning develops.

He smiles benevolently at the small group gathered around him and asks, "Do you know the difference between a buffalo and a bison?" We all search for a reply. He waits patiently, then answers with a smile, a slight tip of his head and a twinkle in his eye, "A buffalo is an animal. A bison is what you wash your face in!" When we hesitate, he hints that an Australian student would probably immediately catch the intended response. We all laugh as we recognize that he is stretching our boundaries by his humorous use of a homonym.

He activates what is of value in common human nature by involving himself and the people in the seminar. "You participate with the patient and then get the patient to start participating with you. Then they'll use their own potentialities." He spins out a story of a woman who was suffering from painful cancer. She doubts that she can control the pain and he explains how he helps her discover her abilities. Then he looks down, turning to our daughter who sits at his feet on the floor and says, "You don't know what hypnosis is, so go into trance to help your mother." (Annellen was pregnant with our son at the time.) The trance he induces not only helps with the comfortable birth of our son, but also illustrates his ideas, using our own motivations and needs, to feel his healing presence in action. He shares what he is and what he does as an opportunity for others to reflect. "I talk about my memories and associations, and you will think about yours," he says. We learned to learn from this, and others can as well.

We met with Erickson regularly for a number of years until his death. He had the unique capacity to be fully present for us and for all others at the same time. Perhaps this was because he brought his presence so wholeheartedly to every seminar and every session with his patients. He helped and taught people until close to the end of his life, giving his time without ambivalence. Practitioners sometimes struggle with feeling bored or distracted during sessions. Erickson was always excited and interested, curious about the moment he was in. When he said, "And you might wonder when you will make that discovery," he really meant it.

We have all known people who are able to draw on unique inner capacities to accomplish the unusual. For example, we were fortunate to discover a seemingly ordinary man who could fix any VCR. Whenever we brought him a VCR, he felt immediately curious: why wasn't it working? He began by looking at the machine very closely. Within minutes, he had figured out how to fix it, ingeniously devising creative methods using parts he already had. Erickson always enjoyed the challenge and the fun of making people function well. He was always curious. By perceiving carefully and fully, he knew what would best trigger people's resources to help them help themselves.

For Zen practitioners, enlightenment is that moment of absolute involvement, so fully engaged that there is room for nothing else. Erickson lived his enlightened life, expressed in each interaction and every intervention. And yet, at the same time, enlightenment is nothing special. It is found in the everyday moments, when we are just being authentically what we are. We saw Erickson invoke everyday, commonplace experiences. As a farmer's son, he knew the earth. He understood that life and health come forth from fertile soil. And he drew from the fertile soil of his patients' everyday lives, working with birth, marriage, sex, death, and sickness. When he assigned a task, such as climbing Squaw Peak, he knew from firsthand experience that going there could be inspiring and a source for learning. Or when he directed the insomniac to scrub his floor, he knew from his own experience the fatigue one gets from hard labor. He opened windows of opportunity through the everyday moments. And his patients would make healing discoveries.

Erickson believed that most of his important insights occurred in an altered state, so he valued the experience of hypnosis. He told us that he would synchronize his breathing with patients, to intuitively attune to them. He often went into trance with patients or between sessions to gain unconscious insights about them.

He had absolute faith in the capacities of the unconscious mind, and he instilled this faith in his patients. This capacity to invoke hope in another by instilling faith in the unconscious mind was Erickson's unique way of stimulating healing. No matter how limited or unhappy a person might be, Erickson always imagined their potential, the valuable quality that needed to be expressed. And he communicated this faith in creative ways: The patient who could not write, could draw a line or a circle. And so what she did know could link to what she did not know, and she didn't need to know how, just trust the process. The woman who lost a child could raise a plant. And so her unconscious could enjoy the miracle of life in a different way.

Erickson was able to heal his patients by giving them some kind of experience, which drew on their own intelligent, supportive, creative unconscious mind. He extended his healing presence by being fully present in himself, accepting his unconscious mind along with his rational mind. We have come a long way from Ma, Ma and yet we are still close. Our children have grown, and we have experienced many trances. We continue to use our unconscious minds, curious in each moment as new, wondering what discoveries will be made! ❋

MICHELE RITTERMAN

A clinical psychologist, Ritterman studied with Milton Erickson for seven years. She authored *Using Hypnosis in Family Therapy*, the first integration of hypnotherapy and family therapy. Active in Human rights, she authored *Hope under Siege* on terror, terrorism, torture, and human dignity. Ritterman runs a managed care free practice in Oakland, California, and has trained thousands of psychotherapists around the world in her methods of what she calls the shared and separate-track trances of couples and families.

I met Dr. Erickson after several years of studying and applying his work—through the classes and writings of Jay Haley, and through the first polished video tape of Erickson's work, "The Artistry of Milton H. Erickson, M.D.," filmed by Herbert Lustig, M.D. I arrived at Erickson's humble office with a great interest in his philosophy of life; his attitude seemed so positive, even though he was often wracked with physical pain. But during my precious time with him, my physiological insight was enhanced as much as my philosophy and realistic attitudes. I experienced with Erickson not so-called psychotherapy, but the essence of healing, which is something the body and the mind of the patient must do, and the therapist/healer may catalyze, if he or she is both skilled and lucky.

I have a kind of skepticism about communications from one person to the physiology of another. No matter how many times I've seen it and been lucky enough to facilitate it in my therapy practice, I always find these physiological responses to be amazing. Erickson was such an expert in these communications because he was a case par excellence of Physician Heal Thyself. And he used talking to his own physiology as a daily survival tool.

In one of my early cases, a lovely young girl came in with a trail of warts over her face. I remembered Erickson's teaching that patients must heal themselves and therapy is not about symptom elimination, so I asked her which wart she would want to save. She answered and I suggested she starve the blood supply to all but that one and the warts vanished within the next week. Erickson understood the need not merely to eliminate symptoms but to teach people to utilize and influence their own physiology and at even more complex levels than blood flow.

As Erickson's subject and student, I know that I hoped to impress him with my competence as a family therapy intern. I know that I sat in his office for what seemed a long time, feeling a bit impatient, but unconsciously belying much more about myself than I was aware of, while he worked with two other female students. But to my surprise and delight, he sent the other two women on one of his prescribed therapeutic adventure experiences. Then he turned to me with his slow abruptness and said, "Now I dismissed those two, so what is it you really want to talk about?"

Erickson did lots of seemingly offensive and outrageous things. That's part of what made his work great. He didn't care much what people thought of him, as long as what he was doing was in the interest of healing. He didn't disrespect the two other students. What he did was show me in one fell swoop, at an unconscious level, that he understood why I was silenced by the symbolic presence of two other women with the father figure in the room. Erickson conveyed that he'd protect me.

The following hours sped by in any clock time sense, and my pain was nearly unbearable. I shook unrelentingly and wept copiously and developed a terrible headache. But in my emotional pain I felt totally accepted by this man who was in a kind of visceral, palpable anguish of his own.

This was how I learned that polio was his mentor. But with pain and physical disabilities, this man had helped so many, produced such great students as Jay Haley and Kay Thompson, had eight children, and had turned Freudian psychology on its head. And he was not wallowing in his discomfort.

He told me many stories while I was going through my physiological changes. I taped the stories and listened years later, only to realize that I, who thought I had a bad memory, remembered almost to the word, every story he told me while I suffered through these psycho-physiological waves. But it was in these waves that the deepest and enduring change took place.

"The salt water will subside," he said.

When it did, and I looked at him from a different state of mind, on the verge of shame for having exposed myself inappropriately, because I'd come as a student of Jay Haley, he said calmly, "Now, we can talk about anything you like." That sentence was a complete transformation of all I'd learned about therapy until that moment. I realized that what we talk about is not the therapy. It is only a vehicle for the therapy, which is in the connection between the healer and the person being healed and in the relationship between the person being healed and his/her untapped resources.

I chattered happily about my difficult case—the young man whose father drew a knife on him in my session, whose mother was molesting him, and who'd been diagnosed schizophrenic. I left feeling very professional.

The next day when I returned with my terrible throbbing headache, he was delighted like a child who has gotten the answer to a question. He had asked something of me, and my body had produced a physiological response. I believe now that his question was about my family—he'd asked me about my parents and my sister and he'd suggested I develop a physical response that would tell me and him on an unconscious level, in code, what I felt about my family.

And then he worked with me to find my own skin, where I started and finished, my boundaries from family members, my rights to autonomy and freedom. He worked with the physiological context.

After one seven-hour session, he said, "Now it feels like someone's been rolling a baseball bat up and down my spinal column. So I think we're done for the day."

I'd never suffered physical pain, yet my body experienced a kind of sympathetic unrelenting pressure while I discussed my cases with Dr. Erickson that I believe was related to the pain he was distancing himself from in order to attend to the work at hand. In this way I felt he exposed and shared his own vulnerability and pain, again, protecting me from having so exposed my own vulnerability.

Much of my healing was about my having children. I was under what I would later write about fluently as a family trance that culminated in my feeling that I was doomed to be a bad parent and wasn't cut out to have children. Erickson told me many stories about his children, but especially the three girls who were closest to my age. In so doing, in the way he did it, he gave me a kind of honorary child status. He told me about Betty Alice who he'd done trance demonstrations with—how one night she refused to cooperate with the suggestions he made during a group demonstration. He used this story to help me feel I had the right not to live up to parental expectations. At the conclusion of the Betty Alice story, he said dramatically, "Anything expected should be denied." I realized from that dramatic phrase, that a father could take pride in his daughter's autonomy. He told me about how his daughter Roxie was offered a high-level nursing job, a real plum, but she realized that she'd be understaffed and thereby doomed to failure. So she rejected that job offer. He told me lots of Kristi stories, because she and I are "the babies." We both knew how to be good and bad, so we knew twice as much as the kid who just knew how to be good. He showed me a card from Betty Alice that said on the front "When you look out into the night sky and see the stars and envision the planets and watch the big moon, doesn't it all make you feel tiny and insignificant?" and inside it says, "Me, neither."

So now I was with my pain and the feelings that I was unworthy to parent, and I was laughing. And I was loving these brassy daughters I hadn't met yet. And I was getting some honorary daughter status as well. And I got to be good in the eyes of a very critical parent. Now that is healing

I say critical parent because Erickson went to great lengths to show me he was no milk-toast. I might have interpreted easy acceptance as meaning he'd missed all my dreadful qualities. By demonstrating his high standards throughout our time together, when he did accept me, I knew he really accepted me, the good and the bad, and that in fact he greatly admired daughters, like me, who stood up for what they believed.

Somehow Erickson broke a spell I'd fallen under from the hypnosis of my family. His instruction to my unconscious was seminal and had a visceral effect. After one session, while I was swimming at the hotel pool, my brain fired like the fourth of July. I felt my synapses firing. I had needed to feel a kind of new connection with my own body, my own sense of myself as a woman, my independence from my family in order to move on to the next stage of development, and I got it.

Erickson told me that his doctor had once told him he'd never move again, so to get movement, he remembered swinging from an apple tree. As he recalled his gripping motion, a finger in his right hand moved! As with much of Erickson's research, he preferred to prove the exception rather than the statistical likelihood of a thing. Once he'd proved the doctor wrong, he was determined to reclaim his own body.

I made a first embroidered gift for him and Betty, when, after a remarriage ceremony he did with my then husband and me, I was on the trip where I got pregnant with my first child, Miranda. After I got pregnant with my son, Judah, I embroidered an apple tree in purple thread on a purple background, with apples made of Indian fabric mirrors, and the whole tree an exact replica of the veins and arteries of the human heart, upside down. Below it was a basket with eight apples—one for each of his and Betty's children—inscribed with the words "Memory Awakens Physiology." Just as Erickson had made me an honorary daughter, he and Betty are the honorary godparents for my children.

Erickson helped me remember—to find where my memory had stored—the happiness and hopefulness I needed to break free from people who could not wish me well, so I could enjoy my life.

Memory Awakens Physiology—that was one of Erickson's many healing lessons. ✵

RONALD H. BOYLE, M.D.

Boyle earned a B.S.M., allowing him to teach, concurrently with his M.D., which included honors in psychiatry, at the University of Arkansas School of Medicine in 1964. After medical school, he became a captain in the USAF, where he served as a flight medical officer. After a residency in psychiatry at the University of Arkansas in 1967–70, he established the Ozark Clinic in Arkansas in 1976, and founded the Milton H. Erickson Institute of Arkansas at Halycon Ranch in Paron, Arkansas in 1993.

WHEN I WAS FIRST INTRODUCED to Erickson's work, I was a resident in psychiatry. I found him too difficult to understand and even wondered why I should be interested in an elderly person confined to a wheelchair. I wanted the young, vital, new psychiatry!

A decade later, after I witnessed his work on video and audio tapes. I immediately decided to arrange a visit. To my surprise he answered the phone and asked, "Why do you want to see me?"

At my first visit, Erickson asked what I wanted and I replied, "I want to be you!"

"Don't do it," he said. "You can be yourself so much better."

I followed Erickson's instructions to go into a trance. I didn't think I was going into a trance. I just didn't want to disappoint him. And initially I felt no awe.

I asked him if he would help me experience anxiety; I rarely consciously felt fear because I was so aggressive. He seemed to ignore me, focused on other people in the group, and I soon forgot my request. Six weeks later, I began to experience relentless free-floating anxiety! After our second meeting, I felt a resolution of this feeling.

I often cautioned my peers that it they visited Erickson, they should be very careful what they asked for. Now I certainly had a strong feeling of awe.

But my most common and consistent feeling with Erickson—one that has endured—was trust. I know many people will not consider trust a true feeling. However I evaluate the world initially with my gut, my muscles, my bones, and then check it out with my brain. Trust is a basic feeling to me. My perception was that Erickson acted and responded according to what was best for the other. He helped me take risks in therapy and life. And my essential learning was to trust the patient's capacities and abilities to move forward.

Once I was approached about treating a good friend's mother who had remained depressed after the death of her husband. I was told I couldn't tell her that I was there to assess or treat her, nor could I tell her if I recommended anti-depressants. In the Ozark Mountains, a psychiatrist can be as much "feared of."

Ozark Mountain culture ensured me an invitation to visit the woman as well as an offer of something to drink. As she fixed coffee, she asked how I was doing. She knew I was going through a personal loss. I responded that I was depressed and began to describe my authentic symptoms, which were exactly like hers.

She immediately began to tell me what to do—to get over it, not to let my depression get me down. She said I needed to get up and let go and get on with it as I still had a life to live. And that is exactly what she did, after doing her own therapy on herself. I could not charge her a fee; after all, she was the one who gave me advice.

Utilize what's available because there are unlimited capacities in your patient and in yourself—this is what Erickson taught me.

His presence then and now has encouraged me to keep my ego

out of conflict, to do at any given moment what is best for the other. This has been a very painful, albeit successful, journey, requiring a long and persistent effort.

After Dr. Erickson's death, he came to me in a dream. He was standing over me as I lay in bed. The place was my cabin in the Ozark Mountains near the Buffalo River. My question to him was, "What do I need to change or do about myself?"

Dr. Erickson answered in a typical way. "Nothing. You are okay. Just as you are."

Dr. Erickson, the healer was—and is—consistently validating the other person.

I want to thank Mrs. Erickson and the Erickson family for sharing him with all of us! His spirit is always with me. I consider him a guardian angel. ✴

RICK LANDIS

A clinical psychologist, Landis is the executive editor for the Milton H. Erickson Foundation *Newsletter* and the director of training for the Southern California Society for Ericksonian Psychotherapy and Hypnosis. Board certified in traumatology, he holds diplomate status in the areas of integrated medicine, behavioral medicine, and psychopharmacology. He has been a well-received faculty member for numerous Ericksonian conferences as well as for other organizations.

WHEN I FIRST MET ERICKSON, I was primarily a causal linear thinker; step-by-step, digital, one straight line from beginning to end. Now, I am more systemic in my thinking; every direction provides the possibility of a different view. Therefore, my musings on Erickson as a healer and how he affected my life will have the flight path of a mildly deranged butterfly. Each thought opens me to other thoughts. They all fit. Like a box of specialty Lego® pieces that can be put together in countless, marvelous ways to reveal different aspects of the puzzle that was Erickson.

I first met him when a group of colleagues and I attended one of the small seminars at his home in Phoenix. Before we met, Erickson asked us to write what we wanted to accomplish at the seminar. At that time, I needed certainty. I was looking for the TRUTH in therapy: how to know what was the RIGHT thing to do with each patient. Rather than being filled with certainty by the end of the seminar, I remember being filled with feelings of confusion. I left no longer knowing what it was that I wanted.

As the weeks and months passed, I found I had an insatiable desire to understand what Erickson did with us during that and subsequent meetings. Gary Ruelas, Terry Argast, and I, from the original seminars group, met once a week for over 10 years just to analyze the hours of video and audio tape and related materials we acquired in those meetings with Erickson. We were obsessed with his technique and elegant deliveries. Each tone and inflection was overanalyzed. We were "men on a mission." We were still trying to understand how to do it RIGHT. However, my feelings of confusion only got worse as I focused on the techniques. I understood more of what Erickson was doing, but I felt that I was still missing something big.

Over the years, I have come to realize why clinicians who have the Erickson techniques mastered but lack the Erickson heart have so much less success than Erickson had. The techniques were important, but the heart was the magic. Erickson did not do therapy; he was therapy. He inspired people to activate their own inner healing and growth by his being. Erickson gave total acceptance of what it meant to be human. When I was in his presence, I felt total acceptance of who I was and who I could be.

In retrospect I can see how Erickson taught and attempted to instill that magic in me. I remember a time when I asked him why he had accepted me as a student, since he had greatly reduced his one-to-one contacts as his health was diminishing. He said he accepted me because he enjoyed working with a student who looked at the world through the eyes of an eight-year-old (a comment that my colleagues often said about me). In what was to be my last meeting with him before he died, I again asked Erickson if I had improved at all. He said, "Yes, you now looked at the world through the eyes of a six-year-old. You're getting there." He sponsored and nurtured my perspective of wonder, fascination, and seeing old things with new eyes more than just my competency in learning the techniques.

At some point in my life, all of Erickson's teachings came together for me and static certainty was no longer a desired goal. I was able to internalize the Erickson I knew who was never wedded to his conclusions. As soon as a person responded to an intervention, Erickson would readjust his thinking to accommodate the new information. The nature of the interaction determined the truth of the interaction. That was the core of his acceptance. With my internalization of that, I no longer had that tension-reducing release of energy that comes with reaching a conclusion. I once heard someone say that we reach a conclusion at the point that we are tired of thinking. I was curious to discover whether the answers explain all aspects of the question or if they merely stopped my thinking and avoided the deeper aspect of the question. As a result of Erickson's gentle (and not always so gentle) influences, there is now just a constant and gentle hum where all conclusions are experienced as beginning points for further clarifications and understandings. And, there is an excitement at discovering a new beginning with each conclusion. There is an infinite variety of points-of-view and perspectives on any thought. There is no place for a final conclusion in understanding what it means to be human and the infinite ways that people express their humanness.

The Erickson I knew valued observing without having expectations. In the same way the nature of the question biases the answers, so expectations bias the observation. It is human nature to have confirmation biases: As I have often observed, some things have to be believed in order to be seen. In our interactions with other humans, the less "believed" about them, the more we can learn and be delighted by their uniqueness.

I have three friends that I acquired from Erickson: Confusion,

Doubt, and Curiosity. Confusion reminds me that I do not have enough information to understand that which I want to understand. Doubt keeps me from being satisfied with my current answers. And Curiosity gives me the positive energy to move through the confusion and doubt to find something I had not understood before.

Over the years, I've continued to try to view the world through the eyes of a child. With each layer of age I peal off, I see things with fewer expectations and still have the older aspects of myself with all their resources left intact. It is as though I can look through the faceted eyes of a dragonfly, seeing many perspectives at the same time. I learned that from Erickson by his example. Erickson had both the wisdom of the patriarch and the guilelessness of the child. He was ageless. I remember when Terry Argast, my colleague, was sitting in "the hot seat" during one of Erickson's seminars and Erickson was trying to induce arm levitation. Dr. Argast was resisting mightily and the hand refused to budge. Erickson just paused and turned his head to face Dr. Argast. Erickson then tilted his head in a look of expectation and a child-like twinkle sparkled from his eyes. Dr. Argast laughed and the arm took flight with a mind of its own.

Each age has its own developmental lens. Each builds from an experiential and neurological platform and interprets the environment to help satisfy a particular developmental task. By being able to identify with any age, it is easy to resonate with the developmental level of my patients and to immediately be there with them. It is not a technique. There is only the being. Erickson embodied a respect for the natural progression of human development, which manifests not so much as a decision as a realization. The child within me wants to play with the patient's child. Instant acceptance and understanding. And the next older child within me knows where the patient needs to go. Gentle urgings and awakenings with the help of occasional confusion to move the logjams are all that is needed. Each patient has the natural pressure to move to the next level. And I hear Erickson's voice say to me, "That right." ✳

ERIC GREENLEAF

The first recipient of the Milton H. Erickson Award of Scientific Excellence for Writing in Hypnosis, Greenleaf is a clinical psychologist with a private practice in Albany, California. He is the director of the Milton H. Erickson Institute of the Bay Area and teaches hypnosis throughout the world. Greenleaf has extensively researched trance and healing in Bali. His book, *The Problem of Evil: Ancient Dilemmas and Modern Therapy*, was published in 2000.

DR. ERICKSON ONCE SAID: "When you look back in your life, you'd like to see that you've left a trail of happiness behind you." Coming to know Dr. Erickson meant coming to know my own family and friends in a different way; it has also meant coming to know myself.

My first experience with hypnosis was at age eight at summer camp when my father stretched a volunteer between the backs of two chairs. Impressive! I never remember my mother giving me a direct order. Years later, I realized she was an expert at distraction and indirect suggestion. My grandmother, who lived with us, taught with stories and taught me how to observe people and value their individual struggles to live their lives well. When I was a graduate student I took a hypnosis course from Erika Fromm. I couldn't remember a thing from those classes but I would race home to put my roommate into trances. A year later another student, knowing I'd taken a course in hypnosis, gave me an article by Dr. Erickson. I read it and said, "Oh, that's how you do therapy!"

In 1970, my doctoral dissertation, "Developmental Stage Regression Through Hypnosis," was published in shorter form in the *American Journal of Clinical Hypnosis*, and Dr. Erickson chose it (and me) to receive the first Milton H. Erickson Award for Excellence in Scientific Writing in Hypnosis. He was ill during the time of the award ceremony, so I didn't meet him.

That same year I began a private practice in Berkeley, and a couple of years later started a private consultation group in my home to teach

Ericksonian hypnotherapy. One of my students was Jeff Zeig, who later left to study with Dr. Erickson and who gave him the great gift of The Milton H. Erickson Foundation and the worldwide Institutes.

My first meeting with Dr. Erickson took place in 1979, during the last months of his life, when I joined a group of Kaiser therapists for a week-long seminar at his home in Phoenix. I had read large portions of Erickson's work in Jay Haley's compilation of his papers, *Advanced Techniques in Hypnosis and Therapy*, but somehow I would drift off into trance while reading them. I always thought them exceptionally clear, perceptive, witty, and inventive papers, written with a thick and apt vocabulary. They were like an alchemical mix of the best of Jung, Sullivan, and Bruner, and, of course, distinctly and deliciously Erickson. I loved his way of mixing truism and eccentric observation, individual feeling and social relations into the stock-pot of trance.

Meeting Erickson was wonderful! Despite being in pain, confined to a wheelchair, tiring easily, despite having lost most of the use of one of his hands and much of his articulation, he embodied strength, presence, humor, and loving attentiveness.

Erickson had huge stacks of stuff all over his office. I remember seeing a 100,000-mile airline passenger certificate. I remember seeing (although I don't think I could have) a mounted deer head. And he had stacks of papers and letters and photos. He told us that he would hallucinate the oval hooked rug at his feet spiraling up, flying up beside him, to distract him from his pain.

For the week we were with him, he told stories for four or five hours a day, and people would go in and out of trance as he spoke. Then he would reach into one of the piles and say, "And here is a picture of the child she had," or show some other incontrovertible "proof" of a reality changed through imagination and healing. Once he asked for a volunteer to read a letter. I volunteered and found myself reading a letter from a patient who had come to see me after Dr. Erickson had dismissed him. I couldn't get anywhere with the patient. Dr. Erickson had refused to see the man, knowing he couldn't help him. I resisted the chance to think that Dr. Erickson was tele-pathic or clairvoyant.

But what was clear was the intense feelings of the people Erickson worked with. These feelings set them into new motion, new patterns from which inner healing and social resolution flowed. When we left at the end of the week with Dr. Erickson, many of us cried, some kissed him. We all received inscribed books, signed in his shaky hand. I think mine said, "May you get what you wish." In all the years since then, I have, with much halting, backing, and filling, gotten much of what I wished.

In 1988, however in an event far from what I wished, I was hit by a car while walking. My recovery was greatly influenced by having read Dr. Erickson's physician's story of a similar sudden injury. The physician, Dr. Robert Pearson, wrote that he wished Milton Erickson were there, but since he wasn't, Pearson had to "do it himself."

This is close to my understanding of healing. We each do it ourselves in the background atmosphere formed by all the teachers in our lives.

The concept of the benign unconscious mind leads almost directly to the useful notion of trust in oneself; this "doing it yourself, in your own way in your own good time," as Dr. Erickson often advised, is healing in itself.

He liked to say, "No one knows the future." I like to imagine he said it in impossible situations of high stakes and low odds where he wished to say something that might mobilize a reorganization leading to possible healing. I say it to my patients when they are in those situations. You have to live. You have to celebrate what needs celebrating. You have to prune unnecessary things and people, the deadwood, so you can grow. You have to say what you need to say. You have to keep on living while you're living.

That is how Dr. Erickson approached life too. I am glad he was so clear in everything he said to people so that each person could make their own deep sense of what he said and use it to their own good purposes. That is healing.

A friend of mine, a Zen priest, was asked at her induction into office the traditional question, "Who is this I see before me?" Dr. Erickson often asked that question of people in trance. "Who are you now?" and, "Who am I to you now?" My friend answered, "Can't help it!"

Dr. Erickson had that quality—that intense, caring, "Can't help it!" about being the person he happened to have become, through all his lived experience. And he transduced this sense to his patients and students: to utilize their unconscious learning, rely on themselves, meet an unknown future, enjoy living life. Best of all, his healing was not solipsistic. It was and is always in the presence of family, friends, teachers, and our ancestors. It and he and the healing itself, and the rich, powerful effects his teaching has had on my life, are best expressed in his most famous saying, delivered in his effort to help heal another person's pain: "And my voice will go with you. And my voice will change into that of your parents, your neighbors, your friends, your schoolmates, your playmates, your teachers." ✶

STEPHEN GILLIGAN, PH.D.

A student of Milton Erickson from 1974–1977, Gilligan earned his doctorate from Stanford University. In addition to private practice, he teaches Ericksonian hypnotherapy and his own approach of Self-Relations psychotherapy integrating Erickson's work with aikido, Buddhism, and performance arts throughout the world. Author of seven books, including *Therapeutic Trances*, *The Courage to Love*, *The Legacy of Erickson*, and *Walking in Two Worlds*, he received the Lifetime Achievement Award for Outstanding Contributions to the Field of Psychotherapy from the Milton H. Erickson Foundation in 2004. His website is www.StephenGilligan.com.

And it was at that age…poetry arrived
in search of me. I don't know, I don't know where
it came from, from winter or a river.
I don't know how or when,
no, they were not voices, they were not
words, not silence,

but from a street it called me,
from the branches of night,
abruptly from the others,
among raging fires
or returning alone,
there it was, without a face
and it touched me.

> —Pablo Neruda, "Poetry" from *Isla Negra: A Notebook*
> (1982), Alastair Reid translation

I was without a face and it touched me: Milton Erickson as a healer
I WAS AWAKENED by the healing presence of Milton Erickson in
1974. A young man of 19 years, I was a confused but intensely curious undergraduate student in psychology at U.C. Santa Cruz. The
previous year had seen me drop out of college and descend into a
dark pit of depression and suicidal thoughts, which led to a sort of
death and rebirth process. When I returned to college, I met Gregory
Bateson, an old colleague and friend of Erickson's, and then John
Grinder and Richard Bandler. Through these connections, I soon had
the luck of meeting Milton Erickson.

That meeting changed my life forever, and Erickson's legacy has
absorbed much of my life path over the past 30 years (e.g., see
Gilligan, 1987; 2002). One thing about Erickson is clear: Like most
people, he had many different identities—psychiatrist, father,
researcher, journal editor, mentor, practical joker, lover of nature, and
more. He had a keen intellect and was deeply grounded in social
realities; he was an exceptional communicator and a therapist without peer. He taught in medical school, founded and edited an
academic journal, and worked tirelessly with psychiatric patients for
close to five decades. But along with these rational and worldly
achievements, Milton Erickson was also a great healer.[1] Given his
heroic efforts to distinguish hypnosis as a reputable therapeutic
modality, it is understandable that this aspect of Erickson has been

1. In using the term "healer,"
I wish to make it clear that
I am not invoking super-
natural forces or ascribing
magical powers to Erickson.
He worked all his life to
emphasize his work in terms
of basic (though usually
unconscious) processes,
accessed by certain states of
attention and intention. On
the other hand, by using the
term "healer" I deliberately
hope to extend an under-
standing of Erickson beyond
merely mechanistic or mate-
rialistic notions.

338

relatively ignored. However, this oversight has led, in my view, to an incomplete understanding of his work and the possible paths it illuminates for other serious therapeutic practitioners. What I would like to do in the following pages is sketch a few aspects on the path of the healer, and how Erickson walked it, in hopes that others may discover the courage and capacity to find their own paths as healers.

Walking in two worlds: The ground of the healer's gift
One of Erickson's greatest skills was his capacity to operate in two "realities" simultaneously: the interior world and the exterior world. His "inner work" (with a dazzling array of naturalistic trance experiences) showed the infinite possibilities of consciousness; his "outer work" (with all sorts of directives to act differently in the social world) showed many creative paths for shifting a person's identity; and his skill at holding both worlds simultaneously gave him a special capacity as a healer.

I think none of his students have come close to emulating Erickson's remarkable "bi-nocular" balance—this beautiful capacity to operate at the intersection of the two worlds, and in so doing, have a greater depth of vision. Part of the problem, in my view, is that Erickson has been primarily viewed from the traditional Western "mono-nocular" view of external reality being the only viable and "real" world. Bateson pointed out the dangers of this limited understanding, especially in understanding Erickson's work, in an interview with Brad Keeney (1977):

KEENEY: *You're saying that people who go to see Erickson come away with a craving for power?*
BATESON: *Yes! They all want power.*
KEENEY: *Is there something about seeing (Erickson) that induces this power hungriness?*
BATESON: *Well, it's the skill which he has of manipulating the other person which really in the long run does not separate him as an ego*

dominant to the other person. He works in the weave of the total complex and they come away with a trick which is separate from the total complex, therefore goeth counter to it, and becomes a sort of power. I think it's something like that. (p. 49)

The capacity to work within the "weave of the total complex" suggests an experience of "internal relatedness," a process of mindfully entering within the interior of a communal field of consciousness. In their remarkable book, *A General Theory of Love*, Lewis, Amini, and Lannon (2000) describe this process of an interpersonal neural hook-up as "limbic resonance":

"To the animals capable of bridging the gap between minds, limbic resonance is the door to communal connection. Limbic resonance supplies the wordless harmony we see everywhere but take for granted—between mother and infant, between a boy and his dog, between lovers holding hands across a restaurant table. This silent reverberation between minds is so much a part of us that, like the noiseless machinations of the kidney or the liver, it functions smoothly and continuously without our notice." (p.64)

By intentionally and mindfully using this process of "limbic resonance," I think Erickson was able to enter a person's interior consciousness, expand it and relocate it within a more vast, resourceful field of which he was a part, and then work within this healing field for therapeutic purposes.

Initiation of Others into the Deeper World

This sense of a communal healing field was present in my first meeting with Erickson. I had some strange sense that this is what I had been waiting for all my life. I surely went into a sort of trance, the first of many with Erickson. I felt in his presence something wondrous, vibrating, and alive. I vividly remember an image arising from deep within me, an image of an "American Freud"—a sort of conventional, uptight, dissociated analyst-type with patches on a

340

tweed jacket, pipe in mouth, and massive emotional constipation. It was an image of who I thought I should be when I "grew up"— you see, I knew from an early age that I would be a therapist. (I sometimes joke that one look at my family would make it clear that somebody in that mess needed to be a therapist!)

I surely assumed that to be a good professional or, for that matter, a responsible citizen, you needed to embody that disconnected, emotionally constipated, up-in-the-head consciousness. Erickson, with his sparkling shaman-like presence, coupled with his exceptional professional achievements and talents, exploded that image into a thousand pieces, never to be reassembled again. In its place was a deep encouragement to be myself, to go deep within and find happiness in my own unique ways while also helping others. This was my first healing with Milton Erickson.

Other deep learnings soon followed. Milton Erickson was the first person I met who was clearly better at trance than I. I wasn't good at much else, but I learned a lot about living in a trance while growing up in a violent, alcoholic, Irish Catholic family (some would say that's redundant). Meeting Erickson was a little like the scene in the movie, *Close Encounters of the Third Kind*, where the simple musical pattern offered to the extra-terrestrial spaceship is met with an incredibly more complex and beautiful pattern. Erickson could dance circles around me in the inner space of consciousness, and I felt like I had finally met my teacher. More importantly, he was using trance in a fundamentally different way than I had ever imagined. Rather than using trance to dissociate "away from" the living world of human connection, which is the only way I had ever used it in the trauma-field of my boyhood, Erickson was using trance to "move into" human connection. In other words, he was using it as a healing process.

As I attuned to his hypnotic rhythms, I found myself in a vast, seemingly infinite, inner space. I felt surrounded by a loving presence, and touched by an inner spirit. This spirit offered freedom to explore anything, to be open to everything, and to be curious about all the possibilities. Later, I realized that this was the spirit of healing, the spirit that Erickson embodied that touched many lives in profound ways.

This connection awakened something in me that I don't think I will (or can) ever forget, despite my periodic efforts to do so. It showed me that however big problems seem to be, there is always a deeper, wider space of possibility and healing that is available. (Most importantly, the latter is a generative field for the former.) It showed me that when I feel too restricted, too limited, or too upset, that I am forgetting my membership in an infinite world of spirit. And that when a wound or trauma needs healing or an identity calls for transformation, there is an inner world with immense intelligence and wisdom that can absorb, hold, guide, and allow such a journey. In short, these trance experiences with Milton Erickson initiated me into an awareness of a great consciousness far beyond what we usually settle for.

The Path of the Wounded Healer

In many ways, Erickson's personal life followed the classic profile of the wounded healer as described by many writers (Campbell, 1949, 1973; Moore & Gillette, 1993; Eliade, 1958; Turner, 1969), summarized by Campbell (1973):

"The usual pattern is, first, of a break away or departure from the local social order and context; next, a long, deep retreat inward and backward, as it were, in time, and inward, deep into the psyche; a chaotic series of encounters there, darkly terrifying experiences, and presently (if the victim is fortunate) encounters of a centering kind, fulfilling, harmonizing, giving new courage; and then finally, in such fortunate cases, a return journey of rebirth to life (p. 208)."

In Erickson's case, this departure from the normal social order began early. Life dealt him an interesting nervous system. He experienced an unusual form of color blindness (so that he could only "enjoy" purple); he was arrhythmic and tone deaf, so what we experience as music was not available to him; and he was dyslectic.

One aspect of his dyslexia was that he didn't realize that the dictionary was alphabetized until he was a teenager![2] In a deep sense, all these early experiences placed him in a position "at the edge of the village," the classic place of the shaman/healer.

This pattern of separation intensified with a severe polio attack at the age of 17. A major wound to a young man right around the time of initiation into adulthood is a classic sign of the healer in traditional cultures (cf. Eliade, 1958; Moore and Gillette, 1994). Erickson's body lay paralyzed (except for his eyes), and he was told by doctors he would never walk again. This prompted an intensive series of "experiments in learning," what he would later call "deep self-hypnotic trances," to explore the possibilities of inner healing. Extraordinarily, he found through the connection to inner resources and a "creative unconscious" a way to rehabilitate his body (see Erickson and Rossi, 1977). He walked again with the aid of a cane, and was physically very active. At 46, he was felled by severe serum sickness from a tetanus shot, nearly dying from it. From then until he died in early 1980 at the age of 79, he was periodically bedridden and chronically pain-afflicted with various ailments, perhaps as part of a post-polio syndrome.[3] Throughout all of these immense challenges, he used his connection to the interior world not only to survive but to continue to enjoy life.

As an example of his journeys through strange interior worlds, he recounted to me how when he was paralyzed from polio, he couldn't sense his body in space. He knew he had a left arm, but he could not for the life of him sense where it was in space. Maybe it was over there, no, maybe over there, oh, perhaps over there. He knew he had a left foot, but he couldn't image where it was in space or in relation to his right hand. As Erickson described this sort of jumbled syntax of body parts, I thought of the Scarecrow in the The Wizard of Oz, his limbs thrown every which way.

What was amazing about this experience, and all the others described above, was his relation to them. He was not a bitter or

2. For a fuller description of Erickson's personal challenges and his creative ways of dealing with them, see Erickson and Rossi (1980e), Rossi, Ryan, & Sharp (1983), and Zeig (1985).

3. A more complete description of Erickson's long struggle with physical ailments is given by his wife, Elizabeth Erickson, in Zeig, 1985.

defeated man. On the contrary, his eyes would twinkle as he described them as opportunities for learning. Life threw so many strange things at him, and he responded by going "deeper and wider," by finding a deep place of interior consciousness ("trance") where he could allow a wise intelligence ("the unconscious") to join him and help him accept all these realities as opportunities for learning.

The Return of the Healer into the Community

It was this hard-won acceptance and curiosity about using difficult experiences to grow and develop as a human being, especially with inner trance states as a resource, that Erickson brought back into the community. This capacity to skillfully enter and transform painful states of suffering was the basis for his success as a healer and psychiatrist. For the first several decades of his psychiatric career, he worked primarily with psychotic patients in inpatient hospital settings. He found out pretty fast that they couldn't enter his reality, so if he wanted to establish communication he would need to enter their realities. His collected works (Erickson, 1980a, b, c, d) reveal a breathtaking capacity to intuitively work with severely disturbed patients. With a patient who could only speak "word salad," Erickson spent months studying recordings of the man's speech patterns and then spoke "word salad" to develop rapport, gradually adding other types of communications over the course of therapy. With another patient who believed he was Jesus Christ, Erickson put him to work as a carpenter on a hospital building project.

With all of his patients, Erickson exhibited a remarkable compassion and understanding of non-rational states of consciousness, and was exceptionally skillful at guiding people through such inner realms for therapeutic gains. He used the traditional tools of a healer/ shaman: deep trances, metaphorical stories, temporal/spatial disorientation, confusion and surprise, non-rational communications, intense interpersonal absorption, and many other experiential-symbolic methods. He believed in the value of disrupting the social order of ordinary consciousness as a pathway into deeper realms, and then finding ways to integrate these learnings back into the consensus world. He was not interested in intellectual understanding so much as the experiential transformation of consciousness so that new realities and possibilities could emerge. These are all essential aspects of a healer.

But while he had dazzling technical prowess and mesmerizing presence, at the heart of his healing capacity was his love and compassion for his patients. This is often overlooked in the published accounts of Erickson, partly because it is difficult to convey in words. But I believe that his exceptional ability to enter and gently affirm a person's deepest identity was responsible for much of his success. Patients and students trusted him and thus opened to his influence in no small part because his heart was kind and generous. This "discerning heart of compassion" is an integral part to the healer's approach, and I think Erickson embodied it thoroughly.

Passing on the Lineage

Like other young students who studied with Erickson in his final years, I never paid him any money. This was good, since I was a very poor college student and my family had no money to speak of! Of course, I fully expected to pay him, and asked him how much it would cost to study with him, confident that I could secure a student loan. He looked at me intensely with twinkling eyes and said, "Oh, that's all right. You don't have to pay me anything. The way you can repay me is that whatever you find helpful for yourself here, pass it on to others. That's how you can repay me!" I sometimes joke that I wish I would have just paid the old man off to satisfy my debt once and for all, but it is only a joke. I feel that Erickson embodied a certain lineage of healers that is so needed in the world today, and I am grateful to have "received the transmission" and in my own small way, to try to pass it on.

That's my intent in writing this paper. There is a general consensus that Milton Erickson was one of the great psychotherapists of the last century. He was unorthodox but highly effective and ethical. In seeking to understand the nature of his work, we need to appreciate that there were many facets to the jewel: scientific rigor, steely determination and commitment, endless delight in the complexities of human behavior, exceptional commitment to professional standards, remarkable mentorship of students, and a deep connection to the archetypal path of the healer. I have focused on this "healer" facet, suggesting it was deeply present in Erickson but not sufficiently emphasized by his students. I have noted a few crucial aspects of the healer's path, especially in terms of the "hero's journey" of (a) connection to the regular order of consciousness, (b) the "break" and descent into a deeper "unconscious" where many thresholds and challenges are navigated, and (c) the return back to the community with the new expanded identity of self. I suggested that in going through this hero's journey, Erickson had the healer's skill to help many others on their own "hero's journey."

The point of all of this is not to deify Erickson, but to encourage others to find their own "hero's journey." My intent is to nurture an archetype whose presence is needed in today's difficult times. Those of us who feel a "calling" to help others can be encouraged by Erickson's example to go deeply through our path and to help others to do the same. We can experientially realize that "reality" is much richer and more alive than we often sense; that there is a vast and deep interior space ("the unconscious") that can be safely explored for therapeutic gains; and that there is great intelligence within and around us, far beyond the disembodied intellect with which we too often become identified. We can realize that problems are not to be feared; that wounds are openings to a deeper consciousness; that symptoms and other's non-rational expressions can be seen as natura-listic attempts at healing; and that life's setbacks and challenges are great opportunities for learning and healing. In engaging with these challenges, we are guided by Erickson's "utilization" principle that encourages deep acceptance of difficult experiences; a safe and effec-tive absorption of them into a deeper realm of a healing consciousness; and then skillfully engaging with them with a consciousness imbued with a fierce/tender/playful presence that is curious about how they may be transformed. From the healer's perspective, we can see that this "utilization" principle is not just an intellectual concept to be flatly applied, but a relational process that requires the presence of all of our heart, mind, and soul. It is indeed a hard and difficult path requiring great commitment and ongoing learning, but also a rewarding path that allows us to truly enjoy life, to sense it as sacred and precious, and to enjoy the possibilities of healing and transformation that are always present.

In seeing the healer in Erickson, we can begin to claim it within ourselves. In doing so, we understand more deeply the wise words of the great Sufi poet, Rumi:

> *The inner being of a human being*
> *Is a jungle. Sometimes wolves dominate,*
> *Sometimes wild hogs. Be wary when you breathe!*
>
> *At one moment gentle, generous qualities,*
> *like Josephs' pass from one nature to another.*
> *The next moment vicious qualities move in hidden ways.*
>
> *At every moment a new species arises in the chest—*
> *now a demon, now an angel, now a wild animal.*
>
> *There are also those in this amazing jungle*
> *Who can absorb you into their own surrender.*
> *If you have to stalk and steal something,*
> *steal from them.*

BETTY ALICE ERICKSON

AS I HAVE WORKED ON THIS BOOK, I have been excited, humbled, awed, joyful, tearful, weary, sometimes discouraged, but most of all grateful. The previous chapter of contributions from Dad's colleagues and friends has given me even more appreciation of his incredible abilities, of the way he was able to touch and give to so many. I feel even more enriched by him.

Dad was just a man, but what a man! He was a profoundly complex person, but paradoxically, he was also quite uncomplicated. He was very human, with very human flaws and failings but a person who truly enjoyed every day of his life. Despite multiple physical limitations, despite health problems some of which were extremely painful, he liked life and he loved being alive.

Over the years, I have been told many wonderful things about my dad. Many I am sure are absolutely true, others, I believe are the oft-told stories true in the heart of the person telling me. I do know, however, that many of the ways in which Dad connected with others are un-understandable—true to that person, un-understandable to others.

I don't know how he could have an apparently casual conversation with someone about a seemingly innocuous topic, and that person's life would be changed dramatically and they wouldn't even know why. But they would absolutely know that Dad had been the catalyst, the mechanism, for why they had changed.

I don't know how within a minute or two of meeting, he could inspire a person to trust him totally. But he did that. And I sure don't know how he achieved some of the extraordinary healing within his patients.

This is not the fond but biased recollection of his daughter. Tales illustrating these points have been comprehensively reported and studied and analyzed. People have attempted to describe, explain, label, quantify, and teach what Dad did in such a seemingly effortless way. The field of psychotherapy is richer for that dedicated work.

I know that a great deal of what Dad did is teachable and learnable. "Listen, listen, listen," "observe, observe, observe" are bedrocks which too many of us ignore too often. Utilization. Acceptance of others. We must read, study, expand our minds. All of these are integral parts. but there's more.

I don't think anyone professes to know exactly how the remarkable healing and changes were accomplished. I've heard a lot of guesses and listened to a lot of people tell me what they think. Nothing resonates as even part of the answer. So maybe there is no answer that we can understand, with our limited means of communication, with our partial and inadequate knowledge of mankind's true abilities. That resonates the most.

People forget that my father was an ordinary man. He made mistakes, he was too strict—and not strict enough—a father. He hated to say he had made a mistake, disliked saying he was sorry. He argued when he was wrong, took people for granted, and made bad decisions. Some people didn't like him, and he didn't like them back. And he had therapeutic failures.

Brad Keeney notes that Gregory Bateson called Dad the Mozart of communication. He was a genius, a master of creativity, understanding nuances, evoking emotions, blending differences to make a brilliant combination; Dad—and Mozart—were each one of a kind. I think Dad was also an improvisational artist, playing on the theme, enhancing the overriding melody, changing it sometimes subtly and often dramatically, but the essence of the music was always there. I've been told more than once that Dad played life as if he were conducting a symphony.

Daddy did know when to let the violins sing solo, the trumpets play their chorus, the drums take center stage, and the flutes add their delicate contributions. He knew when silence emphasized and when to bring the various parts together softly or loudly, producing so

much more than the sum totals of the individual notes. He was dedicated to the symphony of life, played at it, with it, in it and was
happy to take turns with the myriad people who wanted to join him.
Odd analogies for a tone-deaf man, but how apt they are.

As a girl, I regarded him with puzzlement. So many people held
him in such high regard! I was always a bit bewildered by the flocks
of students who gathered around him, always felt a little amazement.
Didn't they know this was just Daddy? He told corny stories, played
practical jokes, liked limburger cheese and insisted on keeping it in
the refrigerator where it wafted its foul odor into everything. Didn't
they know he got mad when the dog got on the furniture and that
we'd better not misplace the new comic book before he read it?
Didn't they understand he woke me up in the middle of the night
for a serious and lengthy discussion about why I had left the lawn
tools in the yard? He would inquire with great earnestness about
how he could help me learn to be more thoughtful about my tasks.
We had to discuss each proposed solution in tedious detail while the
clock continued to tick away the night.

The students clearly didn't care about the limburger cheese or the
dog on the couch—and I clearly didn't recognize that his innovative
way of discussing forgetfulness about responsibilities was one of the
reasons they did gather about him.

People ask me when I first knew he was famous. I'll never forget.
I was a teacher on an air base in Okinawa, and one of my friends
worked as liaison between the military and civilians. He began talking
with total awe about a wonderful, gifted, extraordinary and almost
magical psychiatrist who was "into hypnosis." He was excited because
he had attended an all-day seminar teaching fundamentals of hypnosis
to medical personnel and the instructor had studied with this
phenomenal psychiatrist. My friend had already read a great deal
about this fabulously talented doctor, who could do absolutely
miraculous things. The seminar was just incredible, he continued.
After several moments of listening to his enthusiastic praise of the

psychiatrist, I idly asked who the miracle worker was. "A guy named Milton Erickson," he replied. I was stunned. "That's my father," I said.

"That's your father?" he responded, equally stunned. It took us each several minutes to communicate anything beyond amazement. He could not believe my father was actually *the* Milton Erickson and I could not believe Daddy inspired such awe, such admiration in anyone, especially a man who had never met him, who had merely read about him. My husband and I were then invited to the dinner honoring the psychologist who was teaching the seminar. It was a surreal evening. Dad was really the guest of honor; my husband and I were the astonished substitutes.

How much that says about the kind of man Dad was. He was my father—an ordinary, everyday, familiar father. First and foremost, second and third he was just Dad. He didn't want to be seen as anything but just that. That gave us children the freedom to be us. We didn't have to "live up" to anybody—only to the values and ethics that parents always give children. We were just us, as he was just Daddy. How freeing that was!

Dad regarded himself as a man soundly grounded in the observable, measurable and replicable results of science. I do too. But he also was more; he was a healer. A healer works with other people in ways that don't seem scientific. Yet something happens; the other person changes, gets well, feels and is stronger. No one can really define or analyze how it all happens but it just does. It is undeniable that something occurred and people changed in advantageous ways. For us Westerners schooled in traditional ways and understandings, it's almost a leap of faith to have faith that the healer opened the other to that change.

When my brother Allan met with Brad, they discussed healing and healers. Brad asked Allan if his father would have had the same abilities of astute observation, of communication, the same dedication to helping others, the same ability to initiate change with the people who interacted with him if he had been born in a Balinese village.

Allan thought and then agreed, "Yes. Probably so. Different, but yes."

Brad pointed out that Erickson couldn't have been called a psychiatrist. What would he have been called? How would he have been regarded by villagers? The only answer that Allan could think of was "Healer." Dad's abilities to give, to help, to teach, to connect, to love, to heal transcend his cultural origins, cultural limits, and cultural language.

Since beginning this book, I have been asked if Dad would approve of being called a healer. There is no doubt in my mind that he would first thoughtfully consider exactly what he did and how people responded to him. He would think about the advances of science as it begins to move in uncharted directions. Then, what other answer is there?

"Healer" does not detract from science or research, from Dad's foundation of work in hypnosis and psychotherapy. It adds to the assessment of his work. The framework of Ericksonian Hypnosis and Psychology is deliberately without limiting theories; so individualistic and so open that it is able to expand as our knowledge of life expands. I think Dad would accept the term "Healer"—adding a caveat, perhaps even with a twinkle in his eye: "There is a whole lot we don't know about what we think we know a lot about."

As my mother said in her preface, she felt lucky to have had him. So do I feel lucky to have had him as my father. More importantly, I think that good fortune transcends the family. I think we were all lucky to have had him. And he continues to be a healing presence to us, in our memories, dreams, and reflections.

References

For a more extensive understanding of Erickson's orientation to psychotherapy, hypnosis, healing, and pathology, an excellent overview is given in: *The Wisdom of Milton H. Erickson: The Complete Volume* by Ronald A. Havens, Ph.D. This book includes carefully selected quotations from Erickson's own works, categorized in broad concepts with references to the original material. Re-published in 2003, by Crown House Publishing, P.O. Box 2223, Williston, Vermont 05495-9922; **www.crownhouse.co.uk**

Campbell, J. (1949). *The hero with a thousand faces*. New York: Pantheon Books.

Campbell, J. (1973). *Myths to live by*. New York: Bantam.

Eliade, M. (1958). *Rites and symbols of initiation: The mysteries of birth and re-birth*. New York: Harper & Row.

Erickson, M.H. (1980a). *The nature of hypnosis and suggestion: The collected papers of M. H. Erickson*, Volume 1. (Edited by E. L. Rossi). New York: Irvington.

Erickson, M.H. (1980b). *Hypnotic alteration of sensory, perceptual, and psychosocial processes: The collected papers of M. H. Erickson*, Volume 2. (Edited by E. L. Rossi) New York: Irvington.

Erickson, M.H. (1980c). *Hypnotic investigation of psychodynamic processes: The collected papers of M. H. Erickson*, Volume 3. (Edited by E. L. Rossi). New York: Irvington.

Erickson, M. H. (1980d). *Innovative hypnotherapy: The collected papers of M. H. Erickson*, Volume 4. (Edited by E. L. Rossi). New York: Irvington.

Erickson, M. H., & Rossi, E. L. (1977). "Autohypnotic experiences of Milton H. Erickson." *American Journal of Clinical Hypnosis*, 20, 36-54. (Reprinted in Erickson, 1980a.)

Erickson, M.H. (1952). "Deep hypnosis and its induction," in L. M. LeCron (ed.), *Experimental hypnosis*. New York: Macmillan.

Gilligan, S.G. (1987). *Therapeutic trances: The cooperation principle in Ericksonian hypnotherapy.* New York: Brunner/Mazel.

Gilligan. S. G. (2002). *The legacy of Milton H. Erickson: Selected papers of Stephen Gilligan.* Phoenix, AZ: Zeig Tucker Thiesen.

Keeney, B. (1977). *On paradigmatic change: Conversations with Gregory Bateson.* Unpublished manuscript.

Lewis, T., Amini, F., and Landon, R. (2000). *A general theory of love.* New York: Random House.

Moore, R., & Gillette, D. (1993). *The magician within: Accessing the shaman in the male psyche.* New York: William Morrow.

Rossi, E. L., Ryan, M. O., & Sharp, F. A. (Eds.) (1983). *Healing in hypnosis: The seminars, workshops, and lectures of M. H. Erickson.* New York: Irvington.

Short, D, Erickson, B.A., & Klein, R. E. (2005). *Hope & Resiliency: Understanding the psychotherapeutic techniques of Milton Erickson.* Williston, Vermont: Crown House Publishing.

Turner, V. (1969). *The ritual process: Structure and anti-structure.* Chicago: Aldine.

Zeig, J. K. (1985). *Experiencing Erickson: An introduction to the man and his work.* New York: Brunner Mazel.

Zeig, J. K. (1980). *A teaching seminar with Milton H. Erickson.* New York: Brunner Mazel.

Also from Ringing Rocks Press

in association with Leete's Island Books

PROFILES OF HEALING SERIES

Edited by Bradford Keeney, Ph.D.

An ongoing book series, with digital recordings, presents the world's traditional shamans' and medicine people's first-person life stories, visions, training, and complementary medical practices. The series, unfettered by Euro-American analysis, is a unique encyclopedia of alternative healing practices and spirituality.

Gary Holy Bull: Lakota Yuwipi Man ISBN 0-9666509-0-5

Ikuko Osumi: Japanese Master of Seiki Jutsu ISBN 0-9666509-1-3

Kalahari Bushmen Healers ISBN 0-918172-23-3★

Guarani Shamans of the Forest ISBN 0-918172-25-X

Vusamazulu Credo Mutwa: Zulu High Sanusi ISBN 0-918172-24-1★

Walking Thunder: Diné Medicine Woman ISBN 0-918172-30-6★

Shakers of St. Vincent ISBN 0-918172-33-0★

Ropes to God: Experiencing the Bushman Spiritual Universe ISBN 0-918172-39-X★

Hands of Faith: Healers of Brazil ISBN 0-918172-37-3★

Balians: Traditional Healers of Bali ISBN 0-918172-35-7★

Casebound in a slipcase with digital recordings U.S. $39.95, CAN. $59.95
★Available in paperback with digital recordings U.S. $18.95, CAN. $22.95

To order, call: 1-800-888-4741 or visit www.frontdesk@ipgbook.com
For more information visit www.ringingrocks.org